MECHANICS' INSTITUTE LIBRARY
57 Post Street
San Francisco, CA 94104

MECHANICS' INSTITUTE
MECHANICS'
MERCANTILE LIBRARY

Landmarks in Linguistic Thought
The Western Tradition From Socrates to Saussure

Roy Harris is Emeritus Professor of General Linguistics in the University of Oxford, and is the author of *The Language Makers* (1980), *The Language Myth* (1981), *The Origin of Writing* (1986), *The Language Machine* (1987), *Reading Saussure* (1987) and *Language, Saussure and Wittgenstein* (1988). His translation of Saussure's *Course in General Linguistics* was published in 1983.

Talbot J. Taylor is an Associate Professor in the Department of English, College of William and Mary, Williamsburg, Virginia, and is the author of *Linguistic Theory and Structural Stylistics* (1981) and *Analysing Conversation* (with Deborah Cameron, 1987).

Routledge History of Linguistic Thought Series

Series Editor: Talbot J. Taylor, College of William and Mary,
Williamsburg, Virginia

Published

Landmarks in Linguistic Thought: From Socrates to Saussure
Roy Harris and Talbot J. Taylor
Language, Saussure and Wittgenstein
Roy Harris

Forthcoming

Change in Language: Whitney, Bréal and Wegener
Brigitte Nerlich
Language, Man and Knowledge
Hans Aarsleff
Linguistics in America 1769–1924
Julie Andresen
A World of Words: Language in Eighteenth-Century France
Pierre Swiggers

Landmarks in Linguistic Thought

The Western Tradition From Socrates to Saussure

Roy Harris and Talbot J. Taylor

MECHANICS' INSTITUTE

Routledge
London and New York

First published 1989
by Routledge
11 New Fetter Lane, London EC4P 4EE
29 West 35th Street, New York, NY 10001

© 1989 Roy Harris and Talbot J. Taylor

Printed and bound in Great Britain by
Butler & Tanner Ltd, Frome and London

All rights reserved. No part of this book may be reprinted or reproduced
or utilized in any form or by any electronic, mechanical, or other means,
now known or hereafter invented, including photocopying and recording,
or in any information storage or retrieval system, without permission in
writing from the publishers.

Library of Congress Cataloging in Publication Data

Landmarks in linguistic thought: the Western tradition from Socrates
   to Saussure/edited by Roy Harris and Talbot J. Taylor.
      p.   cm.
   "Routledge history of linguistic thought series" — Jacket.
   Bibliography: p.
   Includes index.
   ISBN 0–415–00290–7. ISBN 0–415–00291–5   (pbk.)
   1. Linguistics—History. 2. Languages—Philosophy. I. Harris,
Roy, 1931– . II. Taylor, Talbot J. II. Title: Routledge history
of linguistic thought series.
P61.L36   1989
410′.9—dc 19

88–26528

British Library CIP Data also available

Contents

410
L25

JAN 2 6 1990

Preface   vii

Acknowledgements   x

Introduction   xi

1 **Socrates on names**   1

2 **Aristotle on metaphor**   20

3 **The Bible on the origin and diversification of language**   35

4 **Varro on linguistic regularity**   46

5 **Quintilian on linguistic education**   59

6 **Thomas of Erfurt on the modes of signifying**   75

7 **Caxton on dialects**   86

8 **The Port-Royal Grammar: Arnauld and Lancelot on the rational foundations of grammar**   94

9 **Locke on the imperfection of words**   108

10 **Condillac on the origin of language and thought**   120

11 **Horne Tooke on etymological metaphysics**   136

v

330954

Contents

12 **Humboldt on linguistic and mental diversity**   151

13 **Müller on linguistic evolution**   165

14 **Saussure on language and thought**   176

Bibliography and suggestions for further reading   191

Index   197

Preface

This book is primarily intended as an introduction for English-speaking students making their first acquaintance with the long, multilingual, European linguistic tradition. That tradition is of importance to a wide range of studies – philological, literary, historical and philosophical. In all these disciplines at least some of the authors we deal with here feature as writers of note. Focusing attention on their role in the history of linguistic ideas may perhaps serve to highlight aspects of their work which would otherwise go unnoticed.

Our aim has been to show, in broad outline, how certain influential ideas about language survived, thrived, developed and were modified within a general framework of linguistic inquiry which lasted more or less intact from the era of the Greeks and Romans, who originally constructed it, down to about the beginning of the present century. However, the book should not be read as an attempt to provide a concise history of European linguistic thought over this period, or as a substitute for one. It is neither. No selection of texts or authors can fully reflect the complexities involved in the evolution of the ideas in question. Nevertheless, as our title indicates, we have opted to concentrate on various landmarks, in preference to giving a historical narrative; and we did so for a number of reasons, which may be summarized as follows.

Students at present have available in English only two kinds of publication suitable for introductory study in this subject area; (i) histories of linguistics, and (ii) anthologies of translated texts and extracts. Neither of these resources, in our experience, satisfies the needs of the current generation of British and American university students. The histories of linguistics tend to combine too much linguistic history with too little analytic interpretation. The anthologies tend to offer too much text with too little commentary. We have tried to steer a middle course. By taking a small number of texts, but discussing their implications at some length, we hope to have achieved a more informative initial presentation of one of the most important themes in Western education: the role of language in human society and human thought.

With this objective in view, we have omitted much which a history of linguistic thought, or even a survey, would have had to include. For example, the Stoic philosophers, who discuss linguistic topics constantly, and Sextus Empiricus, the most devastating critic of the linguistics of his day, do not find a place here. And this is because, in the context of the tradition which is our concern, the ideas of the Stoics and of Sextus Empiricus, intriguing though they may be in their own right, lead nowhere. Except indirectly, they are not taken up and incorporated into the mainstream of our tradition. (To examine why not would itself be a major contribution to our understanding of the tradition, but a contribution which cannot be attempted here.) It will be noted that by far the greater number of works we have selected were composed either before 100 AD or after 1650 AD, which appears to leave a large and disproportionate gap in the middle. This is not for want of linguistic works written during the intervening centuries but because, in our view, to have included a larger number of medieval and Renaissance writers would have promoted the work of those periods to a level of importance which its limited originality does not warrant in Western linguistic thought. Coming forward towards the present day, we have stopped short of Frege, Russell and Wittgenstein, and of the post-Saussurean descriptive linguists, because their work marks the adoption of new frameworks of linguistic inquiry, rather than a continuation of the traditional one. Saussure we have taken as our *terminus ad quem* because he makes the break with the old tradition so consciously and so emphatically.

A second consideration which has determined our presentation of material is that we did not wish to presuppose on the reader's part a detailed knowledge of any language other than English. At the same time, it was obviously desirable that students should have the opportunity of reading for themselves a complete version of the various texts under discussion. This has meant, in the case of foreign-language texts, choosing from the range of those currently available in English translations. The same consideration has largely precluded any detailed discussion of the meanings of technical linguistic terms belonging to other languages. Oversimplifications arising from this latter restriction are inevitable; but it would have been impractical, as well as tedious for the reader, constantly to draw attention to them by larding our discussion with terminological caveats. We have tried to avoid, nevertheless, some of the more misleading assimilations (for example, in grammatical terminology) which are currently found in modern interpretations of ancient and medieval linguistic writings. We have also taken the liberty of altering the passages quoted in translation when we felt that the translator's choice of terminological equivalents was potentially misleading for our purposes.

Landmarks are useful for taking one's bearings. But landmarks are relative to journeys undertaken; and we would not wish to deny that our selection of landmarks has been guided by our own interpretation of the direction to be followed if one wishes to explore this particular domain of ideas. That direction will emerge in our comments on the texts in question, and in the Introduction. We do not claim that ours is the only reasonable orientation, but simply that it is consistent and leads somewhere; which is initially useful for students exploring a range of topics in which it is very easy to flounder and lose one's way altogether.

Other guides might well have chosen a somewhat different shortlist of texts for initial study, although we doubt whether any such selection could be made without including some work by the majority of authors represented here. To that extent we are confident that most of our linguistic landmarks are indeed landmarks. Whether or not the bearings to be taken from them are those we propose is, in the end, a matter for individual travellers to decide. For travellers who in any case wish to go further than this book takes them, we have supplied a short bibliography, including references to editions of the original texts as well as their translations. These references, together with other suggestions for further reading, will be found at the end of the volume.

We wish to acknowledge our gratitude to three scholars whose critical comments have helped in the development of some of the following chapters: George Wolf, Hans Aarsleff, and Pierre Swiggers. The College of William and Mary, the Folger Library, the American Society for Eighteenth-Century Studies, and the Virginia Center for the Humanities each gave generous support to this project in the way of research grants awarded to Talbot Taylor.

Acknowledgements

For permission to reprint material from works in copyright the authors and publisher make grateful acknowledgement as follows:

Extracts from Plato's *Cratylus* (trans H. N. Fowler), Aristotle's *De Interpretations* and *Categories* (trans H. P. Cook) and *Rhetoric* (trans J. H. Freese), Varro's *De Lingua Latina* (trans R. G. Kent), and Quintilian's *Institutio Oratoria* (trans H. E. Butler) are reprinted by permission of The Loeb Classical Library, William Heinemann Ltd and Harvard University Press.

Extracts from Thomas of Erfurt's *Grammatica Speculativa* (ed and trans by G. L. Bursill-Hall) are reprinted by permission of Longman Group UK Ltd.

Extracts from *General and rational grammar: the Port-Royal Grammar* (trans Jacques Rieux and Bernard E. Rollin) are reprinted by permission of Mouton de Gruyter, a division of Walter de Gruyter & Co.

Extracts from the translation of Condillac's *Logic* by Franklin Philip and Harlan Lane, contained in *Philosophical Writings of Etienne Bonnot, Abbé de Condillac* are reprinted by permission of Lawrence Erlbaum Associates Inc.

Extracts from Humboldt's *On Language*, translated by Peter Heath, are reprinted by permission of Cambridge University Press.

Introduction

I The ancient world

The Classical Greek view of language as a human accomplishment is nowhere better expressed than in the following passage from the famous Athenian rhetorician Isocrates (436–338 BC):

> In most of our abilities we differ not at all from the animals; we are in fact behind many in swiftness and strength and other resources. But because there is born in us the power to persuade each other and to show ourselves whatever we wish, we not only have escaped from living as brutes, but also by coming together have founded cities and set up laws and invented arts, and speech has helped us attain practically all of the things we have devised. For it is speech that has made laws about justice and injustice and honor and disgrace, without which provisions we should not be able to live together. By speech we refute the wicked and praise the good. By speech we educate the ignorant and inform the wise. We regard the ability to speak properly as the best sign of intelligence, and truthful, legal and just speech is the reflection of a good and trustworthy soul....

The term here translated as 'speech' is the Greek word *logos*, which designates not merely the capacity for articulate discourse but the rational faculty underlying and informing the spoken word in all its forms. It is *logos* which distinguishes humanity from all other living species, and it is *logos* which provides the basis for the Classical definition of the human being as the 'rational animal'.

The earliest manifestation of the Greek regard for the power of *logos* is the respect accorded to poetry in the Greek cultural tradition;

in particular, the epic poetry of Homer, which was for centuries treated as a repository of moral and historical truths. The first Greek thinkers to focus their entire programme of teaching on language were the so-called Sophists (i.e. 'wise men') of the fifth and fourth centuries BC, who lectured on the techniques of oratory and disputation. Their reputation for being unscrupulously clever with words has bequeathed to the term *sophistry* its modern pejorative sense; but they nevertheless fulfilled an important educational function in their day, and brought linguistic questions to the forefront of Greek consciousness in the Classical period. Socrates' debates with the Sophists, as recorded by Plato, constitute the earliest detailed evidence from which we can reconstruct a coherent picture of the Greek view of language.

Greek culture was linguistically self-centred and monoglot. Although they were well aware that other civilizations had other languages, the Greeks took little interest in studying them. They were, however, very conscious of the dialectal varieties of Greek itself. They were also interested in how words and languages originated. Herodotus recounts the story of how the Egyptian pharaoh Psammetichos attempted to discover which was the original language of the world by isolating two newborn infants in order to determine which words they would first utter if left entirely to their own devices; but no Greek thinker seems to have thought this experiment worth repeating. The Greeks attributed to the Egyptians the invention of writing, and credited Cadmus with the introduction of the alphabet into the Hellenic world. They recognized that languages change in the course of time, but treated etymology not as an inquiry into the history of a word but as a search for the 'true' meaning which had been lost sight of over the years.

The political expansion which resulted from the conquests of Alexander the Great (356–323 BC) brought Greece into closer contact with other civilizations. Alexandria under the Ptolemies became a major centre of Greek literary culture abroad. Here the Septuagint was translated into Greek, thus introducing what was eventually to become an important new element into European linguistic thought, with its very specific account of the origin of language and of the cause of linguistic diversity. By the time this influence made itself felt, however, Greece had long been supplanted by Rome as the dominant military and administrative power of the ancient world.

Roman writers took over the Greek attitude to language as part and parcel of their legacy of Greek culture, and their pursuit of linguistic studies was based in all essential respects on Greek models. In both Greece and Rome high regard for the arts of speech was founded on the fact that public debate played an essential role in government and the courts of law. As education developed in the Graeco-Roman world and the demand for literacy increased, there emerged a three-fold division of *logos* and its related skills into (i) rhetoric, (ii) logic, and (iii) grammar. The three were hierarchically related, rhetoric being of the highest importance, and presupposing competence in reasoning (logic) and correct expression (grammar). Poetry was still of importance in Roman culture (although the Romans had no indigenous oral tradition), but the study of poetic technicalities and composition was subsumed under grammar.

With the expansion of the Roman Empire, Latin became adopted as the spoken language of one conquered population after another, in a way that Greek had never been in the wake of Alexander's conquests. By the time the Roman empire fell, what had originally been an insignificant Italic dialect of the plain of Latium in Central Italy was spoken from the British Isles to North Africa and from the Atlantic to the Black Sea. This was linguistic colonization on a scale quite unprecedented in the history of Europe, and it left a lasting mark on the linguistic mentality of European civilization. Down to the Renaissance and beyond, all thinking about language was to remain dominated by the unique status achieved by this ubiquitous, versatile, all-purpose language, which counted among its monuments the speeches of Cicero, the poetry of Virgil, Jerome's translation of the Bible, and the legal code of Justinian. It was a language which eventually penetrated every level of society and united the largest single linguistic community Europe was ever to see in 3,000 years of continuous social and political development.

The three general questions about language most frequently debated in the ancient world seem to have been: (i) whether language was natural or conventional, (ii) whether or not language was based on a fundamental principle of regularity, and (iii) how many parts of speech there were. The subsequent history of these three questions in the Western tradition is of some interest. Question (iii) had been more or less settled by the grammarians of antiquity, at least to their own satisfaction, by the time Priscian wrote his definitive grammar of Latin (c.500 AD), and it does not re-emerge as a significantly controversial issue for linguists until quite recent times. Question (ii) had divided ancient opinion between 'analogists' and 'anomalists', the former maintaining the essential regularity of language, and the latter denying it. This was another debate which had talked itself to a standstill by Priscian's day, but crops up again in a quite different guise when, first in the later Middle Ages and again in the 17th century, new attempts are made to explain the systematicity of language. Question (i) is in many respects the most durable of the three, and can be interpreted as subsuming the other two. It addresses the fundamental issue of the degree of control which human beings have over language. In one form or another, from Socrates to Saussure, this was to remain a permanent topic of debate throughout the Western tradition.

II The Middle Ages

If the Middle Ages began, as some history books tell us, with the sack of Rome in 410 AD, and ended with the discovery of America in 1492 AD, then the Middle Ages both began and ended with events of great linguistic significance, even though it took a long time in both cases for the results to unfold. The first event was destined to alter the linguistic map of Europe, while the second was destined to alter the linguistic map of the world.

Although the barbarian invasions of the fifth century AD eventually brought new languages to power in the great cities of the former Roman empire, the immediate effect was to impose a lengthy moratorium on the development of linguistic thought. Europe embarked on a millenium during which Latin would bifurcate into learned (i.e. written) and popular (i.e. spoken) versions, the latter eventually winning recognition as independent Romance languages (French, Italian, Provençal, Spanish, Rumanian, etc.). European countries remained united, however, in their acceptance of the Christian church, and made common cause against Muslim armies during the Crusades. Throughout the long period of medieval Latin-Romance bilingualism it was Latin which remained the dominant partner for all administrative, educational and religious purposes. Latin meant for the Middle Ages – ideally, at least – the 'correct' Latin enshrined in the works of the great Classical authors (Cicero, 106–43 BC; Virgil, 70–19 BC) and subsequently codified by the great grammarians of late antiquity (Donatus, c.350 AD; Priscian, c.500 AD): but in practice the Latinity of the period often fell far short of this ideal. Teaching Latin to 'barbarians' was a common motivation of medieval scholars. In England, Bede (672–735 AD) and Alcuin (735–804 AD) wrote Latin grammars, and Aelfric (c.1000 AD) wrote both a grammar and a

Latin–Old English glossary for the benefit of his Anglo-Saxon-speaking pupils.

Scholastic philosophy in the Middle Ages was a battleground for disputes between 'realists' and 'nominalists'. The quarrel turned on the status attributed to words. The nominalists held that only particular physical items constitute reality, and that general or 'universal' terms (such as *man, horse, red*, etc.) designate mere abstractions. The realists, on the contrary, held that these are not abstractions, but have a reality which is prior to that of any physical particulars. The issue had controversial religious implications when applied to certain doctrines of medieval Christianity (in particular the sacrament of the Eucharist).

The schools and universities of medieval Europe offered Latin grammar, rhetoric, and logic as their three 'linguistic' subjects, these constituting the so-called *trivium* of the syllabus. The education provided was primarily intended for those seeking ecclesiastical or administrative careers (which in practice overlapped or coincided). The analysis of Latin provided by Donatus and Priscian remained unchallenged for a thousand years and more. The sole theoretical innovation of genuine originality was the attempt made in the 14th century by the school of 'speculative' grammarians to supplement the analysis Donatus and Priscian had given, by explaining why the structure of Latin took the particular form it did. In retrospect, the major shortcoming of this interesting attempt was its underlying assumption that Latin was a 'typical' language, exemplifying universal linguistic distinctions and categories. This assumption is understandable, given the cultural insularity of Europe throughout the Middle Ages. It was not until the Renaissance that European scholars began to realize that the diversity of languages in the world was far greater than the scholars of antiquity had ever imagined.

III The Renaissance

The linguistic paradox of the Renaissance is a double paradox. It hinges on the historical coincidence that a great 'rebirth' of interest in the Classical languages of antiquity (conventionally dated from the fall of Constantinople to the Turks in 1453 AD, and the consequent emigration of Greek scholars to Italy) overlapped with the demise of Latin as the *lingua franca* of Europe and the concomitant 'birth' of linguistic nationalism. At the same time, overseas expansion began to open up quite new linguistic horizons. The infiltration of the New

World brought in its train during the 16th century the first published grammars of Amerindian languages, while missionary activity in the Far East paved the way for the study of Chinese. By the year 1600 enough new linguistic evidence was available to challenge the entire framework of linguistic inquiry which Donatus and Priscian represented; but instead scholars such as Erasmus (1466–1536), Scaliger (1484–1588), Ramus (1515–1572) and Sanctius (1523–1601) focused attention back on reinterpretation of the Classical tradition. The dead languages were still more important than the living.

This intellectual mould was eventually broken by pressure from economic and technological factors. Europe was rapidly becoming a political chessboard on which rival monarchs could contest one another's power only as representatives of nations. Throughout the Middle Ages, wealth had gradually passed from feudal land-owners to merchants. Wars were now too costly to wage unless backed by the financial resources of economic units larger than any single aristocratic family could command. The advent of printing raised the question for the first time of how many mechanically produced copies of a book could profitably be sold; which in turn depended on how many potential purchasers could read the language in which the book was printed. Johann Gutenberg (c.1398–1460), by setting up Europe's first printing press, eventually had a far greater influence on linguistic thought than Erasmus, Scaliger, Ramus and Sanctius put together.

IV The 17th and 18th centuries

Between 1600 and 1800 strong centralized monarchies were gradually established in England, France, and Spain, and centralized government tended increasingly to promote linguistic unification. The prevailing 17th-century view of language was that although languages differed in vocabulary, pronunciation and idiom they must nevertheless share a basic structure which reflected universal characteristics of human thought. This was the thesis underlying the influential French grammar (1660) produced by the newly established Jansenist educational foundation of Port-Royal; and it remained the basic assumption of other 'general grammars' in this and the following century (for example, James Harris's *Hermes* of 1751). The same assumption was implicit in Descartes' (1596–1650) reassertion of the Greek claim that language was the distinguishing characteristic of *homo sapiens*. Leibniz (1646–1716) speculated about the possibility of devising a 'calculus' which would provide a general linguistic symbolization adequate for the expression of all rational thought. In England similar linguistic projects were proposed by Dalgarno (*Ars signorum*, 1661) and Wilkins (*Essay towards a real character and a philosophical language*, 1668). The most important English contribution to the linguistic thought of the period, however, came from Locke, whose account of language in his *Essay on human understanding* (1st edn 1689, 5th edn 1706) remained influential throughout the 18th century.

The age of the 'Enlightenment', as the 18th century came to be known, saw a prolonged struggle between the linguistic theorizing of followers of Locke, such as Condillac (1715–1780), and those who still sought to reconcile new speculations about the origin of language with the orthodox Biblical account. The problem of the origin of language thus came to occupy a central place in the intellectual history of the period. The Prussian Academy in 1769 offered a prize for the best essay on the subject. It was won by Herder (1744–1803), whose essay, published in 1772, is said to have been a major influence on the thinking of Humboldt (1767–1835). Humboldt is the first linguistic theorist to insist on the continuously 'dynamic' character of languages and their role as expressions of the mentality of different peoples. Further reaction against the linguistic ideas of the 'general grammarians' can be seen at the close of the century in Tooke's *Diversions of Purley* (1786, 1805).

V The 19th century

The gradual progress of universal education through the century brought an expansion of literacy and increasingly favoured standardization of the national languages, a process aided by the publication of new dictionaries and grammars. Commercial prosperity, foreign trade and colonization at the same time strengthened the position of the major European languages overseas.

The Romantic movement of the early 1900s had sparked a new interest in the languages of ancient civilizations and exotic cultures abroad. But the key factor in the academic development of linguistic studies was the discovery of Sanskrit. Already in 1786, Sir William Jones had drawn attention to the importance of this language in a much quoted passage:

The Sanscrit language, whatever be its antiquity, is of a wonderful structure; more perfect than the Greek, more copious than the Latin and more exquisitely refined than either; yet bearing to both of them a stronger affinity, both in the roots of verbs and in the forms of grammar, than could possibly have been produced by accident; so strong, indeed, that no philologer could examine all three without believing them to have sprung from some common source, which, perhaps, no longer exists.

The rise of Comparative Philology during the 19th century may be regarded as providing a long, scholarly gloss on Jones's prophetic observations, and an attempt to reconstruct the presumed 'common source' to which Jones refers – the original language of the early Indo-Europeans. Major roles in this philological endeavour were played by Rasmus Rask (1787–1832), Jakob Grimm (1785–1863) and Franz Bopp (1791–1867). By 1850 the comparative study of the Indo-European family of languages had been established on a definitive, well documented basis, and gave rise to the claim forcefully articulated by Max Müller (1834–1898) that the study of language was at last a 'science'. This claim was taken up in the latter half of the century by the school of German scholars known as the *Junggrammatiker* ('Neogrammarians'), who sought to establish the scientific 'sound laws' governing the evolution of the Indo-European languages. Evolutionary thinking in linguistics was supported by, and itself supported, the acceptance of Darwin's ideas in biology. By the end of the century, however, the theoretical basis of 19th-century evolutionary linguistics had been seriously called in question by Saussure (1857–1913), whose posthumously published *Cours de linguistique générale* (1916) launched 20th-century structuralism on its course. Saussure denied that linguistic change was governed by laws and insisted that linguistic evolution could be observed only with the benefit of historical hindsight: a language was not, for its speakers, in a continuous process of evolution, but was a stable, structured system.

Saussure marks the end of the Socratic tradition of linguistic thought; not because as a result of Saussure's teaching old ways of thinking about language were abandoned overnight, but because Saussure is the first to reject the Socratic question of how words relate to the world as an irrelevant and misleading starting-point for linguistic inquiry.

Chapter one

Socrates on names

HERMOGENES: Here is Socrates; shall we take him as a partner in our discussion?

CRATYLUS: If you like.

HERMOGENES: Cratylus, whom you see here, Socrates, says that everything has a right name of its own, which comes by nature, and that a name is not just whatever people call a thing by agreement, just a piece of their own voice applied to the thing, but that there is a kind of inherent correctness in names, which is the same for all men, both Greeks and barbarians. So I ask him whether his name is in truth Cratylus, and he agrees that it is. 'And what is Socrates' name?' I said. 'Socrates,' said he. 'Then that applies to all men, and the particular name by which we call each person is his name?' And he said, 'Well, your name is not Hermogenes, even if all mankind call you so.'

(*Cratylus* 383)

So begins the earliest record of any extended debate on linguistic questions that survives in Western literature. Like all Plato's dialogues, *Cratylus* presents an imaginatively reconstructed discussion between Socrates and his interlocutors on a philosophical topic of some importance to the Greeks of the late fifth and early fourth centuries BC. In this instance Socrates is represented as debating 'the correctness of names' with Hermogenes and Cratylus. Hermogenes was a follower of the school of Parmenides, and Cratylus a philosopher who, according to legend, came to mistrust language

1

so profoundly that eventually he renounced speech altogether and communicated to others by means of gesture only.

Plato (427–347 BC) was born and brought up during the thirty-year Peloponnesian war, in which Sparta eventually defeated Athens, and Athenian democracy itself was put on trial as an effective form of government. These political circumstances shaped Plato's life and work in three ways: (i) by leading to the death of his revered teacher, Socrates, condemned in 399 BC for his subversive views by the democratic leaders then in power, (ii) by occasioning Plato's own twelve-year exile from Athens, to which he returned only in 387 BC, and (iii) by inspiring his rejection of democracy and his intellectual search for the best form of government and of personal conduct. On returning to Athens, Plato founded his own Academy school, and lectured there for the remainder of his career. As the first philosopher whose writings have all survived, as the principal source of our knowledge of Socratic doctrines and methods, and as the teacher of Aristotle, Plato has three claims on the attention of historians, and any one of the three would have guaranteed him a unique position in the development of Western thought. In Plato's quasi-fictional dialogues, culminating in the *Republic* and the *Laws*, Socrates usually appears as the spokesman of Plato's own views. To what extent these conform in detail to the teachings of the historical Socrates it is, understandably, difficult to determine with any accuracy. Exactly when in Plato's career the dialogue *Cratylus* was composed is not known.

Why Cratylus and Hermogenes are interested in the correctness of names does not become apparent until the arguments on both sides have unfolded. In order to follow them, two general points concerning (i) Greek puns, and (ii) Greek parts of speech, must be appreciated.

(i) Cultures vary in their attitude to wordplay. The early Greek delight in it will strike any reader accustomed to the norms of present-day Western education as either rather oriental or rather juvenile. In particular, joking about people's names is nowadays regarded as unsophisticated (although not many generations ago writers of the calibre of Dickens still indulged in it). Making fun of a tall person whose name happens to be Short, or twitting a dull-witted one whose name is Bright, is today treated as being in poor taste. But Cratylus' initial jibe in Plato's dialogue falls into this category.

The claim that Hermogenes is not correctly called *Hermogenes* is based on the fact that in Greek the name means 'born of Hermes', and the Greek god Hermes was the patron deity of businessmen and bankers. Hence the implication that one would expect someone called *Hermogenes* to be favoured by fortune in financial matters. This was evidently not the case with the man to whom Cratylus is speaking. This Hermogenes, whose business ventures always fail, Cratylus suggests, has been given the wrong name: he is no true 'son of Hermes'.

This rather feeble pun on the name *Hermogenes* seems a most unpromising point of departure for a serious discussion of the nature of language. But its sole purpose here is to lead to reflection on whether or not there is any sense in which names are 'appropriate' or 'inappropriate'. This is certainly a question which still preoccupies many modern parents when choosing names for their children, and ensures a steady sale for books which purport to explain the 'meanings' of given names such as *John*, *Mary*, *Peter*, *Alice*, etc. If the popular belief that names have meanings is simply wrong, it is nevertheless widespread in many civilizations. On the other hand, if names do have meanings it seems reasonable to expect that their meanings should be apposite to the person or thing or place thus named. And if there are some names which do have meanings, while others have none, it is not absurd to inquire how this comes to be so.

(ii) In reading Plato's dialogue, it is important to bear in mind that the term usually translated into English as 'name' (*onoma*) covers not only proper names such as *Hermogenes* and *Socrates* but also what would nowadays be classified as common nouns (*man*, *horse*, etc.). Furthermore *onoma* was also sometimes used in Greek as the general term for 'word'. In any case, no systematic distinction between proper names and common nouns was drawn at the time when Plato was teaching in Athens. Plato himself appears to recognize only two 'parts of speech'. One is 'names' and the other is *rhēmata* (usually translated as 'verbs' or 'predicates'). So the question as to whether Hermogenes is correctly called *Hermogenes* is treated as being in principle no different from the question of whether, for example, water is correctly called *water*, or gold rightly called *gold*. All 'names' are in this respect on a par.

Hermogenes states his own position in the debate as follows:

For my part, Socrates, I have often talked with Cratylus and many others, and cannot come to the conclusion that there is any correctness of names other than convention and agreement.

For it seems to me that whatever name you give to a thing is its right name; and if you give up that name and change it for another, the later name is no less correct than the earlier, just as we change the names of our servants; for I think no name belongs to any particular thing by nature, but only by the habit and custom of those who employ it and who established the usage.

(*Cratylus* 384)

Hermogenes' allusion to servants reminds us that Athens in the time of Plato was a slave society. It was a common Greek custom to give slaves new names when they entered the service of a new master. Here it is interesting that Hermogenes cites this social practice not only as evidence bearing on the argument, but as a model which reveals more clearly than anything else the pure conventionality of names. His implied reasoning is: if names were not purely conventional, how would it be possible for me to change a slave's name merely by an arbitrary decision? The fact that we can do this shows that names are in the end decided by the whim of individuals.

Socrates disagrees. His first contribution to the debate is to attack the thesis that names are given or changed by acts of individual volition. What is interesting is the argumentative strategy which Socrates chooses. He does not point out to Hermogenes that changing a slave's name is an exceptional and marginal case. Nor does he point out that Hermogenes is not at liberty to change names like *water* or *gold*. Instead he opts for a more subtle and powerful argument.

SOCRATES: It may be that you are right, Hermogenes; but let us see. Whatever name we decide to give to each particular thing is its name?

HERMOGENES: Yes.

SOCRATES: Whether the giver be a private person or a state?

HERMOGENES: Yes.

SOCRATES: Well, then, suppose I give a name to something or other, designating, for instance, that which we now call 'man' as 'horse' and that which we now call 'horse' as 'man', will the real name of the same thing be 'man' for the public and 'horse' for me individually, and in the other case 'horse' for the public and 'man' for me individually? Is that your meaning?

HERMOGENES: Yes, that is my opinion.

SOCRATES: Now answer this question. Is there anything which you call speaking the truth and speaking falsehood?

Hermogenes agrees that there is, and thereby closes the trap which Socrates has carefully laid for him. The thrust of Socrates' question is to point out that the volitional theory of names which Hermogenes champions leads directly to a conclusion which conflicts with common sense. For it validates the recognition of as many private languages as there are individuals. This, for one thing, makes nonsense of our normal understanding of the difference between truth and falsehood. Normally, when someone says 'A horse has four legs' we take this to be a true statement. But if Hermogenes is to be believed, we could be mistaken: for all we know, the speaker might be speaking a private language in which *horse* is the name for what we call *man*. Consequently 'A horse has four legs' could be false.

Now once we admit that the word *horse* could mean 'man', or that *Socrates* could be the name of Hermogenes, then language as we normally understand it simply breaks down. We are unable to judge whether such statements as 'A horse has four legs' or 'Socrates is married to Xanthippe' are true or false. Worse still, it becomes unclear even how we would go about establishing their truth or falsity, if Hermogenes' theory of names is correct.

Hermogenes is thus forced to beat a hasty retreat. Already by this stage in the discussion Socrates appears to have established incontrovertibly that whatever the relations may be between the person Hermogenes and the name *Hermogenes*, or between a horse and the word *horse*, one thing is at least clear: it is not a relation either established by or at the mercy of volitional acts by particular individuals. But now the question arises: 'What, then, *does* establish this relationship?' The remainder of the dialogue is devoted to exploring various possibilities.

First, says Socrates, we must inquire what kind of correctness a name might be expected to have. And in order to establish this, we must ask what purpose names serve. He persuades Hermogenes to agree that

things have some fixed reality of their own, not in relation to us nor caused by us; they do not vary, swaying one way and another in accordance with our fancy, but exist of themselves in relation to their own reality imposed by nature.

(*Cratylus* 386)

Actions too are 'a class of realities':

actions also are performed according to their own nature, not according to our opinion.

(*Cratylus* 387)

For example, we cannot cut this piece of wood or burn it unless we proceed in accordance with the nature of cutting and burning: we shall fail to cut anything unless we use a sharp instrument, and we shall not burn anything by pouring water on it. For such actions are not determined by human volition: rather, human volition must conform to the nature of the action if we wish to accomplish it successfully.

Then comes the crucial move in Socrates' argument. Speaking is also an action; and names are the instruments of speech. To speak correctly is to use the instruments of speech in the proper way, just as the proper use of other implements is essential to the particular types of activity they are designed for.

How, then, do names function when properly used in the activity of speaking? Their function, Socrates claims, is to divide up reality for us; to distinguish one thing from another, one person from the next. The name *Hermogenes* distinguishes the individual Hermogenes from other individuals. Socrates draws an imaginative comparison between the activities of speaking and weaving. He describes a name as 'an instrument of teaching and of separating reality, as a shuttle is an instrument of separating the web' (*Cratylus* 388).

In order to perform this function, a name must be designed in the right way, just as a shuttle must be appropriately designed for the purpose of weaving. It must have the right form: otherwise it will not work. The efficiency of a shuttle, as of any other instrument, depends on its shape. Here Socrates begins to attack the second principal idea in Hermogenes' theory: that *it does not matter* which name is given to a person or a thing. That, according to Socrates, is not only a rash assumption but a ridiculous one.

The language we speak was already established long before we were born. We do not know who invented it, any more than the weaver knows who invented the loom. But in both cases we can to a certain extent tell what was in the inventor's mind, simply by examining the design of the invention. For purposes of the discussion Socrates here introduces a mythical inventor of language, whom he calls simply 'the name-maker'. The name-maker did not merely choose names at random, any more than the inventor of the loom assembled a random collection of objects and made them into a machine for weaving. If we wish to inquire into the correctness of names, therefore, we must try to discover how the name-maker originally designed them. For he knew 'how to embody in the sounds and syllables that name which is fitted by nature for each object' (*Cratylus* 389).

Before proceeding further, it is worth noting how the analogy with weaving enables Socrates to introduce in one move a number of quite separate ideas about language: (i) that it is purposeful, (ii) that its purpose is reflected in its design, (iii) that it was invented, (iv) that its parts are fitted for their function, (v) that it would not work otherwise, and (vi) that in order to operate it properly we need to understand its design. The connecting thread in all these ideas is that of *functionality*, which in turn is assumed to presuppose *rationality*. By implication, Hermogenes' theory of names is cast in the role of a theory which represents language as irrational, fortuitous and contingent.

This is why Socrates does not need to rebut directly Hermogenes' point that any master can change the name of his slave. The analogy with weaving shifts the whole argument to a different level. It would be a mistake to suppose that Socrates expects the analogy to be taken literally: a language is neither a loom, nor any other kind of physical contrivance. But Socrates is in effect saying: 'If we want to inquire into language, we have to *assume* that it is functional. Otherwise there is nothing to inquire into. Similarly, unless we assume that a loom is functional, it makes no sense to ask why it is put together as it is. So it is silly to start with a theory like Hermogenes'. For to claim that names can be changed at random and by individual whim is simply to deny in advance the functionality of language: and that leaves us with no basis of inquiry at all.'

Functionality, then, implies that form is *not* fortuitous, but is designed to serve a purpose. What would make the form of one name more apt for a given purpose than the form of another name? This takes us to the next step in Socrates' argument. It introduces the notion that speech *represents* or depicts reality. Thus a name will be well designed to the extent that it correctly represents what it designates. (This follows from the original premiss that speech requires names in order to 'divide up' and distinguish the different parts of reality we wish to talk about.) For example, says Socrates, Homer tells us that Hector's son was known by two names, *Astyanax* and *Scamandrius*. But the former is more appropriate than the latter, because *Astyanax* means 'lord of the city', and *Hector* means 'holder'. They are both names appropriate for kings; for the nature of kingship entails the possession of the cities over which a king rules, and which his son in turn will possess after him. Socrates proceeds to illustrate this principle with a discussion of other Homeric personal names. But personal names are not invariably reliable guides, being given by parents, who themselves are liable to error. Therefore the examination must be extended to other Greek words. Socrates says:

> we are most likely to find the correct names in the nature of the eternal and absolute; for there the names ought to have been given with the greatest care, and perhaps some of them were given by a power more divine than is that of man.
>
> (*Cratylus* 397)

There follows a long and rambling etymological discussion in which Hermogenes tests Socrates' ingenuity by asking him to explain the meanings of all kinds of words. Some of the etymologies canvassed are very unconvincing. The word *hero*, for example, is explained by associating it with the god of love (Eros), on the basis that heroes were the offspring of love between gods and mortals. How seriously Socrates takes the etymologies he proposes is not at all clear: some of them are evidently offered with tongue in cheek. In other instances Socrates is merely repeating a traditional explanation of a name. In explaining the name *Aphrodite* as appropriate to the goddess who was born from the foam (*aphros*) he is simply citing the account already given by Hesiod. Etymologizing, it seems, was just another aspect of the traditional Greek fondness for wordplay. Sometimes Socrates mentions conflicting etymologies, and does not know which one to choose. In the course of this discussion it becomes apparent that the Greeks of Plato's day were fully aware that Greek pronunciation and spelling had altered over the centuries. Socrates always appears to assume that an earlier form of a word is more 'correct' than a later form. No explanations are given for the changes noted, other than the suggestion that sometimes the pronunciation has altered for reasons of 'euphony'. Socrates is also aware that not all Greek words are of Greek origin, and acknow-

ledges that the original meanings of these would have to be accounted
for by reference to the language from which they were borrowed.

In these respects Socrates' etymological inquiry is not lacking in
self-criticism. He notes that it is all too easy to claim that a word
must be of foreign origin if one cannot find an obvious Greek
etymology for it. He also notes that there are limits to invoking
phonetic change to bolster one's explanation and discount awkward
consonants or vowels.

SOCRATES: ... I think that sort of thing is the work of people
             who care nothing for truth, but only for the shape of
             their mouths; so they keep adding to the original
             words until finally no human being can understand
             what in the world the word means...

HERMOGENES: Yes, that is true, Socrates.

SOCRATES: And if we are permitted to insert and remove any
             letters we please in words, it will be perfectly easy to
             fit any name to anything.

                                                    (*Cratylus* 414)

(Socrates here anticipates Voltaire's sarcastic criticism of etymology
as a science in which consonants count for little and vowels for
nothing at all.)

By this time the reader may begin to suspect that the very facility
with which Socrates produces etymological explanations of the
meanings of words is intended as a *reductio ad absurdum* of his own
thesis, and that the unfortunate Hermogenes is being led by the
nose. Socrates himself comes close to admitting this. Eventually, he
concedes, such explanations come to an end. The etymologist will
have to abandon his search and another technique of inquiry must
take its place.

SOCRATES: Now at what point will he be right in giving up and
             stopping? Will it not be when he reaches the names
             which are the elements of the other names and
             words? For these, if they are the elements, can no
             longer rightly appear to be composed of other names
             ... if we ever get hold of a word which is no longer
             composed of other words, we should be right in
             saying that we had at least reached an element, and

that we must no longer refer to other words for its derivation.

HERMOGENES: I think you are right.

SOCRATES: Are, then, these words about which you are now asking elements, and must we henceforth investigate their correctness by some other method?

(*Cratylus* 422)

The long-suffering Hermogenes is thus eventually brought to agree that in the end we cannot hope to explain the correctness of words simply by reference to other words. Ultimately this form of explanation would be circular. Furthermore, it would not come to terms with the relationship between the name and the physical reality of the object named. We have to look for some further explanatory principle which does not already presuppose connections between one word and other words. But what could such a principle be?

SOCRATES: Well, then, how can the earliest names, which are not as yet based upon any others, make clear to us the nature of things, so far as that is possible, which they must do if they are to be names at all? Answer me this question: If we had no voice or tongue, and wished to make things clear to one another, should we not try, as dumb people actually do, to make signs with our hands and head and person generally?

HERMOGENES: Yes. What other method is there, Socrates?

SOCRATES: If we wished to designate that which is above and light, we should, I fancy, raise our hand towards heaven in imitation of the nature of thing in question; but if the things to be designated were below or heavy, we should extend our hands towards the ground; and if we wished to mention a galloping horse or any other animal, we should, of course, make our bodily attitudes as much like theirs as possible.

HERMOGENES: I think you are quite right; there is no other way.

SOCRATES: For the expression of anything, I fancy, would be accomplished by bodily imitation of that which was to be expressed.

HERMOGENES: Yes.

SOCRATES: And when we wish to express anything by voice or

tongue or mouth, will not our expression by these means be accomplished in any given instance when an imitation of something is accomplished by them?

HERMOGENES: I think that is inevitable.

SOCRATES: A name, then, it appears, is a vocal imitation of that which is imitated, and he who imitates with his voice names that which he imitates.

(*Cratylus* 422)

By imitation in names, however, Socrates says that he does not mean the echoic replication of the calls of animals or birds, but something quite different. He means a representation of the essential nature of each thing by means of a combination of appropriate sounds:

just as painters, when they wish to produce an imitation, sometimes use only red, sometimes some other colour, and sometimes mix many colours, as when they are making a picture of a man or something of that sort, employing each colour, I suppose, as they think the particular picture demands it. In just this way we, too, shall apply letters to things, using one letter for one thing, when that seems to be required, or many letters together, forming syllables, as they are called, and in turn combining syllables...

(*Cratylus* 424)

Socrates then embarks upon a speculative analysis of Greek names in order to test the assumption that their composition is based upon mimetic principles. In defence of this programme he says:

It will, I imagine, seem ridiculous that things are made manifest through imitation in letters and syllables; nevertheless it cannot be otherwise. For there is no better theory upon which we can base the truth of the earliest names, unless you think we had better follow the example of the tragic poets, who, when they are in a dilemma, have recourse to the introduction of gods on machines. So we may get out of trouble by saying that the gods gave the earliest names, and therefore they are right. Is that the best theory for us? Or perhaps this one, that we got the earliest names from some foreign folk and the foreigners are more ancient than we are? Or that it is impossible to investigate them because

11

of their antiquity, as is also the case with the foreign words? All these are merely very clever evasions on the part of those who refuse to offer any rational theory of the correctness of the earliest names.

(*Cratylus* 425)

Socrates begins his analysis with the consonant *r*, which he takes to be 'an instrument expressing all motion', and points out that it occurs in the Greek words meaning 'flow', 'current', 'trembling', 'run', etc. The reason for this appropriateness, says Socrates, is that 'the tongue is least at rest and most agitated in pronouncing this letter'. The consonants *d* and *t*, on the other hand, by reason of 'the compression and pressure' of the tongue are naturally fitted 'to imitate the notion of binding and rest'. In the consonant *l* 'the tongue has a gliding movement', and this consonant is found in the Greek words meaning 'glide', 'level', 'sleek', etc. The vowel *o* is appropriate to the expression of roundness. And so on. In this way, Socrates supposes, the name-giver originally made

by letters and syllables a name for each and every thing, and from those names he compounds all the rest by imitation. This, Hermogenes, appears to me to be the theory of the correctness of names...

(*Cratylus* 427)

In its final form, then, we have a two-stage theory. The primary names are built up by a mimetic process through combinations of sounds which copy the essential nature of the thing named, and this mimetic process is based upon the physiological articulations of the individual sounds in question. Once these primary names are established, the repertory is then extended by combining them into meaningful compounds according to their primary senses.

Having expounded this theory in outline, Socrates now proceeds to question it; and at this point in the structure of the dialogue Hermogenes is replaced by Cratylus as Socrates' chief interlocutor. The discussion reverts to Cratylus' original contention that Hermogenes is not correctly called *Hermogenes*, and Socrates again begins by arguing from the necessity of recognizing the distinction between truth and falsehood.

SOCRATES: How about the name of our friend Hermogenes, which was mentioned a while ago? Shall we say that it is not his name at all, unless he belongs to the race of Hermes, or that it is his name, but is incorrect?

CRATYLUS: I think, Socrates, that it is not his name at all; it appears to be his, but is really the name of someone else who possesses the nature that makes the name clear.

SOCRATES: And when anyone says that our friend is Hermogenes, is he not even speaking falsely? For perhaps it is not even possible to say that he is Hermogenes, if he is not.

CRATYLUS: What do you mean?

SOCRATES: Do you mean to say that it is impossible to speak falsehood at all? For there are, my dear Cratylus, many who do so, and who have done so in the past.

CRATYLUS: Why, Socrates, how could anyone who says that which he says, say that which is not? Is not falsehood saying that which is not?

SOCRATES: Your reasoning is too clever for me at my age, my friend. However, tell me this: do you think it is possible to speak falsehood but not to say it?

CRATYLUS: Neither to speak nor to say it.

SOCRATES: Nor utter it or use it as a form of address? For instance, if someone should meet you in hospitable fashion, should grasp your hand and say, 'Well met, my friend from Athens, son of Smicrion, Hermogenes,' would he be saying or speaking or uttering or addressing these words not to you, but to Hermogenes – or to nobody?

CRATYLUS: I think, Socrates, the man would be producing sounds without sense.

SOCRATES: Even that reply is welcome; for I can ask whether the words he produced would be true, or false, or partly true and partly false. Even that would suffice.

CRATYLUS: I should say that the man in such a case was merely making a noise, going through purposeless motions, as if he were beating a bronze pot.

(*Cratylus* 429–30)

But Socrates is not satisfied with this reply, and he pursues the question by elaborating the analogy between language and painting. Just as we can wrongly assign a portrait to an individual (because it is actually a likeness of someone else) so too we can make a mistake in assigning a name. The correct assignment in both cases is that 'which attributes to each that which belongs to it and is like it'.

SOCRATES: I call that kind of assignment in the case of both imitations – paintings and names – correct, and in the case of names not only correct, but true; and the other kind, which gives and applies the unlike imitation, I call incorrect and, in the case of names, false.

CRATYLUS: But it may be, Socrates, that this incorrect assignment is possible in the case of paintings, and not in the case of names, which must always be correctly assigned.

SOCRATES: What do you mean? What difference is there between the two? Can I not step up to a man and say to him, 'This is your portrait,' and show him perhaps his own likeness or, perhaps, that of a woman? And by 'show' I mean bring before the sense of sight.

CRATYLUS: Certainly.

SOCRATES: Well, then, can I not step up to the same man again and say, 'This is your name'? A name is an imitation, just as a picture is. Very well; can I not say to him, 'This is your name,' and then bring before his sense of hearing perhaps the imitation of himself, saying that it is a man, or perhaps the imitation of the female of the human species, saying that it is a woman?

(*Cratylus* 430–1)

This argument quells Cratylus' migivings, and he concedes that Socrates is right.

Socrates now follows up the analogy. Some portraits of a person may be better than others; and the same is presumably true in the case of words.

SOCRATES: If, then, we compare the earliest words to sketches, it is possible in them, as in pictures, to reproduce all the colours and shapes, or not all; some may be wanting, and some may be added, and they may be too many or too large. Is not that true?

CRATYLUS: Yes, it is.

SOCRATES: Then he who reproduces all, produces good sketches and pictures, and he who adds or takes away produces also sketches and pictures, but bad ones?

CRATYLUS: Yes.

SOCRATES: And how about him who imitates the nature of things by means of letters and syllables? By the same principle, if he gives all that is appropriate, the image – that is to say, the name – will be good, and if he sometimes omits a little, it will be an image, but not a good one; and therefore some names are well and others badly made. Is that not true?

(*Cratylus* 431)

Cratylus, however, is inclined to doubt it. He argues that correct spelling is not a matter of approximation: for there is only one way to spell a name correctly.

CRATYLUS: But you see, Socrates, when by the science of grammar we assign these letters – alpha, beta, and the rest – to names, if we take away or transpose any letter, it is not true that the name is written, but written incorrectly; it is not written at all, but immediately becomes a different word, if any such thing happens to it.

SOCRATES: Perhaps we are not considering the matter in the right way.

CRATYLUS: Why not?

SOCRATES: It may be that what you say would be true of those things which must necessarily consist of a certain number or cease to exist at all, as ten, for instance, or any number you like, if you add or subtract anything is immediately another number; but this is not the kind of correctness which applies to quality or to images in general; on the contrary, the image must not by any means reproduce all the qualities of that which it imitates, if it is to be an image. See if I am not right. Would there be two things, Cratylus and the image of Cratylus, if some god should not merely imitate your colour and form, as painters do, but should also make all the inner parts like yours, should reproduce the same flexibility and warmth, should put into them motion, life, and intellect, such as exist in you, and in short, should place beside you a duplicate of all your qualities? Would there be in such an event Cratylus and an image of Cratylus, or two Cratyluses?

CRATYLUS: I should say, Socrates, two Cratyluses.

SOCRATES: Then don't you see, my friend, that we must look for some other principle of correctness in images and in names, of which we were speaking, and must not insist that they are no longer images if anything be wanting or be added?

(*Cratylus* 431–2)

The problem is that once we admit degrees of likeness, either in names or in pictures, it becomes unclear what criteria of similarity are to be applied in particular cases. Worse still, it seems we have to admit the existence of dissimilarities between the representation and what it represents. For example, if the consonant *l* represents a gliding movement, it presumably has no business to be present in the Greek word meaning 'hard' (*sklēron*): yet it is.

SOCRATES: However, do we not understand one another when anyone says *sklēron*, using the present pronunciation, and do you not now know what I mean?

CRATYLUS: Yes, but that is by custom, my friend.

SOCRATES: In saying 'custom' do you think you are saying anything different from convention? Do you not mean by 'convention' that when I speak I have a definite meaning and you recognize that I have that meaning?

(*Cratylus* 434)

The moment Cratylus concedes this, however, it seems that he is committed to a conventional theory of names just as much as Hermogenes is. Socrates immediately presses home the point by arguing that it is difficult in many cases to see how a likeness could possibly be captured in sounds.

SOCRATES: For, my friend, if you will just turn your attention to numbers, where do you think you can possibly get names to apply to each individual number on the principle of likeness, unless you allow agreement and convention on your part to control the correctness of names? I myself prefer the theory that names are, so far as is possible, like the things named; but really this attractive force of likeness is, as Hermogenes says, a poor thing, and we are compelled to employ in addition this commonplace expedient, convention, to establish the correctness of names. Probably language would be, within the bounds of possibility, most excellent when all its terms, or as many as possible, were based on likeness, that is to say, were appropriate, and most deficient under opposite conditions.

(Cratylus 435)

The final topic discussed in the dialogue is whether, in view of these uncertainties, it is ever safe to assume that a name is a reliable guide to the nature of the thing named. Socrates argues that we cannot take it for granted that the original name-giver was always right in his understanding of the world.

SOCRATES: For if the giver of names erred in the beginning and thenceforth forced all other names into agreement with his own initial error, there is nothing strange about that. It is just so sometimes in geometrical diagrams; the initial error is small and unnoticed, but all the numerous deductions are wrong, though consistent.

(Cratylus 436)

Furthermore, we cannot suppose that the investigation of names is the sole approach to discovering the nature of reality: for the original name-giver, at least, must have used some other method, having no previous names to guide him. This alternative method can be none other than the direct investigation of the things themselves.

SOCRATES: Then if it be really true that things can be learned either through names or through themselves which would be the better and surer way of learning? To learn from the image whether it is itself a good imitation and also to learn the truth which it imitates, or to learn from the truth both the truth itself and whether the image is properly made?

CRATYLUS: I think it is certainly better to learn from the truth.

(Cratylus 439)

Many commentators have been puzzled by this dialogue, being unable to assign it a place in Plato's overall philosophical system, or to see what its vacillating discussion is driving at. For in the end neither of the theories put forward by Cratylus or Hermogenes is approved, and the eventual compromise can hardly be taken as intended to be satisfactory as an answer to the original question.

It would be a mistake, however, to treat *Cratylus* as a minor or exploratory work in which Plato had not yet formulated his own views on language. Socrates' conspicuous reluctance to come down either on the side of Cratylus or on the side of Hermogenes is itself our best clue to Plato's intentions. We must not forget that throughout Plato's dialogues Socrates is constantly engaged in verbal battles with the Sophists, the 'clever talkers' of the Greek world, and is especially concerned to discredit the Sophistic view, associated in particular with Protagoras, that truth is an illusion. Socratic inquiry is nothing else but a relentless pursuit of truth by the method of question and answer: if truth were an illusion this inquiry would be worthless.

The Sophists offered an educational programme quite different in spirit and aim from Socrates'. In many respects it fulfilled the functions which later devolved upon the universities of medieval and modern Europe. Those who attended the Sophists' lectures were essentially seeking a training which would stand them in good stead in public life; and in Plato's Greece the key to this lay in the skills of public speaking. Plato's basic attitude to the Sophists has to be placed in the context of his political views. The two main civil institutions of the democratic city-state, the Assembly and the Law Courts, were both institutions in which success depended on verbal persuasion. In this sense, democracy appeared to Plato as a system which valued consensus above objectivity and intellectual honesty. The death of Socrates was the philosophical lesson which Plato never forgot. The trial and condemnation of Socrates represented for Plato the unacceptable face of democracy and democratic values; and furthermore represented democracy in its true colours.

Language is therefore of importance in Plato's philosophy for one overriding reason. If Protagoras' doctrine were right, Socrates' death would have been a sacrifice in vain. Verbal inquiry can hardly claim to yield truth if truth is an illusion. The best one could hope for would be to persuade others to accept one's own opinion. This would be the ultimate vindication simultaneously of both Sophistry and democracy. Therefore it becomes important for Plato to show that language – which is the essential instrument through which both Sophists and democratic politicians alike conduct their affairs – itself demands our recognition of truth as independent and non-illusory. And this is the point of *Cratylus*.

When Hermogenes takes his intransigently individualist stand on the correctness of names, Socrates does not oppose him in the way we might expect; that is, by arguing that it is for the linguistic community and not the individual to decide what things are called. For that would be to play straight into the hands of the Sophists and those who treat consensus as the highest form of corroboration which human beings can value (as the Democrats claim). To the individualism of Hermogenes Socrates opposes a 'realist' view of language: names are answerable to reality, not to the community. But likewise when Cratylus advances the view that names have some kind of inherent correctness, Socrates counters with the possibility that whoever decides on names may simply be mistaken in their reasons for assigning any particular name. So in so far as a name expresses a judgement, that judgement too is answerable to reality and not to the community.

Language is thus for Plato the guarantee that truth must be valued over consensual agreement. If it were otherwise, then there would be nothing for us to agree or disagree about, and our efforts to convince others would be meaningful only as attempts to trick, browbeat or bully. Plato's point is that it does not matter whether language is conventional or mimetic, or to what extent it is a mixture of both. Since these are the only possibilities we can imagine, we are driven in the end to realize that language reaches both beyond our opinions and beyond itself. Or else we renounce rational discussion altogether (as the legendary Cratylus in the end did).

Where 'beyond' does language reach to? The answer to this is not given in *Cratylus*. It is supplied by Plato's quasi-mystical doctrine of 'forms' or 'ideas' (Cornford 1935). The things and properties we perceive, or believe we perceive, in this world are merely imperfect 'copies' of their corresponding 'forms' or 'ideas'. These latter are the sempiternal realities whose existence supplies the ultimate foundation for all human knowledge. Language connects us across the limbo from this absolute reality to its shadowy reflection, which is the familiar everyday world in which mortals live.

Chapter two

Aristotle on metaphor

Metaphor consists in giving the thing a name that belongs to something else; the transference being either from genus to species, or from species to genus, or from species to species, or on grounds of analogy.

(*Poetics* 21)

Aristotle's concept of metaphor is clearly based on Socrates' concept of names. A name is a word which 'belongs to' something or someone. The debate which Socrates referees in Plato's dialogue is a debate about how names 'belong to' the objects, persons, actions, qualities, etc. with which they are correlated. (According to Cratylus, names 'belong' by nature to whatever it is they belong to; whereas according to Hermogenes names 'belong' merely by convention.) Aristotle's definition of metaphor bypasses this controversy, and rests content with identifying metaphor as the transference of a name to something it does *not* 'belong to'. But this definition would hardly make sense without the Socratic assumption that names *do* (either by nature or convention) 'belong to' something or other in the first place. Metaphor is thus characterized straight away as an 'exceptional' case, involving a transgression or setting aside of the normal correlations which govern the everyday use of words. It is significant that Aristotle discusses metaphor as a feature of poetry, as if it were not part of ordinary language. The reasons underlying Aristotle's treatment of metaphor in this way are intimately connected with his philosophy of language, which differs in certain crucial respects from Plato's.

Aristotle (384–322 BC), Plato's most distinguished pupil, was the son of a doctor and in all probability began by studying medicine. If so, this may well explain to some extent the characteristic difference between his philosophy and Plato's: the greater emphasis on specific topics and details, the preference for practical solutions, and the reliance on empirical observation. (There is nothing in Plato, for instance, to match the meticulous description Aristotle gives in his *Historia animalium* of the day-by-day embryonic development of a chicken in the egg during incubation.) These down-to-earth qualities, together with his encyclopedic range of knowledge, may in turn explain why Aristotle was chosen in 342 BC by Philip of Macedon to educate his son, the future Alexander the Great. In 335 BC Aristotle returned to Athens, opened his own school at the Lyceum, and taught there for twelve years. He was identified by Alexander's political opponents as the conqueror's mentor, although relations between the two men were never easy. It has been remarked that Alexander had greater success with Bucephalus (his reputedly untameable horse) than Aristotle with Alexander. However, when Alexander died in 323 BC Aristotle could no longer rely on political protection and prudently retired. He died in the following year, possibly by his own hand. His works have survived in a less satisfactory form than Plato's. They are manifestly incomplete and riddled with textual problems. It has sometimes been suggested that what survived was simply a version of lecture notes taken by his students. This did not prevent the (alleged) pronouncements of Aristotle from acquiring oracular authority in Western philosophy for a thousand years and more.

Aristotle's basic position on language is clear enough.

> Words spoken are symbols or signs of affections or impressions of the soul; written words are the signs of words spoken. As writing, so also is speech not the same for all races of men. But the mental affections themselves, of which these words are primarily signs, are the same for the whole of mankind, as are also the objects of which those affections are representations or likenesses, images, copies.
>
> (*De Interpretatione* I)

It would be difficult to give a more concise but at the same time a more lucid summary of a whole theory of language than this statement which occurs right at the beginning of *De Interpretatione*. Aristotle apologizes for the brevity of the statement, saying that he has already dealt with these matters 'in my treatise concerning the soul'. If this means *De Anima*, all one can say is that the text as it has come down to us contains no such discussion. Nor is any of the works of the Aristotelian canon which have survived devoted explicitly to language as such.

This apparent lacuna calls for comment. In fact, to regard it *as* a lacuna is already to look back at Aristotelian thought through modern spectacles. The first point to grasp is that Aristotle *does* give what he sees as a detailed analysis of how language works: but this analysis is what we now call 'logic'. Language for Aristotle is simply the manifestation of *logos*, that distinctive mental faculty which makes man 'the rational animal'. Those who bewail the presumed 'loss' of a complete Aristotelian treatise on language are almost certainly lamenting the disappearance of something that never was.

This makes perfectly good sense once we realize that Aristotle, unlike Plato, is a committed conventionalist as far as words are concerned. He does not believe in the Platonic doctrine of eternal 'forms' or 'ideas' underlying human thought and speech. He holds that there is no colour 'red' which exists over and above the red things our eyes can see, and no archetypal 'horse' but only particular horses. Consequently, many of the discussions which he would have heard as a student at Plato's Academy must have struck him (unless he was at that stage in his career still very much under Plato's influence) as quite pointless arguments about worthless abstractions. From his physician father he would already have learned that theory is all very fine, but in real life health and illness only affect particular persons, and the diseases to be cured occur only in individual cases. Medicine is in the end about cases, not about generalizations. Generalization may indeed be useful, but the ultimate test of its usefulness will be application to particular instances.

If this is a fair assessment of the temper of Aristotle's mind, one may assume that the kind of etymological speculation that occupies a great deal of the discussion in Plato's *Cratylus* would have been regarded by Aristotle as simply irrelevant to any general understanding of language that would ever be of practical use. If someone argues that Socrates should be condemned to death, what matters is not the etymology of the name *Socrates*, or whether his parents gave him the correct name, but how the conclusion that Socrates must die was reached. Neither from the condemned man's point of view, nor from that of his accusers, would it have made the slightest difference what name Socrates had been given at birth. No one ever argued that Socrates' guilt or innocence had anything to do with his being called *Socrates*. He would still have been condemned, whatever his name. This line of thought clearly leads to a linguistic conventionalism which is subtly different from the conventionalism defended by Hermogenes in Plato's dialogue.

The difference is twofold. On one level, it bypasses the terms of the debate between Cratylus and Hermogenes altogether. The question is no longer whether the 'correctness' of a name is determined by Nature or by human decision. For it makes no difference. On another level, however, the question of the correctness of names re-emerges as a question about the identity of the individual or individuals thus named. What matters as regards the condemnation of Socrates is that the name *Socrates* shall not give rise to a problem about mistaken identity. The person who eventually drinks the hemlock must be *the same* as the person found guilty by the trial. This is where Aristotle's conventionalism parts company with the conventionalism of Hermogenes.

All that matters for Aristotle is that somehow there shall be an assurance that the name *Socrates* identifies the same individual on two separate occasions: the individual found guilty and the individual who consequently drank the poison. For only then can we (truly) say: 'Socrates was condemned and executed.' And if we cannot make that true statement, then language breaks down, or else our understanding of what is said breaks down (which amounts to the same thing). So this, from an Aristotelian point of view, is the very *first* question about language. It has nothing to do with etymologies or affinities with Nature. Nor is it relevant to point out that in one sense the Socrates who was condemned was a different man from the Socrates who drank the hemlock (the latter being an older man than the former, and perhaps a wiser man too). Given *this* formulation of the question, there is simply no room for Hermogenes' argument that a name can be altered voluntarily by individual whim. It would have availed Socrates nothing to attempt to evade the death sentence by changing his name.

So we have first to understand what guarantees the *stability* of a name. And this has to be a stability which is impervious to the vagaries of individual whims about name-changing. The source of this stability, for Aristotle, is – and can be nothing other than – convention: but convention understood not as an arbitrary decision to adopt one name rather than another, but as part of an ongoing social process with its own momentum. It is the momentum of this social process which in the end provides the assurance that the man who drank the hemlock was the man who had been condemned and, simultaneously, that both were the man called *Socrates*. If there was any miscarriage of justice, it was not because 'the wrong Socrates' died, or that language proved inadequate in any other way for carrying through the social process which began with Socrates' accusers. *That*, as far as Aristotle is concerned, is the linguistic mechanism we need to understand. For that at least is real, in the 'here-and-now' everyday sense of reality. And any generalization about language which can help us understand this mechanism is not a fanciful abstraction; for it bears upon the very specific fate of particular individuals, such as Socrates.

If this reconstruction of Aristotle's thinking about names is thus far correct, it may appear to have no profound originality, but to be simple common sense of a rather banal kind. But we must be careful here not to do Aristotle a double injustice. In the first place, what now seems merely common sense to us is doubtless so in part because the Aristotelian view of language was incorporated lock, stock and barrel into the Western educational tradition which has shaped our own assumptions about linguistic 'common sense'. To dismiss Aristotle as a purveyor of commonplaces about language would be to make a mistake of the same order as accusing Newton of making a song and dance about a gravitational principle obvious to every country bumpkin who had ever been hit on the head by a falling apple. In the second place, Aristotle saw a connection involving the stability of names which no previous thinker had seen. He saw that the guarantee which ensures that the bearer of the name *Socrates* is both the individual condemned to death and the person who later drank the hemlock is simultaneously the guarantee which underwrites the validity of the syllogism:

> All men are mortal.
> Socrates is a man.
> Therefore Socrates is mortal.

The realization of this connection was the basis on which Aristotelian logic is founded.

The syllogism does not work unless the Socrates mentioned in the minor premiss is identical with the Socrates mentioned in the conclusion. If they are different, then the conclusion is invalid. Thus human rationality itself demands a stability in names which at the very least does not collapse between one line of a syllogism and the next. So the convention which guarantees this continuity is not *merely* a social custom or habit, such as adopting a certain style of dress, or following a certain cycle of annual feast days. Naming-conventions, and their stability, are *necessary* if language is to be an expression of *logos* and human speech behaviour is to be that of a rational creature.

Aristotle saw logic as the *organon* or instrument used in every branch of human knowledge, and consequently as taking priority over all more specific fields of inquiry. This view of logic as the neutral, all-purpose foundation common to every rational investigation passed into the Western educational tradition and was reflected in the position assigned to logic in the common curriculum of the European universities. In that respect, Aristotle must take the credit not merely for being the first philosopher to systematize the processes of human reasoning, but also, by so doing, for laying down the ground plan for the entire edifice of higher education in the Western world. What concerns us here, however, is simply to trace the linguistic implications of Aristotle's position.

The Greeks were perfectly well aware that different languages are spoken in different parts of the world and also that languages gradually change in the course of time. But it follows from Aristotelian conventionalism that there is nothing much to be gained by studying either the geographical or the chronological differentiation of language. For whatever linguistic conventions may be adopted by different communities at different times or places, these conventions all serve exactly the same purposes, which are to provide a stable basis for the articulation of rational thought and, simultaneously, a means of expressing and communicating thought which will be comprehensible to those who share the same verbal conventions. In that sense, it is of no importance that the Greek word for 'horse' is quite different from the Persian word for 'horse', any more than it matters whether Hermogenes is called *Hermogenes* or some quite different name. The important thing is not the sounds or letters the name is composed of, but the connection between the name and what it stands for. The difference between the Greek and Persian word for 'horse' is exactly on a par with the fact that Hector's son is sometimes called *Astyanax* and sometimes *Scamandrius*. But Hector's son is the same person, regardless of which name is used to refer to him on any given occasion. In effect, Aristotelian logic is an attempt to deal with language simply by abstracting from the verbal differences which separate one language from another.

Particular languages (such as Greek) thus emerge in an Aristotelian perspective as being essentially *nomenclatures*, sets of names by means of which it is possible to identify different persons, places, animals, species, qualities, properties, etc., and to say something about them. For this purpose, one name is as good as another *provided* everybody is clear about which name stands for what. The name itself is of no consequence: Aristotle would doubtless have agreed with Shakespeare that a rose by any other name would smell as sweet. *If* there is anything further to the 'correctness' of a name, as Cratylus maintained, for Aristotle it is something which we do not have to take into account for ordinary human purposes in *using* names.

Nor is Aristotle interested in the classification of words and their combinatorial possibilities beyond what is necessary to elucidate their functions in the articulation of rational thought. Hence his classifications are based on meaning, as in the following passage from his *Categories*.

Each uncombined word or expression means one of the following things: – what (or Substance), how large (that is, Quantity), what sort of thing (that is, Quality), related to what (or Relation), where (that is, Place), when (or Time), in what attitude (Posture, Position), how circumstanced (State or Condition), how active, what doing (or Action), how passive, what suffering (Affection).

(*Categories* IV)

He gives the following examples of his ten categories of expression (some of which it is necessary to render in English by a phrase instead of the single Greek word).

Man and *horse* are expressions of Substance; *two cubits long, three cubits long* of Quantity; *white* and *grammatical* of Quality; *half, double* and *greater* of Relation; *in the market place* and *in the Lyceum* of Place; *yesterday, last year* of Time; *is lying* and *sitting* of Posture; *is shod* and *is armed* of State; *cuts, burns* of Action; and *is cut, is burnt* of Affection.

These ten categories of expression are for Aristotle the verbal building bricks to be used in the construction of any simple statement. He says:

> Not one of these terms in itself will involve any positive statement. Affirmations, as also denials, can only arise when such terms are combined or united together. Each positive or negative statement must either be true or be false – that, at least, is allowed on all hands – but an uncombined word or expression (for instance, 'man', 'white', 'runs' or 'conquers') can neither be true nor be false.
>
> (*Categories* IV)

It should be noted that Aristotle's ten categories are not 'parts of speech' in our modern sense of the term. But they are, perhaps, 'parts of the sentence'; or at least of the kind of sentence used to make a simple statement ('Fish swim', 'It was raining here yesterday', etc.).

Aristotle also takes over from Plato the traditional distinction between *onoma* and *rhēma*; but again he is interested in this distinction principally for its utility in analysing the structure of propositions and syllogisms. Consequently, although these terms are often rendered as 'noun' and 'verb' in English translations of Aristotle, this is potentially misleading. For example, in *De Interpretatione* we find *onoma* defined as: 'a sound having meaning established by convention alone but no reference whatever to time, while no part of it has any meaning, considered apart from the whole', and *rhēma* defined as 'a sound which not only conveys a particular meaning but has a time-reference also. No part by itself has a meaning. It indicates always that something is said or asserted of something' (*De Interpretatione* II–III). Clearly what Aristotle has in mind here is not the modern distinction between nouns and verbs but something much closer to that between the simplest subjects and the simplest predicates (*John laughed, the sun shone, birds fly*, etc.).

However, Aristotle does not draw a clear distinction between sentences and utterances. He is more interested in distinguishing between the 'sentence/utterance' and what can be said with it. Thus he defines *logos* (which English translations often render misleadingly as 'sentence') as 'significant speech, of which this or that part may have meaning – as something, that is, that is uttered but not as expressing a judgement of a positive or negative character' (*De Interpretatione* IV). Every *logos*, he continues, 'has meaning, though not as an instrument of nature but, as we observed, by convention'.

However, 'not all can be called propositions. We call propositions those only that have truth or falsity in them.' Here, evidently, he wishes to distinguish between a *logos* such as 'Let's go to Athens', which merely expresses a wish, and a *logos* such as 'We went to Athens', which expresses a report and must thus, in his view, be either true or false. But he finds no room for distinguishing the sentence as such (for example, *We went to Athens*); that is, as a form of words which itself is neither true nor false, but which has the potential for being employed on different occasions by different people to make assertions which, *depending on the circumstances*, may then be judged true or false. One way of putting this in modern terms is to say that Aristotle does not see the necessity for distinguishing either between the *logos* as sentence and the *logos* as utterance, or between the *logos* as type and the *logos* as token. This strikes the modern reader as all the more remarkable in that Aristotle's texts are full of 'examples' (in the sense that sentences written in inverted commas, or by the teacher on the blackboard, are examples). Linguistic examples of this kind must be presumed to be meaningful (otherwise it would be pointless to cite them); but it is unclear that it makes much sense to ascribe truth or falsity to the words *We went to Athens* when written on the classroom blackboard; or to the act of writing them; or to any 'proposition' (what proposition?) they are alleged to express.

Aristotle does not restrict his discussion of words to languages considered as an instrument of rationality. He also considers language as an instrument of persuasion, and in particular of literary persuasion. These points of view predominate in the treatises on rhetoric and his *Poetics*. The latter work contains Aristotle's highly influential account of metaphor. Unfortunately, it also contains, in the version which has come down to us, much about language which is simply garbled.

Of the three chapters in the *Poetics* devoted to general remarks about language, the first (Chapter 19) draws a general distinction between *lexis* ('language, diction') and *dianoia* ('thought'). Here Aristotle discusses how it is possible for the poet to represent what is going on in the mind of a fictional personage.

The thought of the personages is shown in everything to be effected by their language – in every effort to prove or disprove, to arouse emotion (pity, fear, anger and the like), or to maximize or minimize things. It is clear, also, that their mental procedure must be on the same lines in their actions likewise, whenever they wish them to arouse pity or horror, or have a look of importance or probability. The only difference is that with the act the impression has to be made without explanation; whereas with the spoken word it has to be produced by the speaker, and result from his language. What, indeed, would be the good of the speaker, if things appeared in the required light even apart from anything he says?

(*Poetics* 19)

This last question invites the more general query: 'What good would speech itself be if we could communicate by actions without the support of words?' Clearly, it would be redundant. But Aristotle evidently does not believe this to be the case. The passage is of interest in connection with the account of language given at the beginning of *De Interpretatione*. For here in the *Poetics* Aristotle is considering the same question at one remove: that is, he is looking at the poet's problem of representing human behaviour by means of the words and actions attributed to the characters in the poem. The relevance of this cannot be grasped without realizing that for Aristotle poetry is inherently mimetic: and, moreover, the sole art 'which imitates by language alone'. So in poetry we see, as it were, language reduced to its functional essence.

Epic poetry and Tragedy, as also Comedy, Dithyrambic poetry, and most flute-playing and lyre-playing, are all, viewed as a whole, modes of imitation. But at the same time they differ from one another in three ways, either by a difference of kind in their means, or by differences in the objects, or in the manner of their imitations.

Just as form and colour are used as means by some, who (whether by art or constant practice) imitate and portray many things by their aid, and the voice is used by others; so also in the above-mentioned group of arts, the means with them as a whole are rhythm, language, and harmony – used, however, either singly or in certain combinations. A combination of rhythm and harmony alone is the means in flute-playing and lyre-playing, and any other arts there may be of the same description, e.g. imitative piping. Rhythm alone, without harmony, is the means in the dancer's imitations; for even he, by the rhythms of his attitudes, may represent men's characters, as well as what they do and suffer. There is further an art which imitates by language alone, without harmony, in prose or in verse, and if in verse, either in some one or in a plurality of metres. This form of imitation is to this day without a name.

(*Poetics* 1)

Aristotle goes on to deplore the misconception which attaches the term 'poetry' simply to compositions in verse, thus obscuring the more fundamental criterion, which is that of imitation through language.

For Aristotle the primary purpose of speech is to express what is going on in the speaker's mind; but this can also be expressed non-verbally by means of gestures, looks, posture, movements, etc. What, then, is the relation between these alternative modes of expression? From what we are told in the *Poetics*, it appears that speech and action stand in the same relation to 'thought' (*dianoia*), inasmuch as both are modes of externalization. Both make manifest, and there-fore communicable, what is internal and would otherwise remain concealed and uncommunicated. But whereas a person's actions can express hope, fear, pity, acceptance, rejection, etc., as well as various responses to present events and circumstances, it seems that action has no way of expressing a simple statement. This requires recourse to language. If human communication did not require facts to be stated (as distinct from conveying attitudes, emotions and responses), it seems that language would indeed be superfluous. This, one may infer, explains Aristotle's evident preoccupation with language as a means of making statements. (For it is the one thing which language can do, which non-verbal communication cannot.)

Chapter 20 of the *Poetics* distinguishes eight units of *lexis*: they are the letter, the syllable, the conjunction (*sundesmos*), the article (*arthron*), the *onoma*, the *rhēma*, the inflectional form (*ptōsis*), and the *logos*. This chaotic taxonomy has been the despair of com-mentators, who have nevertheless taken it seriously instead of reject-ing it as spurious, as it probably deserves. The definitions and examples given of the eight units are problematic on various counts, and the relevance of the whole analysis to the art or techniques of poetry is quite obscure.

Chapter 21, which attempts to classify words on the basis of composition, usage and gender, is only a little less of a muddle, and is certainly incomplete in the version which has come down to us. It does contain, however, the famous Aristotelian analysis of metaphor, which there are good theoretical reasons (see below) for accepting as genuine.

Metaphor consists in giving the thing a name that belongs to something else; the transference being either from genus to species, or from species to genus, or from species to species, or on grounds of analogy. That from genus to species is exemplified in 'Here stands my ship'; for lying at anchor is the 'standing' of a particular kind of thing.[1] That from species to genus in 'Truly ten thousand good deeds has Ulysses wrought',[2] where 'ten thousand', which is a particular large number, is put in place of the generic 'a large number'. That from species to species in 'Drawing the life with the bronze', and in 'severing with the enduring bronze'; where the poet uses 'draw' in the sense of 'sever' and 'sever' in that of 'draw', both words meaning to 'take away' something.[3] That from analogy is possible whenever there are four terms so related that the second is to the first as the fourth to the third; for one may then metaphorically substitute the fourth for the second or the second for the fourth. Now and then, too, they qualify the metaphor by adding on to it that to which the word it supplants is relative. Thus a cup is in relation to Dionysius what a shield is to Ares.[4] The cup accordingly will be metaphorically described as the 'shield of Dionysius', and the shield as the 'cup of Ares'. Or to take another instance: As old age is to life, so is evening to day. One will accordingly describe evening as the 'old age of the day' – or by the Empedoclean equivalent;[5] and old age as the 'evening' or 'sunset of life'. It may be that some of the terms thus related have no special name of their own, but for all that they will be metaphorically described in just the same way. Thus to cast forth seed-corn is called 'sowing'; but to cast forth its flame, as said of the sun, has no special name. This nameless act, however, stands in just the same relation to its object, sunlight, as sowing to the seed-corn. Hence the expression in the poet, 'sowing around a god-created flame'.[6]

1. This metaphor occurs twice in Homer's *Odyssey*.
2. The quotation is from the *Iliad* 2.272.
3. The example, which is somewhat obscure as quoted, probably comes from Empedocles.
4. Dionysius, the god of wine, was usually represented as bearing a cup, and Ares, the god of war, as bearing a shield.
5. The quotation from Empedocles is lost.
6. The poet quoted is unknown.

There is also another form of qualified metaphor. Having given the thing the alien name, one may by a negative addition deny of it one of the attributes naturally associated with its new name. An instance of this would be to call the shield not 'the cup of Ares', as in the former case, but a 'cup that holds no wine'.

(*Poetics* 21)

This passage repays attention for a number of reasons, not least being that it is probably the first attested instance of an original piece of empirical linguistic analysis, produced in response to a need for theoretical consistency. Aristotle does not appear to be drawing on any earlier account of metaphor. The examples he quotes all come from poetry he knew. In short, he has tried to explain the fact, observable in the evidence of poetic usage, that in certain cases we find words perfectly comprehensible *even when they are not used in their conventional meanings*. As a conventionalist Aristotle was bound to see this as potential counterevidence to his view of language; and therefore he endeavours to explain it away by constructing a theory of semantic transference. In effect, he claims that meanings can be transferred from one word to another without establishing a special convention, *provided that* certain regular patterns of relationship hold between the words in question. He manages to do this by reducing all metaphors to dependence either on the relationship between species and genus, or on the relationship of proportionality. Whether this reduction is successful need not concern us here: the subsequent history of controversy over metaphor right down to the present day suggests at least that Aristotle's reduction is open to question. More relevant to our present purposes is to consider whether Aristotle's theory, even if it succeeds in covering all attested types of metaphor, does not conflict nevertheless with his basic conventionalist account of meaning.

This takes us back again to the theory outlined at the beginning of *De Interpretatione*, where Aristotle has taken a position which differs from Plato's in two respects. First, he has jettisoned Platonic eternal 'forms' as the ultimate sources of knowledge and meaning, and assumed that it is the immediate 'real world', as perceived by our senses, which supplies examples of the things we talk about. But he holds that the relationship between words and the real world is only indirect: it is mediated through the human mind. Second, although agreeing with Plato that the mind stores 'likenesses' of the things we perceive, he does not agree that there is any mimetic relation between these likenesses and the words which stand for them. This latter relationship is purely conventional. Thus he maintains (i) that the world is the same for all its inhabitants, (ii) that the 'mental representation' of the world is the same for all its inhabitants, but (iii) that language is not the same for all *because* it is conventional, and different communities have different conventions.

This entails that people will understand one another's speech if, and only if, they base their speech on the same conventions. For since everybody's perception of the world is the same, it is only a difference in verbal conventions that can prevent universal communication. There is no other barrier or source of difficulty. So for Aristotle it is the conventional nature of language which simultaneously explains both why we understand people who speak our own language and also why we cannot understand people who speak a foreign language, even though they are speaking meaningfully and correctly. It is clear that Aristotle presupposes that communication is telemental; in short, that words 'transfer' thoughts from one person's mind to another person's mind because – and in so far as – the words are associated with the same thoughts in both minds. And that, precisely, is the role of convention; to establish in a person's mind the connections between words and thoughts. Words, *De Interpretatione* tells us, are signs or symbols of the 'affections of the soul' (i.e. what is stored in the mind); whereas the 'affections of the soul' are *not* signs or symbols of things in the real world, but *copies* of them (although *natural* copies and therefore identical for the whole human race). So the chain which connects words to the world is one which Aristotle divides into two sections. There is a section of natural, universal processes (linking the world via our sense perceptions to our mental representations of the world); and there is a section of conventional non-universal processes linking mental representations to language.

Metaphor is a phenomenon which threatens this picture, for the following reason. The poet does not need to give us any prior warning of intention to use a term metaphorically. Nevertheless, when he refers to the 'shield of Dionysius' we understand that the object in question is a cup. Unvarnished conventionalism is at a loss to explain this, for there is no convention which links the word *shield* with cups. So a strict conventionalist, it seems, would be forced into a position of claiming that *by* referring to Dionysius' cup as a 'shield' a convention is *eo ipso* established which gives the word *shield* a new meaning. But this is a quite implausible account of the matter, and self-defeating for conventionalism into the bargain. For it would then seem that any new use of a word is automatically sanctioned as 'conventional'.

Aristotle tries to avoid this by maintaining that the transference of meaning is only possible if certain conceptual relations hold between the items involved in the transfer.[7] But even this concession undermines the conventionalist position, and does so on at least two counts. First, the conceptual relations appealed to for the validation of metaphor are not themselves conventional; that is to say, no one has established a general linguistic convention by which the meaning of a species term may be transferred to a corresponding genus, etc. So the mechanism involved must be a 'natural', non-conventional mechanism of some kind. Second, if the transfers of meaning involve such broad and pervasive relationships as species to genus, it is difficult to see that conventionalism offers any persuasive account of how we understand one another. In other words, if the word *horse* may stand not only for a horse, but for any one of an indefinite number of other things which may stand in a metaphorical relation to horses, or to some particular horse, this is tantamount to declaring that the term *horse* has not only its conventional meaning, but many other non-conventional meanings as well; and how hearers decide which meaning to choose from this potential plethora of meanings becomes a problem. Aristotle gives no explanation of how we ever know whether a word is being used with a transferred meaning or not.

These problems did not, in the end, bother Aristotle's pupils and followers. But that was because, like Aristotle, they failed to see to what extent metaphor is simply one example of a more general phenomenon in language. This more general phenomenon, of which conventionalism fails to give a satisfactory explanation, is analogy.

7. Although Aristotle himself does not describe it as 'semantic transfer', this is the effect produced, as is clearly shown by examples such as *leg of the table* and *foot of the mountain*, where a metaphor has become established in common usage as a customary designation.

Chapter three

The Bible on the origin and diversification of language

And out of the ground the Lord God formed every beast of the field, and every fowl of the air; and brought them unto Adam to see what he would call them: and whatsoever Adam called every living creature, that was the name thereof. And Adam gave names to all cattle, and to the fowl of the air, and to every beast of the field ...

Genesis II, 19–20

The definitive study of the influence of the Bible on Western linguistics has yet to be written, and it would be a brave scholar who attempted to write it. But there is no doubt that the Biblical pronouncements on the subject of language for many centuries limited the kinds of questions – and the kinds of answers – which were regarded as legitimate. The most often quoted reference to the origin of language in the Western tradition is the story in Book II of Genesis about how the animals got their names.

It is interesting to compare this account with that given in Plato's *Cratylus*, where Socrates speaks of a mythical 'name-giver' inventing the first names. Many cultures have myths about the origin of language, which are of interest because they reveal deeply entrenched assumptions concerning the human faculty of speech. The Bible story is no exception.

The first point to note is the assumption in Genesis, as in *Cratylus*, that the first names were created. This is by no means a belief universally held. In the Indian linguistic tradition one of the topics debated by the Sanskrit grammarians was this very question: are words created or not? But it is a question which never arises in early

Greek or Hebraic discussions. The presupposition is always that language is the product of a creative act of some kind, and that words have no independent existence as natural objects. Inquiry then immediately focuses on the questions of by whom, or how, or why, the first words were made. This leaves no room for discussion of whether that initial question about the origin of language is correctly posed.

The answer which Genesis gives to the question of the origin of language is in certain respects a more straightforward answer than we get from Plato. Whether the Greek 'name-giver' was a wise man or a divinity is not altogether clear; but the Bible account leaves us in no doubt that language is of human origin and began with the first man, Adam. In the Bible there is no problem of the kind discussed in Plato's dialogue: that is, there is no question as to whether Adam named the animals 'correctly'. On the contrary, what the Bible tells us seems to imply that, far from every animal having, by nature, a right name of its own, it had no name at all until Adam, at God's instigation, gave it one. According to the writer of Genesis, God never refused to accept what Adam called any of the animals, or rebuked him for misnaming them, or considered some of Adam's names better than others. This was apparently not a quiz which God devised in order to see whether Adam could get the names right. On the contrary, 'whatsoever Adam called every living creature, that was the name thereof'. The names are created by a human decision that this is how something shall be called.

This may initially sound like support for the position maintained by Hermogenes, who holds that 'whatever name you give to a thing is its right name'. However, this would be to read back into the Bible story a controversy which is not there. The point of Cratylus' argument in Plato's dialogue is that there are natural connections between words and things which transcend particular languages. Whereas in the context of the Biblical account there are no particular languages to be transcended. We are present at the birth of language itself, when hitherto nameless animals are first given names. The possibility of the same creature having different names in different languages does not yet arise. That belongs to a later phase of linguistic history, which is dealt with subsequently in the Bible by the story of Babel.

What Genesis does not tell us, unfortunately, is the information which might have settled the debate between Cratylus and Hermogenes: namely what principle of nomenclature Adam adopted in naming the animals. Did Adam just call the animals whatever first came into his head? If so, that could be argued to support Hermogenes. Or did he somehow attempt systematically to choose an appropriate name for each animal? If so, that could be argued to support Cratylus. But the Biblical account gives us no information about this. That did not stop later scholars from speculating about exactly how Adam did name the animals.

According to Leibniz (1646–1716), Adam must have named the animals on the basis of a natural analogy between the sound of each name and the mental impression prompted by his perception of the animal in question (Aarsleff 1982: 91). This is a somewhat different theory of natural appropriateness from the one put forward by Socrates in Plato's *Cratylus*. Locke (1632–1704), on the other hand, assumed that Adam was free to impose names entirely arbitrarily, in the manner claimed by Hermogenes. Locke imaginatively improves upon the story in Genesis, and depicts scenes in which Adam coins various new words. Two of these are words for abstract ideas: 'jealousy' (*kinneah*) and 'adultery' (*niouph*). Locke contrasts these cases with what happens when Adam is called upon to name a piece of metal brought to him by one of his children.

One of Adam's children, roving in the mountains, lights on a glittering substance which pleases his eye. Home he carries it to Adam, who, upon consideration of it, finds it to be hard, to have a bright yellow colour, and an exceeding great weight. These perhaps, at first, are all the qualities he takes notice of in it; and abstracting this complex idea, consisting of a substance having that peculiar bright yellowness, and a weight very great in proportion to its bulk, he gives the name *zahab*, to denominate and mark all substances that have these sensible qualities in them. It is evident now, that, in this case, Adam acts quite differently from what he did before, in forming those ideas of mixed modes to which he gave the names *kinneah* and *niouph*. For there he put ideas together only by his own imagination, not taken from the existence of anything; and to them he gave names to denominate all things that should happen to agree to those his abstract ideas, without considering whether any such thing did exist or not; the standard there was of his own making. But in the forming his idea of this new substance, he takes the quite contrary course; here he has a standard made by nature; and therefore, being able to represent that to himself, by the idea he has of it, even when it is absent, he puts in no simple idea into his complex one, but what he has the perception of from the thing itself. He takes care that his idea be conformable to this archetype, and intends the name should stand for an idea so conformable.

(Locke 1706: III, Chapter 6, Section 46)

Locke's theory of ideas will be discussed in a later chapter. What may be noted here is Locke's assumption that Adam did not have any special knowledge to guide him in giving names, but relied simply on his human sense perceptions (in the case of concrete objects) or on his own ideas (in the case of abstractions). Unlike Locke, however, many people assumed that since the Bible narrative places the naming of the animals before Adam's fall, these original names must have been the 'true' names of the creatures in question. In the 17th and 18th centuries, the notion that a rediscovery of the first language spoken by Adam would reveal long-lost truths about the world of nature was widespread.

Between Adam and Plato's 'name-giver' there are at least two parallels worth pondering. First of all, both inventors treat their task as deciding on names for things that are already present in the world. What is to be named is antecedently given. God brings to Adam the animals He has previously created, but which are so far nameless. Plato's 'name-giver' is imagined as choosing names which are articulatorily appropriate to 'imitate' various natural objects and processes he is already acquainted with. There is no case in which either of them invents a name for something which does not as yet exist. The act of naming does not create anything *other than* the name: it leaves the world exactly as it was before names were invented. In this conception of naming there are two closely related ideas which it is nevertheless important to distinguish: (i)*priority* of the thing named: things can exist without names, but not vice versa, (ii) *independence* of name and thing: names do not alter anything, because reality is already complete without them.

These two ideas are an important source of support for the linguistic doctrine sometimes called *nomenclaturism*, or, in its more general form, *surrogationalism*. This doctrine is based on the assumption that the words we use are vocal surrogates (that is to say, substitutes) for meanings: the meaning is what the word 'stands for'. Hence words are superfluous if other ways of conveying meanings are available. For example, a traveller abroad does not need to learn the foreign names for fruit and vegetables if it is possible, when shopping in the market, simply to point to the fruits and vegetables required. The name is merely a substitute for a direct indication of the thing itself. Hence there would be no need for language at all if human beings could always point to what they wanted, or could convey thoughts telepathically from one person's mind to another's.

This surrogationalist view of language, which is merely latent in the Biblical account of Adam's activities as the first nomenclator, we find overtly expressed in the Aristotelian definition of words as 'symbols or signs' of our mental impressions of the external world (see Chapter 2). Surrogationalism is also implicit in early Western explanations of how a child learns its native language. Perhaps the most famous of these is the account given in the fourth century AD by St Augustine. According to Augustine, the significance of words first dawned upon him as a child in the following way.

> When they (my elders) named some object, and accordingly moved towards something, I saw this and I grasped that the thing was called by the sound they uttered when they meant to point it out. Their intention was shewn by their bodily movements, as it were the natural language of all peoples: the expression of the face, the play of the eyes, the movement of other parts of the body, and the tone of voice which expresses our state of mind in seeking, having, rejecting or avoiding something. Thus, as I heard words repeatedly used in their proper places in various sentences, I gradually learnt to understand what objects they signified; and after I had trained my mouth to form these signs, I used them to express my own desires.
>
> (*Confessions* I.8.)

Augustine's retrospective narrative of this experience clearly owes a great deal both to the Bible and to Aristotle. What he says would scarcely make sense without the basic assumption that the primary function of words is to stand for objects in the external world, which we perceive by means of our senses of sight, touch, etc. Already Augustine is not only writing within the surrogationalist tradition but also extending it. For, as Wittgenstein later pointed out (Wittgenstein 1953:1), Augustine does not appear to recognize any difference between various kinds of word. The Augustinian picture does not take into account the fact that many words we use have no corresponding things we can point to as the objects they 'stand for'. Nor does Genesis explain the origin of any words other than the names of the various species of animals and birds. Between the use of such names and the use of sentences there is an explanatory gap which both the Bible's account and Augustine's fail to fill.

The longevity of the surrogationalist account of language-learning in the Western tradition is remarkable. It is interesting to compare St Augustine's version with that given in 1927 by Bertrand Russell. Russell writes:

> If you always say 'bottle' when you give a child his bottle, he presently reacts to the word 'bottle', within limits as he formerly reacts to the bottle . . . When the association has been established, parents say that the child 'understands' the word 'bottle', or knows what the word 'means'. Of course the word does not have *all* the effects that the actual bottle has. It does not exert gravitation, it does not nourish, it cannot bump on to the child's head. The effects which are shared by the word and the thing are those which depend on the law of association or 'conditioned reflexes' or 'learned reactions'.
>
> (Russell 1927: 51–2)

This account is based upon exactly the same Biblical premiss as Augustine's; namely, that the key to language-learning is to grasp that things have names. The main difference between Augustine and Russell is that Augustine represents the child as working this out by a process of inference, whereas Russell opts for a behaviourist explanation of how the word comes to be a vocal surrogate for the object.

A second parallel between Adam and Plato's 'name-giver' hinges on the question 'What are names for?' In neither myth are names created because of a prior communicational need for them. When Adam names the animals he is the only human being alive. Eve has not yet been made from Adam's rib, and Adam does not know that he will soon have a partner. Similarly, when Socrates discusses the activities of the 'name-giver', there is no suggestion that he has to devise names that will be readily understood by his peers, or take any considerations of social utility into account. The result in both cases is that the invention of names is presented as something which takes place independently of any social context, and prior to any consideration of what needs to be named, or of how, once invented, names are to be used. Thus language and language-use are treated as quite separate questions from the very beginning. Questions of language-use can only arise once words are already available for human beings to employ.

This has far-reaching implications on various counts. In the case of Adam, it is clear that God does not feel the need to explain to him what names are, *even though* they serve no immediate purpose for Adam's existence in the Garden of Eden. In other words, Adam's name-giving is conceived of as the spontaneous exercise of a natural faculty, with which he had presumably been endowed at his creation. Something similar must be assumed to hold for Plato's name-giver, since the question never arises as to why the name-giver embarks on the invention of names in the first place, or how he understands what a name is. Given this 'naturalistic' assumption about the human capacity or propensity for naming, it becomes comprehensible that the whole rationale of names should be reduced to a search for the answers to two basic questions: (i) what is it that this name designates? (ii) why does it designate this, rather than something else? (This is precisely the point at which the discussion in Plato's dialogue starts.) A no less important corollary is that language is seen as something which originates in advance of society, and makes social intercourse possible; rather than as something which arises in response to social needs and is to be explained in terms of how it can satisfy these needs.

Finally, both Genesis and Plato offer accounts of the origin of names which, if correct, would lead one to assume that in the beginning there was only one language, which was the same for all people. Yet clearly both Jews and Greeks were well aware of the actual diversity of human languages and their mutual incomprehensibility. Consequently, in both traditions of thinking about language, there arises a need to explain this discrepancy by introducing a theory which will account for how an originally monoglot society became polyglot. This is the explanatory task specifically addressed in the Bible by the story of the Tower of Babel.

And the whole earth was of one language and one speech. And it came to pass, as they journeyed from the east, that they found a plain in the land of Shinar; and they dwelt there. And they said to one another, 'Go to, let us make brick, and burn them thoroughly.' And they had brick for stone, and slime had they for mortar. And they said, 'Go to, let us build us a city and a tower, whose top may reach unto heaven; and let us make a name, lest we be scattered abroad upon the face of the whole earth.'

And the Lord came down to see the city and the tower, which the children of men builded. And the Lord said, 'Behold, the people is one, and they have all one language; and this they begin to do: and now nothing will be restrained from them, which they have imagined to do. Go to, let us go down, and there confound their language, that they may not understand one another's speech.' So the Lord scattered them abroad from thence upon the face of all the earth: and they left off to build the city. Therefore is the name of it called Babel; because the Lord did there confound the language of all the earth: and from thence did the Lord scatter them abroad upon the face of all the earth.

(Genesis II, 1–9)

On the face of it, this sounds like a story invented to explain why a certain place was called 'Babel'. The legends of every continent in the world abound in such stories, and the question 'Why is this called such-and-such?' must be a very primitive one in human linguistic consciousness. In this instance, the etymological explanation rests upon the Hebrew verb *bālal* 'to confound', from which the name *Babel* is supposedly derived. More sophisticated Biblical commentators, however, have seen this, like the story of Adam naming the animals, as an aetiological myth: indeed, according to some, it represents a fusion of two originally separate aetiological myths, one a diaspora myth and the other a language myth, which have somehow got jumbled up. Whether or not this is the correct explanation, what the commentators have failed to see is that if the Tower of Babel is an aetiological myth, it is an extremely subtle one; because it uses the one name *Babel*, meaning 'confusion', as a pretext for presenting a general account of the confusion or diversity of names. Now either there was in fact a place called *Babel*, of which the name was traditionally explained in this way; or else the whole story is a fabrication. Either way, the aetiological mythmaker had a sense of humour. Explaining the origin of just one name becomes a peg on which to hang an account which tells us, in effect, that there is no explanation for the various names things have other than God's intention to cause confusion.

What the Biblical commentators have been slow to grasp is the connection between the Tower of Babel and Adam's naming of the animals. This connection, once grasped, transforms the two stories into a single riddle or conundrum, of the kind which more than once in the history of civilization marks an intermediate step in the sophistication of linguistic consciousness. An apparently legitimate question about language is answered by showing, in effect, that it is unanswerable. In Genesis, the conundrum is presented in the following form. Question: why are, say, sparrows called *sparrows*? Answer: because that was what Adam called them. ('Adam' here being the personification of our ancestors.) Second question: but why then don't other nations, who are also descended from Adam, also call sparrows *sparrows*? Answer: because if everybody called sparrows *sparrows* we should all be able to understand one another. The conundrum hinges on the paradox that, on the face of it, understanding one another ought to be the prime reason for calling sparrows *sparrows*: that is, communication is the prime reason human beings *think* they have for using words. But the words they use, being different from one language to the next, effectively constitute a hindrance to communication. The lesson of Genesis, in short, is that our limited human vision leads us to think that there must be an answer to questions like 'Why are sparrows called *sparrows*?' because we are under the illusion that it is human beings who decide what sparrows are called. But in fact there is no answer other than that God decided not to allow all human beings to call sparrows by the same name. The use of the word *sparrow* is simply one facet of that divinely ordained diversity. So the human being's question is wrongly posed. There is no reason – in human terms – why words are as they are. Language is something we think we create (if not individually, at least collectively): but in reality it is a gift from God, which we do not understand because, precisely, it was God's intention that we should not have control over it.

The Tower of Babel, seen in this light, is the allegorical explanation of why God did not want our ancestors to understand one another. It would put human beings in control of what the Greeks called *logos*: and that, in the Hebraic tradition, was the divine attribute above all others. As a later writer put it: 'In the beginning was the Word, and the Word was with God, and the Word was God' (John I, 1). This is the first and clearest statement of the synthesis of Greek and Hebraic linguistic traditions. It seems, as New Testament scholars have recognized, that the Gospel of St John must have come from a part of the world where Jewish and Hellenic culture interpenetrated (most probably Asia Minor about 100 AD). St John expresses the Hebraic mystical view of the origin of language, somewhat outlandishly, in the only available Greek terms (themselves perhaps originally no less mystical, but coming from a quite different line of mysticism).

Thus the Tower of Babel is the Biblical sequel to the story of Adam's naming. In the sequel, God overrides Adam's original decison to establish a one–one correspondence between names and what they stand for. What this means, allegorically, is that it is in man's interests to have one language, a primeval and universal Esperanto; but it is just not God's will that it should be so. Linguistic diversity is consequently seen as a brute fact of life which men are powerless to alter: but this brute fact of life precludes any ultimate answer to why things are named as they are. The divine confusion of tongues means that we can never get back to that Adamic situation in which we might properly raise the question: 'How did our primeval ancestors originally give names to things?'

For centuries the Tower of Babel was regarded by many – as was everything else in the Bible – as historical fact. To doubt the literal truth of the story would have bordered on heresy. It is interesting, for example, to find an Enlightenment grammarian like Beauzée in eighteenth-century France, who does not really believe the Tower of Babel account, forced nevertheless to come to terms with it in case outright rejection of what the Bible says should be too scandalous. The compromise Beauzée reached was an ingenious one. He accepted the historicity of the Tower of Babel, but interpreted God's intervention on that occasion as merely accelerating a process of linguistic diversification which would have taken place anyway in the natural course of events.

The Tower of Babel myth re-emerges in many subtle disguises in Western culture. One of the most significant twentieth-century versions is Wittgenstein's parable of the builders in *Philosophische Untersuchungen* (1953). Wittgenstein's builders have a language consisting of only four words: but so long as they agree on what those four words mean, it suffices them to erect any construction they wish. Wittgenstein does not explicitly say they are building a Tower of Babel; but it is no coincidence that he uses this example to make the point that in language all depends on communicational agreement between the users. That is exactly what the threatened God of Genesis wished to thwart, and did. The confusion of tongues leaves language with its nomenclature function intact, but its communicational function is left dependent on the hazards of history. We communicate if and only if our nomenclatures coincide.

It is a measure of the hold of religion over linguistic inquiry in the

Western tradition that the linguistic scholars of medieval, Renaissance and post-Renaissance Europe seem retrospectively to have conspired in a gross failure to understand the parable spelt out in Genesis. They became absorbed in the problem of determining what language Adam originally spoke; or, failing that, of getting back to the 'earliest' known language of man. Their motivation, as Hans Aarsleff has pointed out, was undoubtedly the Biblically-inspired theory that a return to primitive linguistic origins would cast light on many modern mysteries of the mind and of Nature. Nor can anyone suppose that this motivation did not survive in a more secular form into the nineteenth century, the heyday of historical linguistics, and the quest for a lost historical Atlantis called 'primitive Indo-European'. The historical reconstruction of languages, as the nineteenth century pursued it, is perhaps best understood as a serious pursuit of the Adamic myth minus Adam.

MECHANICS' INSTITUTE LIBRARY
57 Post Street
San Francisco, CA 94104
(415) 421-1750

Varro on linguistic regularity

But those who give us advice in the matter of speaking, some saying to follow usage and others saying to follow theory, are not so much at variance, because usage and regularity are more closely connected with each other than those advisers think.

For Regularity is sprung from a certain usage in speech, and from this usage likewise is sprung Anomaly. Therefore, since usage consists of unlike and like words and their derivative forms, neither Anomaly nor Regularity is to be cast aside, unless man is not of soul because he is of body and of soul.

But that what I am about to say may be more easily grasped, first there must be a clear distinction of three sets of relations; for most things are said indiscriminately in two ways, and of them some ought to be referred to one principle and others to other principles. First, the distinction of the relations of nature and use; for these are two factors which are diverse in the goals toward which they direct themselves, because it is one thing to say that Regularities exist in words, and another thing to say that we ought to follow the Regularities. Second, the distinction of the relations of extension and limitation, whether the use of the Regularities should be said to be proper in all words, or only in a majority of them. Third, the distinction in the relations of the speaking persons, how the majority of persons ought to observe the Regularities.

For some words and forms are the usage of the people as a whole, others belong to individual persons; and of these, the words of the orator and those of the poet are not the same, because their rights and limitations are not the same. Therefore the people as a whole ought in all words to use Regularity, and if it has a wrong practice, it ought to correct itself; whereas the orator ought not to use Regularity in all words, because he cannot do so without giving offence, and on the other hand the poet can with impunity leap across all the bounds.

For the people has power over itself, but the individuals are in its power; therefore as each one ought to correct his own usage if it is bad, so should the people correct its usage. I am not the master – so to speak – of the people's usage, but it is of mine. As a helmsman ought to obey reason, and each one in the ship ought to obey the helmsman, so the people ought to obey reason, and we individuals ought to obey the people. Therefore, if you will take notice of each principle on which I shall base my argument in the matter of speaking, you will appreciate whether Regularity is said merely to exist, or it is said that we ought to follow it; and likewise you will appreciate that if the practice of speech ought to be reduced to Regularity, then this is meant for the people in a different sense from that in which it is meant for individuals, and that that which is taken from the entire body of speakers is not necessarily meant in the same form for him who is only an individual in the people.

(De Lingua Latina IX, 2–6)*

This passage is the earliest example in the history of European linguistic thought where an attempt is made to reconcile two apparently contradictory facts about language: liberty of the individual versus uniformity of collective usage. It is the same opposition which, two thousand years later, will emerge as the basis for Saussure's distinction between *parole* and *langue* (Chapter 14), although Varro's solution of the problem is by no means the same as Saussure's. Varro here acknowledges, as Hermogenes had claimed in Plato's *Cratylus*, that as individuals we are absolutely free to use any words we choose; but, he argues, it would be foolish for us to exercise this freedom indiscriminately. A poet may take liberties which an orator cannot afford; for all linguistic freedom is relative to the regimentation of established usage. The norms of established usage, according to Varro, are vested in the collectivity, 'the people'; and 'the people has power over itself'. So ultimately the question is why the people chooses to exercise its power in the way it does; that is, in such a way that language exhibits both Regularity (*analogia*) and Anomaly (*anomalia*). For to Varro the most indisputable and conspicuous general fact about language is that it is only partially and incompletely systematic.

Marcus Terentius Varro (116–27 BC) was one of the great polymaths of antiquity to whom posterity has done less than justice; in the first place by failing to preserve so much of what he bequeathed to it. Apart from being a soldier and politician, actively involved in the great Roman power struggle between Caesar and Pompey, Varro studied and wrote about a wide range of subjects, from agriculture to mathematics. The twenty-five books of his monumental treatise on the Latin language, *De Lingua Latina*, were dedicated to Cicero. Only six of these books have survived, and even in these there are gaps.

Varro's linguistic reputation unfortunately came to be associated, even in antiquity, with the sponsorship of absurd etymologies (see Chapter 1), of which *De Lingua Latina* contains a good number. A typical example is his claim that Latin *pretium* 'price' is derived from *periti* 'experts', because in commercial affairs it takes an expert to determine the right price (*De Lingua Latina* V, 177). Thus Varro came to be the butt of later critics, and on this particular count rightly so; but as a result it tends to be forgotten that Varro was in other respects a highly original linguistic theorist, and the first to treat syntax as an integral part of linguistic structure. No less than six books (regrettably lost) of *De Lingua Latina* were devoted to syntax. This shows on Varro's part linguistic insight of a different order from merely acknowledging the obvious fact that words must be put in order to form phrases and sentences.

Varro's interest in syntax and his interest in etymology are two facets of his more general obsession with the problem of systematicity in language. In this connection it is worth quoting the rarely cited justification of etymology which Varro gives in Book VI:

> Democritus, Epicurus, and likewise others who have pronounced the original elements to be unlimited in number, though they do not tell us whence the elements are, but only of what sort they are, still perform a great service: they show us the things which in the world consist of these elements. Therefore if the etymologist should postulate one thousand original elements of words, about which an interpretation is not asked of him, and show the nature of the rest, about which he does not make the postulation [i.e. that they are original elements], the number of words which he would explain would still be enormous.
>
> (*De Lingua Latina* VI, 39)

This is of interest not only for Varro's explicit assimilation of etymological inquiry to inquiry in the physical sciences, but also because it shows why, for Varro, it does not greatly matter that fifty per cent of his etymologies may be wrong or unprovable. For if only fifty per cent are correct, that still constitutes a massive body of evidence; enough to put beyond reasonable doubt the general proposition that one of the permanent, universal mechanisms of language is to construct words from other words.

* * *

Regularity in language was a topic which had come to the fore since the death of Aristotle, and the reasons for its rise to prominence were twofold. In the first place, language had come to be an important subject for philosophers of the Stoic school. In the third century BC, the Stoic philosophers Chrysippus and, a generation later, Diogenes of Babylon are known to have written treatises on a variety of linguistic questions; but none of these has survived. The Stoic starting point, it appears, was the notion that logic (dialectic) as formalized by Aristotle presupposes the existence of the Greek language. Therefore the study of language was seen as being an essential philosophical preliminary (at the very least) to understanding the system of thought which Aristotelian logic revealed. From this position it is no more than a small step to assuming that regularity in thought patterns (of which the Aristotelian syllogism is the classic example) must or ought to be reflected in regularity of language patterns. If language were fundamentally irregular (i.e. if Anomaly ruled rather than Regularity), how could *logos* ever come to be manifest in rational human discourse?

A second and no less important reason why questions of linguistic regularity had become important was that since the death of Aristotle the Greek system of education had changed. The most far-reaching innovation was the introduction of grammar as a component of the educational syllabus. The earliest surviving definition of grammar is traditionally taken to be that of Dionysius Thrax (Dionysius the Thracian), who taught towards the end of the second century BC, and was regarded as the author of an extant grammatical treatise entitled *Technē grammatikē* ('Art of Grammar').

Grammar is the practical knowledge of the general usage of poets and prose writers. It has six parts: first accurate reading (aloud) with due regard to the prosodies; second, explanation of the literary expressions in the works; third, the provision of notes on phraseology and subject matter; fourth, the discovery of etymologies; fifth, the working out of analogical regularities; sixth, the appreciation of literary compositions, which is the noblest part of grammar.

(*Technē grammatikē* 1)

The fifth of these 'six parts of grammar' is stated in terms which leave no doubt as to the importance of the principle of analogical regularity as far as the grammarian is concerned.

Supposedly, Dionysius was a pupil of the Alexandrian scholar Aristarchus. Egypt had become a major centre of learning under the Ptolemies in the period which followed its conquest by the Greeks. The contact between Hellenic, Egyptian and other civilizations of the Near East produced a flowering of scholarship. This was centred, both practically and symbolically, on the great libraries at Alexandria. (The burning of the books by Saracen invaders subsequently became legendary in European culture as an act of vandalism.) Whether Dionysius actually wrote the text which has survived as the *Technē grammatikē* is now regarded as dubious. It seems more likely in its present form to be a compilation dating from the third century AD or later. Nevertheless, it has become traditional to use the name 'Dionysius Thrax' to refer to its author. Whoever wrote it, the text was well known in antiquity. It attracted comments by other grammarians and was translated into Armenian and Syriac, probably in the fifth century AD. In spite of the obscurity surrounding its origin, it epitomizes a new approach to the study of language and reflects interests far removed from those of the Classical period in Greece.

Whatever the intellectual background of the author of the *Technē grammatikē*, it is immediately obvious from the opening statement quoted above that his linguistic concerns are on a different level altogether from those of Plato and Aristotle. Even at this distance of time, we recognize straight away the accents and the atmosphere of the classroom. Grammar, as Dionysius Thrax presents it, evokes a familiar picture of the hesitant pupil called upon to stand up in class, read from a text, and give the right answers to questions about it asked by the teacher. Grammar, in short, is a specific part of an educational curriculum. It has its own pedagogic methods, and it is a topic for rote learning, not for philosophical discussion.

Grammar, as Dionysius presents it, certainly did not originate with the *Technē grammatikē*. The extant treatise is no more than a brief digest (running only to some 3,000 words) setting out a classification of the Greek vowels, consonants, syllables, accentuation and parts of speech. On the contrary, everything about the *Technē grammatikē* suggests that it merely reflects an already established programme of linguistic study. How then, did this programme come into existence, and what was its purpose?

Classical scholars have proposed a variety of answers to these questions. But the term *grammatikē* itself, quite apart from Dionysius' definition, already tells us a great deal about the origins of the subject. Grammar evidently had to do with literacy, with the ability to read and write: it was concerned with the use of letters (*grammata*). And for the Greeks the letters in question were the letters of the alphabet, a system of writing which had been borrowed and adapted from the Phoenicians some time during the first half of the first millenium BC (Diringer 1968). For hundreds of years after it was introduced into the Hellenic world, writing does not seem to have played a very vital part in Greek life. The poetry of Homer was oral poetry and reflected an essentially oral civilization (Ong 1982). Not until Plato do we begin to see signs in Greece of the transition from an oral to a literate culture (Havelock 1963). Even then the important affairs of public life, in the Assembly and the Law Courts, remained in the hands of those who could command the arts of oral discussion. Writing was originally a mere technology, a useful adjunct to speech, especially for the purpose of keeping records. Hence grammar, as the mastery of *grammata*, began as a merely utilitarian expertise, a status still reflected in the term *technē* which the title of Dionysius' treatise bears. Eventually this situation changed, and writing became much more important to the Greeks for a number of reasons.

If grammar as Dionysius Thrax defines it had already been established prior to 350 BC, there is no doubt that this would be evident from the works of Plato or – even more conspicuously – the encyclopaedic Aristotle. Clearly this was not so. Both Plato and Aristotle were taught to read and write, both were familiar with the poets, and both were led to reflect philosophically upon linguistic questions; but neither shows any acquaintance with the grammatical curriculum which Dionysius describes. In *Cratylus* 432 the expression *grammatikē technē* appears to refer to nothing more sophisticated than knowing how to spell. The inference is that there must have been a significant change in patterns of Greek education during the post-Aristotelian period. Various factors suggest that during the latter part of the fourth century BC Greek culture underwent a 'literacy crisis'. Writing, as the most advanced communications technology of the ancient world, was called upon to serve new and pressing social demands, which the running of the old city-state had never placed upon it.

The crisis was brought about in part by the dramatic expansion of the Greek world in the wake of the conquests of Alexander the Great. By the time Alexander died, Greece had acquired an empire of quite unprecedented size. Empires require administration: administration requires bureaucracy: and bureaucracy is based on keeping and checking records, accounts, reports, surveys and authorizations – all written documents. Thus arose, virtually in the space of a single generation, an unforeseen demand for scribes and clerks who were proficient in reading and writing Greek. Greece suddenly needed a new administrative class which was to constitute an important cog in the wheel of imperial machinery.

At the same time, and for the same reasons, there arose a new demand for teaching the rudiments of Greek to foreigners. This came from the non-Greeks who now found themselves, whether they liked it or not, inhabitants of the recently established Greek provinces overseas. Foremost among these was Egypt, where the invading Greeks came into contact with a civilization which could boast a longer tradition of literacy than any which Greece had to offer.

A third factor was that in Greece itself oral transmission and tutorship was no longer perceived as an effective means of handing on from one generation to the next the accumulated sum of Greek wisdom. (Aristotle was the first Greek philosopher who thought it worthwhile to build up his own private library.) In combination with the geographical dispersion of Greek culture, this worked in favour of promoting writing to a new status in the Greek world. The written text, instead of being merely a convenient substitute for the spoken word, became an authoritative form of expression in its own right. (Again, Aristotle was the first philosopher to benefit – or perhaps to suffer – from this revolution. Works attributed to him, even on the most dubious of evidence, subsequently became canonical in European philosophy for centuries.) Even the Homeric poems, which represented the essence of the Greek tradition of oral culture, came to be transmitted in written form. Manuscripts of Homer became prized possessions, and were studied by, among others, the scholars of Ptolemaic Alexandria. For them the question of linguistic 'correctness' thus arose in quite a different context from that presented in Plato's *Cratylus*. They could observe that there were textual divergences between one manuscript of Homer and another. The question which consequently exercised them was: which version was 'authentic'? This is a type of question which is sooner or later bound to arise in any civilization where important texts are handed down from one generation to another by means of writing. Copyists make mistakes. Editors make alterations and 'improvements'. Soon it becomes difficult to establish which version of an ancient text is 'genuine' and which is 'corrupt'.

All this must be borne in mind as historical background against which to assess the contents of the *Technē grammatikē*. For the very thing that strikes us when we read Dionysius Thrax's definition of grammar is that it presupposes a society in which education is based on the study of written texts. The pupil is not expected, as in a primarily oral culture, to recite by heart passages from the poets or the sayings of wise men, but to read them out; which is quite a different matter. That is why it becomes relevant to know which sounds the letters stand for, how to distinguish between long and short syllables, and so on. These are essentially *readers'* problems; and they determine the schema of topics dealt with in the first sections of the *Technē grammatikē*. When Dionysius discusses the Greek letters he does not go into their graphological constitution and peculiarities, nor their origin and development: he is interested only in how one pronounces them. His whole concept of the *grammata* is reader-oriented.

The name 'Dionysius Thrax' and the *Technē grammatikē* became legendary in the annals of Western grammar. They are still invoked today. A contemporary grammarian, discussing the number of parts of speech conventionally recognized in English grammar, raises the question why there should be just eight, and proposes the following answer: 'Probably because Dionysius Thrax had eight.' The answer is interesting, if only because at the time when the *Technē grammatikē* was written the English language had not yet appeared on the linguistic map of Europe. But if the answer is right, it can only be right because Dionysius' system of eight parts of speech was later incorporated into the most widely used grammar book in the history of European education. This was the Latin grammar of Donatus, written in the fourth century AD. Its fame was such that subsequently

53

in both French and English the word *donet* came to be used not only of grammar books in general but also to designate an elementary treatise on any subject whatsoever.

The grammar of Donatus existed in two versions, known as the *Ars minor* and the *Ars major*. The former dealt simply with the parts of speech, while the latter included also sections on pronunciation, metre and figures of rhetoric. The stark question-and-answer format adopted by Donatus reveals beyond any shadow of doubt its design as a classroom manual. The following extract from the beginning of Donatus' chapter on the part of speech which corresponds to Aristotle's *onoma* is typical.

> What is a noun? A part of speech which signifies with the case a person or a thing specifically or generally. How many attributes has a noun? Six. What? Quality, comparison, gender, number, form, case. In what does the quality of nouns consist? It is twofold, for either it is the name of one and is called proper, or it is the name of many and is called common. How many degrees of comparison are there? Three. What? Positive, as *doctus* ('learned'); comparative, as *doctior* ('more learned'); superlative, as *doctissimus* ('most learned'). What nouns are compared? Only common nouns signifying quality or quantity. What case is the comparative degree used with? The ablative without a preposition; for we say *doctior illo* ('more learned than he'). What case with the superlative? Only the genitive plural: for we say *doctissimus poetarum* ('most learned of poets').

It is evident from this that Donatus' 'noun' (*nomen*) includes also what would nowadays be classified as 'adjectives'. More important for present purposes is the illustration of how syntactic features (as in the examples *doctior illo* and *doctissimus poetarum*) are subsumed as properties of the parts of speech. Donatus still simply does not recognize syntax as a separate level of verbal organization in the way Varro had done four hundred years earlier.

*   *   *

Although Varro's work lies outside the tradition of pedagogic grammar represented by Dionysius and Donatus, Varro's view of Regularity (or Analogy) clearly presupposes that tradition. In other words, for Varro the fact that it is possible for grammarians to formulate rules that work (i.e. are pedagogically sound) already shows that certain principles of regularity are operative in language. These principles are implicit in the phenomenon of 'inflection' (*declinatio* – an all-embracing term which for Varro covers both declensional and conjugational paradigms, and derivational morphology as well). Varro claims that every language has 'inflection'.

> Inflection has been introduced not only into Latin speech, but into the speech of all men, because it is useful and necessary; for if this system had not developed, we could not learn such a great number of words as we have learned – for the possible forms into which they are inflected are numerically unlimited – nor from those which we should have learned would it be clear what relationship existed between them so far as their meanings were concerned. But as it is, we do see, for the reason that that which is the offshoot bears a similarity to the original: when *legi* 'I have gathered' is inflected from *lego* 'I gather', two things are clear at the same time, namely that in some fashion the acts are said to be the same, and yet that their doing did not take place at the same time. But if, for the sake of a word, one of these two related ideas was called *Priamus* and the other *Hecuba*, there would be no indication of the unity of idea which is clear in *lego* and *legi*, and in nominative *Priamus*, dative *Priamo*.
>
> (*De Lingua Latina* VIII, 3)

This is an argument which surfaces time and again in different guises throughout the Western linguistic tradition, and even when it does not surface often underlies the controversies which do. It is perhaps an argument which carries more intuitive weight with speakers of highly inflected languages like Greek and Latin than with speakers of a language like English, which, by Varro's standards, would be relatively 'uninflected', or of Chinese, which would not count as inflected at all. Had Varro been acquainted with such languages he might perhaps have placed less emphasis on 'inflection'. Here we see an example of the extent to which linguistic theorizing may be based on extrapolation from the native language of the theorist. The longevity of Latin and Greek as the dominant models for linguistic theory may be measured by the fact that in the nineteenth century languages like Chinese would still be described as having no grammatical structure. A.W. Schlegel's famous typology of the world's languages rests on precisely this misconception, recognizing just three language types: (1) languages with no grammatical structure,

(2) languages with affixes, and (3) inflected languages. Similarly, theorists like Max Müller saw the emergence of inflected languages as marking progress in the linguistic evolution of mankind. Müller thought Latin and Greek more 'advanced' than languages remaining in the 'germinal' state, where only unmodified 'roots' were used for verbal communication. He writes:

> We must not forget that there are languages which have remained in that germinal state, and in which there is to the present day no *outward* distinction between a root and a word. In Chinese, for instance, *ly* means to plough, a plough, and an ox, i.e. a plougher; *ta* means to be great, greatness, greatly. Whether a word is intended as a noun, or a verb, or a particle, depends chiefly on the position which it occupies in the sentence. In the Polynesian dialects, almost every verb may, without any change of form, be used as a noun or an adjective; whether it is meant for the one or the other must be learned from certain particles, which are called particles of affirmation (kua), and the particles of the agent (ko). In Egyptian, as Bunsen states, there is no formal distinction between noun, verb, adjective, and particle, and a word like *an'h* might mean life, to live, living, lively. What does this show? I think it shows that there was a stage in the growth of language, in which that sharp distinction which we make between the different parts of speech had not yet been fixed, and when even that fundamental distinction between subject and predicate, on which all the parts of speech are based, had not yet been realised in its fulness, and had not yet received a corresponding outward expression.
>
> (*Lectures on the science of language* Vol. II: 89–90)

If Varro had been acquainted with as many languages as Müller, he would in all probability have reached exactly the same conclusion. Regularity in language thus comes to be seen as marking an evolutionary advance over a more 'primitive' linguistic mentality, in which *logos* has not yet imposed a fully rational systematization on the forms of expression.

Varro already sees anomalies as *failures* to impose regularity, and language as having a natural tendency towards systematicity. Hence his pronouncement that 'the people as a whole ought in all words to use Regularity'. At the same time, however, he recognizes that no language can be entirely constructed on principles of Regularity, inasmuch as the basis of 'inflection' itself is the existence of a stock of elements which cannot be explained as products of Regularity. However exhaustive etymological inquiry may be, eventually one must reach a point where no further etymological explanation is possible.

> Therefore the man who has made many apt pronouncements on the origins of words, one should regard with favour, rather than find fault with him who has been unable to make any contribution; especially since the etymologic art says that it is not of all words that the basis can be stated – just as it cannot be stated how and why a medicine is effective for curing; and that if I have no knowledge of the roots of a tree, still I am not prevented from saying that a pear is from a branch, the branch is from a tree, and the tree from roots which I do not see. For this reason, he who shows that *equitatus* 'cavalry' is from *equites* 'cavalrymen', *equites* from *eques* 'cavalryman', *eques* from *equus* 'horse', even though he does not give the source of the word *equus*, still gives several lessons and satisfies an appreciative person.
>
> (*De Lingua Latina* VII, 4)

When we reach the point at which the chain of explanation gives out, there is no alternative but to say that certain names were 'given' or 'imposed' upon things thus designated.

> The origins of words are therefore two in number, and no more: imposition and inflection; the one is as it were the spring, the other the brook. Men have wished that imposed nouns should be as few as possible; that they might be able to learn them more quickly; but derivative nouns they have wished to be as numerous as possible, that all might the more easily say those nouns which they needed to use.
>
> (*De Lingua Latina* VII, 5)

Varro's theory of language thus in the end reaches a compromise between an irreducible nomenclaturism and recognition of a pervasive tendency towards systematicity. If we cannot ultimately explain the word *equus*, but have to rest content with accepting that it is the name given in Latin to the species 'horse', we can nevertheless, given *equus*, explain the existence of many related Latin words. For Varro the predominance of systematicity in language far outweighs the nucleus of unsystematic elements, or 'primitives' (*primigenia*) as he calls them. If, he argues, we suppose that a language has one thousand primitives, then

> from the thousand primitives five million different forms can be made inasmuch as from one word there are five hundred derivational forms and when these are multiplied by ten through union with a prefix five thousand different forms are produced out of one primitive.
>
> (*De Lingua Latina* VI, 38)

It was this rationale which, centuries later, was to inspire the invention of 'international languages' such as Volapük (by J. M. Schleyer in 1880) and Esperanto (by L. Zamenhof in 1887). The simplicity claimed for these languages by their advocates was based on principles which might have come straight from *De Lingua Latina*. If a language is well enough supplied with prefixes and suffixes of constant semantic value, then a relatively small stock of roots will suffice to give as many distinct word-forms and ideas as any linguistic community needs for purposes of communication. Volapük and Esperanto had 17th-century precursors in the systems proposed by Dalgarno (*Ars signorum*, 1661) and Bishop Wilkins (*Essay towards a real character and a philosophical language*, 1668). All these were prompted by the persistence of the notion that a language approaches perfection to the extent that it minimizes reliance on vocabulary and maximizes reliance on morphology. It is perhaps the prolific Volapük verb, with its 550,440 separate but regular forms, which should be regarded as the Western linguistic tradition's ultimate tribute to this Varronian ideal.

Chapter five

Quintilian on linguistic education

My aim ... is the education of the perfect orator. The first essential
for such an one is that he should be a good man, and consequently
we demand of him not merely the possession of exceptional gifts
of speech, but of all the excellences of character as well. For I
will not admit that the principles of upright and honourable living
should, as some have held, be regarded as the peculiar concern
of philosophy. The man who can really play his part as a citizen
and is capable of meeting the demands both of public and private
business, the man who can guide a state by his counsels, give it a
firm basis by his legislation and purge its vices by his decisions
as a judge, is assuredly no other than the orator of our quest.

(Institutio Oratoria I Pr., 9–10)

Perhaps the most remarkable sociolinguistic ideal in the whole
history of Western education is given its clearest and concisest statement in the above passage from the Preface to the *Institutio Oratoria.*
Its author, Marcus Fabius Quintilianus, was the son of a distinguished teacher of rhetoric and became an even more distinguished
one himself. He was born in Spain about 35 AD, but was sent to
Rome to pursue his studies. He eventually became head of a public
school for orators, and was appointed professor of Latin rhetoric
by the Emperor Vespasian. During his teaching career, his pupils
included the younger Pliny and members of the Imperial family.
Although he pleaded in the courts himself, none of the speeches he
made has survived. Among his own teachers had been the philosopher and tragedian Seneca, the famous grammarian Remmius
Palaemon, and the rhetorician Domitius Afer. Such an education

was of the highest quality it was possible to have in the Roman Empire of the first century AD; and it might be surmised that the educational programme described in the *Institutio Oratoria* is simply an idealized projection of the education Quintilian himself had received. If so, that gives the view of rhetoric championed in the *Institutio Oratoria* unique importance as historical evidence.

The greater part of the twelve books of Quintilian's treatise is devoted to a somewhat tedious exposition of rhetorical technicalities, as codified by earlier writers on the subject from Aristotle onwards. More interesting in the present context are the sections of the work in which the author explains his general philosophy of rhetoric, and the 'science of correct expression' on which it is based.

Quintilian rejects the scepticism about rhetoric found in earlier Greek writers. He argues that Plato's attitude towards rhetoric has been misinterpreted.

> Athenaeus styles it the 'art of deceiving', while the majority, content with reading a few passages from the *Gorgias* of Plato, unskilfully excerpted by earlier writers, refrain from studying that dialogue and the remainder of Plato's writings, and thereby fall into serious error. For they believe that in Plato's view rhetoric was not an art, but a certain 'adroitness in the production of delight and gratification', or with reference to another passage the 'shadow of a small part of politics' and the 'fourth department of flattery'.
>
> *(Institutio Oratoria* II, xv, 24)

A careful scrutiny of the *Gorgias*, according to Quintilian, shows that these derogatory remarks are intended to condemn only the way rhetoric happened to be practised in Plato's Greece. There is no condemnation of rhetoric as such, which Plato regarded as 'genuine and honourable' (*veram et honestam*).

Aristotle had situated the art of rhetoric by contrasting it with logic (or dialectic).

> Rhetoric is a counterpart of Dialectic; for both have to do with matters that are in a manner within the cognizance of all men and not confined to any special science. Hence all men in a manner have a share of both; for all, up to a certain point, endeavour to criticize or uphold an argument, to defend themselves or accuse. Now, the majority of people do this either at random or with a

familiarity arising from habit. But since both these ways are possible, it is clear that matters can be reduced to a system, for it is possible to examine the reason why some attain their end by familiarity and others by chance; and such an examination all would at once admit to be the function of an art.

(Rhetoric I, i, 1–2)

This empirically oriented approach led Aristotle to formulate his celebrated definition of rhetoric.

Rhetoric then may be defined as the faculty of discovering the possible means of persuasion in reference to any subject whatsoever. This is the function of no other of the arts, each of which is able to instruct and persuade in its own special subject; thus, medicine deals with health and sickness, geometry with the properties of magnitudes, arithmetic with number, and similarly with all the other arts and sciences. But Rhetoric, so to say, appears to be able to discover the means of persuasion in reference to any given subject. That is why we say that as an art its rules are not applied to any particular definite class of things.

(Rhetoric I, ii, 1)

Thus it is the generality of rhetoric which makes it for Aristotle the 'counterpart of Dialectic'. Its principles apply to all forms of verbal persuasion, just as the principles of logic apply to all forms of reasoning.

Quintilian rejects the Aristotelian view of rhetoric entirely. His grounds for this rejection are philosophical and moral (*Institutio Oratoria* II, xv). Persuasion in itself is not a noble goal. Evil men may persuade more effectively than good men. Lies and deceit would be sanctioned as legitimate rhetorical devices if the Aristotelian view prevailed. Thus the practice of rhetoric could lead to a corrupt educational system, a corrupt society and corrupt leaders. The alternative view of rhetoric which Quintilian champions sees rhetoric as essentially concerned with the practice of virtue through speech. It is the 'science of good speech' (*bene dicendi scientia*), which is not to be confused with the art of clever speaking. Good speech is quite the opposite of verbal trickery, which would be bad speech (that is, an abuse of the human faculty of speech). For Quintilian, it is a fundamental premiss that one must 'restrict the name of orator and the art itself to those who are good' (II, xv, i). The first requirement for Quintilian's ideal orator, therefore, 'is that he should be a good man' (II, xv, 33).

Quintilian deplores the dangerous divide which has opened up, as he sees it, between moral philosophy and public service.

> As soon as speaking became a means of livelihood and the practice of making an evil use of the blessings of eloquence came into vogue, those who had a reputation for eloquence ceased to study moral philosophy, and ethics, thus abandoned by the orators became the prey of weaker intellects. As a consequence certain persons, disdaining the toil of learning to speak well, returned to the task of forming character and establishing rules of life and kept to themselves what is, if we *must* make a division, the better part of philosophy, but presumptuously laid claim to the sole possession of the title of philosopher, a distinction which neither the greatest generals nor the most famous statesmen and administrators have ever dared to claim for themselves. For they preferred the performance to the promise of great deeds.
>
> (I, Pr., 13–14)

A naturally virtuous character, however, is not enough to ensure success in oratory. The expertise of the orator is linguistic expertise, and this expertise cannot be acquired without a careful programme of linguistic studies. The orator must not only be a gifted speaker but a trained speaker. In order to achieve eloquence, one must know exactly what one is doing with language.

> As for the special uses and distinctions of words, they should be a subject of study common to all who give any thought to the meaning of language. But it is surely the orator who will have the greatest mastery of all such departments of knowledge and the greatest power to express it in words. And if ever he had reached perfection, there would be no need to go to the schools of philosophy for the precepts of virtue. ... Let our ideal orator then be such as to have a genuine title to the name of philosopher: it is not sufficient that he should be blameless in point of character (for I cannot agree with those who hold this opinion): he must also be a thorough master of the science and the art of speaking, to an extent that perhaps no orator has yet attained. Still we must none the less follow the ideal, as was done by not a few of the ancients, who, though they refused to admit that the perfect

sage had yet been found, none the less handed down precepts of
wisdom for the use of posterity. Perfect eloquence is assuredly a
reality, which is not beyond the reach of human intellect.

(I, Pr., 16–20)

The lofty idealism which is such a conspicuous feature of the
Institutio Oratoria is no less remarkably combined with meticulous
attention to practical minutiae of the most humdrum kind. That is
why we owe to Quintilian the most detailed account of any pedagogic
programme which has survived from the ancient world. His education for the ideal orator is an education from infancy onwards. Of
particular interest in the present context is the role assigned in this
education to the grammarian: for it throws far more light on what
grammar meant in practical terms by the later first century AD than
all the scholarly definitions of a Dionysius Thrax.

Quintilian lays great stress on the importance of acquiring good
habits of conduct and speech in the very earliest years of one's life.

Above all see that the child's nurse speaks correctly. The ideal,
according to Chrysippus, would be that she should be a
philosopher: failing that he desired that the best should be chosen,
as far as possible. No doubt the most important point is that
they should be of good character: but they should speak correctly
as well. It is the nurse that the child first hears, and her words
that he will first attempt to imitate. And we are by nature most
tenacious of childish impressions, just as the flavour first
absorbed by vessels persists, and the colour imparted by dyes to
the primitive whiteness of wool is indelible. Further it is the worst
impressions that are most durable. For, while what is good readily
deteriorates, you will never turn vice into virtue. Do not therefore
allow the boy to become accustomed even in infancy to a style of
speech which he will subsequently have to unlearn.

(I, i, 4–5)

Roman education in the first century AD was a bilingual education,
and a perennial debating point was whether it was better to begin
by teaching the child Latin or Greek. Quintilian comes down decis-
ively in favour of Greek.

I prefer that a boy should begin with Greek, because Latin, being in general use, will be picked up by him (*perbibet*) whether we will or no; while the fact that Latin learning is derived from Greek is a further reason for his being first instructed in the latter. I do not however desire that this principle should be so superstitiously observed that he should for long speak and learn only Greek, as is done in the majority of cases. Such a course gives rise to many faults of language and accent; the latter tends to acquire a foreign intonation, while the former through force of habit becomes impregnated with Greek idioms, which persist with extreme obstinacy even when we are speaking another tongue. The study of Latin ought therefore to follow at no great distance and in a short time proceed side by side with Greek. The result will be that, as soon as we begin to give equal attention to both languages, neither will prove a hindrance to the other.

(I, i, 12–14)

Quintilian next considers the question of when children should be taught to read. A commonly held opinion was that children should not be taught to read before the age of seven, but Quintilian rejects this view as involving a waste of valuable time when the memory is at its most retentive. Why, he asks, since children are capable of learning moral lessons in their very earliest years, should they not be capable of learning their letters as well (I, i, 17)? However, he disapproves of the method commonly used for teaching children the alphabet.

I am not satisfied with the course (which I note is usually adopted) of teaching small children the names and order of the letters before their shapes. Such a practice makes them slow to recognise the letters, since they do not pay attention to their actual shape, preferring to be guided by what they have already learned by rote. It is for this reason that teachers, when they think they may have sufficiently familiarised their young pupils with the letters written in their usual order, reverse that order or rearrange it in every kind of combination, until they learn to know the letters from their appearance and not from the order in which they occur. It will be best therefore for children to begin by learning their appearance and names just as they do with men. The method, however, to which we have objected in teaching the alphabet, is unobjectionable when applied to syllables. I quite approve on the other hand of a practice which has been devised to stimulate children to learn by giving them ivory letters to play with, as I do of anything else that may be discovered to delight the very young, the sight, handling and naming of which is a pleasure.

As soon as the child has begun to know the shapes of the various letters, it will be no bad thing to have them cut as accurately as possible upon a board, so that the pen may be guided along the grooves. Thus mistakes such as occur with wax tablets will be rendered impossible; for the pen will be confined between the edges of the letters and will be prevented from going astray. Further by increasing the frequency and speed with which they follow these fixed outlines we shall give steadiness to the fingers, and there will be no need to guide the child's hand with our own.

(I, i, 24–7)

This passage is of great interest not only for Quintilian's assessment of the most efficacious teaching techniques but also because it reveals so clearly the extent to which educational thinking by his day was already dominated by the alphabet. Here we see a culture which had definitively established writing as the basis for education even though the ultimate objective is still the cultivation of forensic skills. The result is a view of language in which literacy is no longer just a useful but inessential extension of speech. It is the writing system which provides the child from the very beginning with the primary tools for gaining an analytic grasp of the spoken word. Speech is now understood in terms of writing, rather than writing understood in terms of speech.

The importance of this transition for the history of linguistic thought would be difficult to exaggerate. The result is an atomistic conception of linguistic structure which survives down to the present day. Spoken words are treated as complexes built up out of smaller, indivisible phonetic units, through a series of intermediate molecules called 'syllables'. Sentences are then treated as simple sequences of words. This picture of the architecture of language is not merely presented to the pupil envisaged in the *Institutio Oratoria*, but actually inculcated by the pedagogic programme itself, as is clear from the following passage.

As regards syllables, no short cut is possible: they must all be
learnt, and there is no good in putting off learning the most
difficult; this is the general practice, but the sole result is bad
spelling. Further we must beware of placing a blind confidence in
a child's memory. It is better to repeat syllables and impress them
on the memory and, when he is reading, not to press him to read
continuously or with greater speed, unless indeed the clear and
obvious sequence of letters can suggest itself without its being
necessary for the child to stop to think. The syllables once learnt,
let him begin to construct words with them and sentences with
the words.

(I, i, 30–1)

Thus the sequence of familiarization which Quintilian advocates
proceeds rigidly from the smallest units to the largest: letters,
syllables, words, and finally sentences. Each stage must be mastered
before proceeding to the next. Quintilian is insistent that the objective
in this elementary phase of literacy is merely mechanical proficiency.
For example, he recommends the pedagogic use of tongue-twisters.

It will be worth while, by way of improving the child's
pronunciation and distinctness of utterance, to make him rattle
off a selection of names and lines of studied difficulty: they should
be formed of a number of syllables which go ill together and
should be harsh and rugged in sound: the Greeks call them 'gags'.
This sounds a trifling matter, but its omission will result in
numerous faults of pronunciation, which, unless removed in early
years, will become a perverse and incurable habit and persist
throughout life.

(I, i, 37)

*　　　*　　　*

All this is preliminary to the study of grammar, which should begin,
says Quintilian, as soon as the child has learnt to read and write.
Grammar is taught by a specialist teacher, the grammarian (*grammaticus*). Again there is a question as to whether the study of Latin
grammar should precede the study of Greek grammar; and again
Quintilian pronounces in favour of starting with Greek. But in either
case the syllabus is the same, and Quintilian lays it out in considerable
detail.

Unlike Dionysius Thrax, Quintilian regards grammar as divisible into just two parts: (i) a science of correct expression (*recte loquendi scientia*), and (ii) interpretation of the poets (*poetarum enarratio*). As regards the former, one must note that it is not to be equated with *bene dicendi scientia* (which is Quintilian's definition of rhetoric). Nor, on the other hand, is it to be equated with the skills of writing and reading (*scribendi legendique facultas*), which are necessary tools for the study of grammar. Thus it emerges that for Quintilian rhetoric is the culmination of a three-level hierarchy of learning, which might be represented diagrammatically as below.

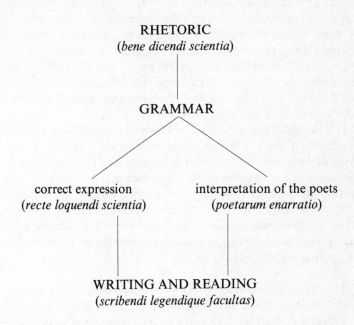

RHETORIC
(*bene dicendi scientia*)

GRAMMAR

correct expression
(*recte loquendi scientia*)

interpretation of the poets
(*poetarum enarratio*)

WRITING AND READING
(*scribendi legendique facultas*)

Quintilian's *grammaticus* is the teacher in charge of the middle tier of this hierarchy. The *rhetor*, or teacher of rhetoric, is in charge of the top tier.

The rationale underlying this hierarchy of language studies is evidently intended to be as follows: pupils cannot be taught rhetoric unless they have already been taught grammar, and they cannot be taught grammar unless they have already been taught to read and write. But as an educational rationale this is, to say the least, curious; for it is by no means obvious why it would not be both possible and fruitful to devise a curriculum in which the teaching of grammar and rhetoric were combined, to the mutual enrichment of both subjects and the advantage of the pupil. Quintilian, however, does not consider this possibility. Nor does he advance any arguments in favour of the separate three-tier system which he advocates. Why not?

The explanation is that by the latter half of the first century AD Graeco-Roman education was already in the hands of professionals, and its structure dominated by interprofessional rivalries. The hierarchical organization which Quintilian adopts for the education of the perfect orator reflects not so much any internal logic of the learning process as the social fact that certain branches of the teaching profession considered themselves superior to others. The rhetoricians ranked above the grammarians, and the grammarians ranked above the elementary teachers. Quintilian, although an idealist, is not an educational reformer. He simply accepts the structure of the teaching profession as it is and builds his educational programme upon it. For he sees that it is no use advocating a radical curriculum which no one will teach in practice.

It is evident from various remarks which Quintilian makes at the beginning of Book II that in his day demarcation disputes between grammarians and rhetoricians were common. In particular, it was not unusual for the *grammaticus* to teach certain forms of declamation. 'Consequently subjects which once formed the first stages of rhetoric have come to form the final stages of a literary education' (II, i, 3). This state of affairs Quintilian regards as unsatisfactory, and he pronounces in favour of a strict separation between the duties of the *grammaticus* and the *rhetor*.

The two professions must each be assigned their proper sphere. *Grammatice*, which we translate as the science of letters (*literatura*), must learn to know its own limits, especially as it has encroached so far beyond the boundaries to which its unpretentious name should restrict it and to which its earlier professors actually confined themselves. Springing from a tiny fountain-head, it has gathered strength from the historians and critics and has swollen to the dimensions of a brimming river, since, not content with the theory of correct expression (*ratio recte loquendi*), no inconsiderable subject, it has usurped the study of practically all the highest departments of knowledge. On the other hand rhetoric, which derives its name from the power of eloquence, must not shirk its peculiar duties nor rejoice to see its burdens shouldered by others. For the neglect of these is little less than a surrender of its birthright. I will of course admit that there may be a few professors of grammar who have acquired sufficient knowledge to be able to teach rhetoric as well; but when they do so, they are performing the duties of the rhetorician, not their own.

(II, i, 4–6)

Quintilian thus emerges as a conservative, who takes an old-fashioned and somewhat restrictive view of the proper province of grammar. What, then, is this province?

The *Institutio Oratoria* maps it out in great detail (I, iv–ix). Here we shall concentrate on what Quintilian has to say about the first of the two divisions, the *recte loquendi scientia*, which is of far greater significance than his remarks about the *poetarum enarratio*. Under the head of *recte loquendi scientia*, the first subject is the correct pronunciation of the letters of the alphabet. The grammarian will explain to his pupils the difference between vowels and consonants, and the division of consonants into semivowels and mutes. He will discuss whether the alphabet is adequate to represent the sounds of the spoken language; whether it contains too many letters or too few. He will point out that the pronunciation of words undergoes change over time, and acquaint his pupils with older spellings which they may encounter in the texts they study. He will teach them what changes in spelling and pronunciation are brought about by the addition of prefixes and by variations of conjugation. Proceeding to morphology, he will explain the various parts of speech, noting the differences between Greek and Latin, as well as the different opinions as to how many parts of speech there are. He will make his pupils decline nouns and conjugate verbs. He will discuss whether the case system is adequate to express all the relational distinctions that are needed in nouns, and will examine problems arising in connection with the use of participles and passives.

Having dealt with pronunciation, orthography, parts of speech, declensions and conjugations, Quintilian proceeds to consider the various kinds of mistake a grammarian must correct. Here he draws a major distinction between barbarisms and solecisms. Although the former term suggests the kind of error a foreigner might make, Quintilian defines it as a fault confined to a single word, as distinct from solecisms, which are faults in word-combination. Both barbarisms and solecisms have four subcategories, since they can be classified as errors of (i) addition, (ii) omission, (iii) transposition, or (iv) substitution. Quintilian gives illustrative examples of all these. The classification is in itself quite unenlightening, being based on a simple comparison of the faulty expression with its correct counterpart, rather than on an analysis of the possible reasons for the commission of the error. Evidently Quintilian's conception of grammar does not extend to a consideration of why speech errors occur. Although it offers a taxonomy of errors, it offers no explanation of them.

Quintilian does, however, offer an interesting and important analysis of the orthological basis for a *recte loquendi scientia*. He identifies four factors which may be taken into account in establishing the grammatical 'correctness' of an expression. The first of these is *ratio* (a term commonly mistranslated in this context as 'reason', but better rendered as 'systematicity'). The systematicity in question may be based either on analogy or on etymology. Etymology, however, gets very short shrift from Quintilian, who ridicules the implausible etymologizing fashionable among Roman scholars.

> But we may pardon anyone after the example set by Varro. For he tried to persuade Cicero, to whom he dedicated his work, that a field was called *ager* because something is done in it (*agitur*), and jackdaws *graculos* because they fly in flocks (*gregatim*)...
>
> (I, vi, 37)

In Quintilian's view, clearly, arguments from etymology cannot claim to establish the correctness or incorrectness of forms unless it is first clear that the etymologies themselves are beyond dispute.

Quintilian also voices serious misgivings about arguments from analogy. He points out that there are cases where different analogical patterns conflict, with the result that a form which appears to be correct in the light of one analogy may equally appear incorrect in the light of another analogy.

> For analogy was not sent down from heaven at the creation of mankind to frame the rules of language, but was discovered after they began to speak and to note the terminations of words used in speech. It is therefore based not on *ratio* but on example, nor

is it a law of expression (*lex loquendi*), but rather a practice which is observed, being in fact the offspring of usage (*consuetudo*).

(I, vi, 16)

In short, arguments from analogy merely express a preference for regularity over irregularity. Systematicity itself cannot be invoked as the justification for such a preference without making the argument circular.

The second factor Quintilian considers is antiquity (*vetustas*). His contention here is that although 'the authority of age' weighs in favour of regarding long established usage as correct, nevertheless it is simply affectation to insist on clinging to usage which is archaic. Language changes over time, and it would be absurd to maintain that only ancient forms are correct; for eventually correct language would become incomprehensible to most of the linguistic community. 'But what a faulty thing is speech, whose prime virtue is clearness, if it requires an interpreter to make its meaning plain!' (I, vi, 41). This is probably the first example in Western linguistic thought of a *reductio ad absurdum* argument based on the inevitability of linguistic change. If linguistic innovations are automatically incorrect, then after a time correct language would be understood by no one.

The third factor is authority (*auctoritas*). Again Quintilian's attitude is one of scepticism. A proper respect for the language of distinguished writers of the past does not mean that we should regard their usage as correct on every point, particularly when it conflicts with more recent linguistic practice.

Finally, there is usage itself (*consuetudo*); and on this Quintilian's remarks must be quoted in full.

Usage remains to be discussed. For it would be almost laughable to prefer the language of the past to that of the present day, and what is ancient speech but ancient usage of speaking? But even here the critical faculty is necessary, and we must make up our minds what we mean by usage. If it be defined merely as the practice of the majority, we shall have a very dangerous rule affecting not merely style but life as well, a far more serious matter. For where is so much good to be found that what is right should please the majority? The practices of depilation, of dressing the hair in tiers, or of drinking to excess at the baths, although they may have thrust their way into society, cannot claim the support of usage, since there is something to blame in all of them

71

(although we have usage on our side when we bathe or have our hair cut or take our meals together). So too in speech we must not accept as a rule of language words and phrases that have become a vicious habit with a number of persons. To say nothing of the language of the uneducated, we are all of us well aware that whole theatres and the entire crowd of spectators will often commit barbarisms in the cries which they utter as one man. I will therefore define usage in speech as the agreed practice of educated men, just as where our way of life is concerned I should define it as the agreed practice of all good men.

(I, vi, 43–5)

A *recte loquendi scientia*, then, must be based on the correctness established by the consensus of the educated (*consensus eruditorum*). The significance of this, it need hardly be stressed, depends on how we identify 'the educated'. In the context of Quintilian's treatise, the answer leaves no room for doubt. The educated are those who have followed the approved educational curriculum, as laid down by educators like Quintilian. The authority for linguistic correctness is thus vested ultimately in the educational system itself. Quintilian's argument sets the seal on a linguistic prescriptivism that was to dominate European culture for two thousand years. The prescriptivism is self-sustaining and pedagogically impeccable. Grammar defines correct usage because it is based on the consensus of the educated; and the educated speak correctly because they have studied grammar.

According to Quintilian, the mere teaching of correct spelling is not the concern of the *grammaticus*, except in so far as orthographic distinctions may mark differences of meaning or of derivation, or inasmuch as acquaintance with archaic spellings may be relevant to understanding the works of writers of past ages. He should, however, draw attention to cases in which orthography does not conform to pronunciation. For an important part of the instruction given by the *grammaticus* will concern the art of reading aloud. The pupil must learn where to pause for breath, how to make breaks in accordance with the sense of what he is reading, when to raise or lower the voice, the modulation which should be given to each phrase, when to increase or diminish the speed of delivery and the energy of delivery. He must be taught to read poetry differently from prose. He must be given a range of reading, beginning with Homer and Virgil, and including tragic verse and lyrics. The passages chosen must be such as to enlarge the mind, develop the intellect, and enrich the vocabulary. After the reading of a passage of poetry, the *grammaticus* will ask the class what parts of speech a verse contains, and how it is divided metrically into feet. He will comment on noteworthy features of language, and on all artifices of style, including tropes and figures of speech. Furthermore, he will explain the allusions contained in the text and the stories with which they are connected, so that the texts read are properly understood. He will school his pupils in paraphrase, beginning with Aesop's fables and proceeding from a simple line-by-line paraphrase to free paraphrase, in which the original text is abridged or even embellished. He will also teach his pupils the art of aphorisms, and how to write simple types of prose composition. All these things, says Quintilian, must be taught by the *grammaticus* before his pupil is ready to be handed on for the next stage of his education to the teacher of rhetoric.

What Quintilian says puts it beyond doubt that what a *grammaticus* of his day concerned himself with was determined primarily by a certain pattern of education for children of a certain social class. The emphasis is on the practical aims to be achieved, although Quintilian does not deny that certain topics are worth pursuing for their own sake. It did not spoil Caesar's eloquence, says Quintilian, to have written a treatise on analogy. Such academic pursuits, he says, do no harm to those who can simply pass through them and go on to other things: only those are worse off who get bogged down in them (*haereo* is the verb he uses: I, vii, 34).

Quintilian's great catalogue of grammatical topics highlights the fact that in the Graeco-Roman world, although grammar may have begun with philosophical speculations about the nature of language, as time went on it became more and more a matter of pedagogic expediency. The concerns of Quintilian's *grammaticus* are not the concerns of Plato and Aristotle or the Stoics. His business was practical classroom efficiency: that, after all, was what he was being paid for. The acid test of his teaching was simply whether or not his pupils acquired certain practical skills; and the practical skills in question were those Quintilian mentions: being able to read aloud correctly from the Classical poets, to parse the lines word by word, and to paraphrase and comment on the text. In brief, the whole of grammar is geared to literacy and to literature. This Quintilian takes simply as axiomatic: 'the art of writing,' he says, when explaining the educational rationale, 'is combined with that of speaking, and correct reading precedes interpretation.' If we want to understand what grammar meant for Quintilian's generation we have to realize that what Quintilian is claiming is nothing less than this: that you cannot speak a language properly without writing. That claim continued to underlie Western attitudes to speech until long after Quintilian's Latin had become a dead language.

Chapter six

Thomas of Erfurt on the modes of signifying

In all science, understanding and knowledge derive from a recognition of its principles . . . ; we therefore, wishing to know the science of grammar, insist that it is necessary to know its principles which are the modes of signifying. But before we enquire into their particular features, we must first set forth some of their general features without which it is not possible to obtain the fullest understanding of them.

Of these, the first and most important is, in what way is a mode of signifying divided and described? The second is, what does the mode of signifying basically originate from? Thirdly, what is the mode of signifying directly derived from? Fourthly, in what way are the mode of signifying, the mode of understanding and the mode of being differentiated? The fifth is, in what way is the mode of signifying subjectively arrived at? The sixth is, what order obtains for the following terms in relation to one another, i.e. sign, word, part of speech and terminus?

(*Grammatica Speculativa*, Preface)

Thomas of Erfurt's *Grammatica Speculativa*, written probably in the first decade of the 14th century, marks the highest achievement of the school of *modistae* (or 'speculative grammarians') which flourished in centres of learning in Northern Europe from the late 13th century onwards. Little is known about its author except that he studied at Paris, taught both there and at Erfurt in Germany, and wrote various commentaries on Aristotle. The Aristotelian inspiration of his work is evident not only from the various references to Aristotle in the

Grammatica Speculativa itself but from Thomas's whole approach to language.

In common with other speculative grammarians, Thomas was less interested in the teaching of grammar than, as he says in his Preface, in 'wishing to know the science of grammar'. By this he means giving a rational analytic account of why language works in the way it does. Although he refers to Donatus, Priscian and other famous grammarians of antiquity, he clearly does not feel that these authorities succeeded in explaining in a coherent, systematic way what grammar is. This is because they failed to see the essential connections between grammatical structure, logical structure and the structure of the world. The term 'speculative' itself indicates how Thomas and his fellow *modistae* view these connections: language is for them a mirror (*speculum*) of the world as reflected in the human mind. As such, it is an integral part of the universal order designed by God.

The basic task of the speculative grammarian, therefore, is to show how, in spite of appearances to the contrary, language systematically reflects reality. This is an essentially surrogationalist enterprise (see Chapter 3). Its point of departure is the Aristotelian concept that our words are sounds standing symbolically for our mental impressions, which in turn are 'images' of a perceived reality in the external world (see Chapter 2). Aristotelian conventionalism, however, does not go nearly as far as the *modistae* would like to go in their explanatory undertaking. On the contrary, to rest content with explaining the relationship between words and what they stand for as merely conventional risks obscuring or even denying the fact that language is all part of the divine plan which the Creator has devised. A strict conventionalist could well argue that the arbitrary nature of the connection between a word and what it stands for shows that language is merely a matter of human agreement, which is therefore subject to all the imperfections and vicissitudes of human affairs. This could lead to the exclusion of language from any serious consideration of God's universal strategy, and hence actually call in question the validity of the sacred text itself (i.e. the Bible).

The *modistae* start from the assumption that the authorities of antiquity failed to discern the evidence for the work of the divine hand in language, and therefore jumped to the conclusion that language was entirely man-made. In showing this to be false, however, the *modistae* had their range of available moves restricted on the one hand by what the Bible says about language (which must, by definition, be true), and on the other hand, by their respect for

Aristotle and ancient learning. Speculative grammar is perhaps best understood as an ingenious medieval compromise between the Biblical and the Graeco-Roman traditions.

That compromise (although Thomas did not acknowledge it as such, and never spells it out as an underlying rationale) attempts to make the best of both worlds. Adam, according to the Bible, was allowed to invent the first words when he named the animals at God's invitation. But God subsequently interfered with human language at Babel, and deliberately confused the accepted correlations between name and thing which had obtained when all the world was 'of one speech'. Translated into Aristotelian terms, that means distinguishing between the communicational functions of speech and its expressive or representational functions. Communication breaks down when there is no agreement as to which words stand for which things: but that disagreement does not necessarily alter in any way the general structure of correlations between words and things. If suddenly *black* means 'white' and *white* means 'black', that will cause communicational confusion for anyone who supposed that *black* meant 'black' and *white* meant 'white'. But all the same, whichever option we choose, there are still the same two colours distinguished and two colour-words to make the distinction. The correlational structure remains the same, even though it is in dispute which word stands for which colour.

Seen from this perspective, it is possible to construe Adam's role in the making of language as follows. Adam was allowed to choose which sequence of sounds should be adopted as the name of any particular species of living creature. But he was not, as nomenclator, allowed to decide which species to recognize as species. That had already been decided in advance by God. So, just as a child may be allowed to colour in an outline already provided in the picture-book, Adam was allowed to fill in the phonetics of a nomenclature whose structure had been predetermined by God. By the same token, God's confusion of tongues at Babel can be interpreted as an intervention which merely scrambled the correlations between words and what they stood for, but did not alter the correlational structure itself. This would have been sufficient to cause communicational chaos over the building of the tower, but at the same time would have left the representational function of language intact. Grammar, for Thomas, is the linguistic level at which those structural properties of language which mirror reality can be analysed.

The *modistae* can therefore agree with Aristotle that meaning is not inherent in the sounds of which a word is composed, and that a sound only becomes a name by becoming a symbol (*De Interpretatione* 16A). For this reason, they exclude phonetics from the province of grammar. 'Sound as such,' says Thomas, 'is not considered by the grammarian.' This would have been a quite unacceptable proposition for the famous grammarians of antiquity. In their view the classification of sounds into vowels and consonants, correct pronunciation, and the representation of sounds by letters of the alphabet were all essential topics for the grammarian. But by the 14th century grammar was no longer simply a propaedeutic to rhetorical and literary studies.

The crucial step which the *modistae* take beyond Aristotle is to claim that in language the role played by sound depends on the possible modes of signifying things (*modi significandi*: hence the term *modistae* for the proponents of this view of grammar). 'Grammar', Thomas tells us 'deals with signs of things' (*Grammatica Speculativa* VI,12). His answers to the six general questions enunciated at the beginning of his treatise run in outline as follows.

There are both active and passive modes of signifying. The active mode of signifying is that by which a given sound signifies the property of the thing it designates; while the passive mode of signifying is that by which the property of the thing is signified by that sound. Thus the sign relationship simultaneously confers significance upon (i) a sound as having a certain meaning, and (ii) a feature of reality as being signified by that sound. This can only occur within the framework of a grammatical system. Outside a grammatical system there is no relation of signifying or being signified: sounds are merely sounds. But within such a system a sound (*vox*) becomes a sign (*signum*). Furthermore, within such a system a sign both signifies (*significare*) and consignifies (*consignificare*). In virtue of the former it has the status of a word (*dictio*), and in virtue of the latter it has the status of a part of speech (*pars orationis*). The consignification of a sign (its classification as a part of speech) determines its combinatorial possibilities. Thus to supply an English illustration, Thomas would hold that the sound we might write with the letters *grod* is not English, even though it is perfectly pronounceable, because it finds no place in English grammar. There is nothing which this sound signifies or which is signified by it. *Trod*, on the other hand, represents a sound which has significance in English (i.e. is an English sign). It both signifies (by designating an action) and consignifies (being a verb, as distinct from a noun).

Grammar is primarily concerned with the active modes of signifying and consignifying. Every active mode of signifying originates ultimately in some property of a thing designated. For the source of our perceptions must lie in the external world. By means of grammar, the mind sets up correlations between a sound on the one hand and some 'property or mode of being of the thing' on the other. It is no objection to this, argues Thomas, that we have words designating non-existent things, or even absences of certain things or properties. A word like *chimaera*, which designates an imaginary beast, gets its significance not from the animal (for there is no such animal) but from the parts (head of a lion, tail of a dragon, etc.) of which we imagine it to be composed, and which do exist. As for words designating negations (for example, *nothing*) although they correspond to no positive entity outside the mind, nevertheless they do correspond to a positive entity conceptualized in the mind itself. For to conceive of the absence of something in the external world is not a negative but a positive mental act.

However, although the external world provides the ultimate origin of the signification of words, it does not provide the immediate source. The active modes of signifying are directly derived from the passive modes of understanding (*modi intelligendi*). This must be so because the active modes of signifying are not derived from the modes of being (*modi essendi*) unless these modes of being have first been taken in by the mind. The schema thus presented is entirely consonant with Aristotle's analysis (see Chapter 2), in which mental representations mediate between our spoken words and the external world.

Thus being, understanding, and signifying, according to Thomas, are all interconnected. The modes of being relate to the thing as it exists in reality on its own account (*absolute*). The modes of understanding relate to the way in which the thing is grasped and represented by the human mind. The modes of signifying relate to the way in which this understanding is systematized within the framework of a grammatical system.

Finally, grammar confers on the sound not only its status as a sign (*signum*), a word (*dictio*) and a part of speech (*pars orationis*) but also its status as a logical term (*terminus*): that is to say, as the subject or predicate of a proposition. In this way, grammar links up with logic and becomes its foundation. For an expression could not function as a component of a proposition unless it were also a grammatical unit, and therefore had a determinate place in a system by means of which the mind expresses its understanding of reality. Without such a system, the processes of rational thought, as captured classically in the Aristotelian syllogism (*All men are mortal. Socrates is a man. Therefore, Socrates is mortal.*) would be impossible. Here the sequence of sounds which are written as *Socrates* constitutes a unit which functions simultaneously as sign, word, noun and lastly, term (being the subject of the propositions *Socrates is a man* and *Socrates is mortal*).

When Thomas comes to elaborating and exemplifying this explanatory framework, however, it becomes very obvious that for the most part he is simply taking over the traditional distinctions of Latin grammar as given by Donatus and Priscian, and redescribing those distinctions in his own modistic terminology.

For instance, he deals with the grammatical distinction between singular and plural as follows.

We shall now discuss number. First of all it must be noted that according to Boethius number in things outside the mind is a multitude of many unities collected together. But unity is of two kinds; one is the undivided entity of the thing, from which the entity is said to be one, i.e. indivisible. From this often repeated unity the multitude is revealed as one out of a very great number... And because multitude of this kind is transformed with the entity, it is called the number of essences, and in terms of the number of essences, the species of things are enumerated.

Material number. The other unity is the unbroken continuity of the thing, by means of which the continuum is said to be one, i.e. indivisible, and by this often repeated unity multitude is revealed, which is called material number, that is, of individuals according to the material differences of the different species. This number is called accidental because individual things are numerated by this number which differ only by accident.

The properties of number. It should be noted that in both kinds of number two properties are found, i.e. the property of indivisibility which is in the thing by virtue of its unity and the property of divisibility which is in the thing by virtue of plurality, and which is revealed by the repetition of the unity; from these properties just stated, number in the noun is derived, which is an accidental mode of signifying.

The definition of number. Number therefore is the mode of signifying the noun by means of accident whereby the noun signifies the property of indivisibility, which is the property of singularity, or the property of divisibility, which is the property of plurality. It is divided into singular and plural. Singular number is the mode of signifying the thing by means of the property of indivisibleness, which is the property of singularity: e.g. *animal* ('animal'), *homo* ('man'). Plural number is the mode of signifying the thing by means of the property of divisibleness which is the property of plurality: e.g. *animalia* ('animals'), *homines* ('men').

In the end Thomas is saying little more here than that the difference between singular nouns and plural nouns expresses the numerical difference between 'one' and 'more than one'. He fails entirely to explain why this 'real world' distinction should find a grammatical expression, whereas equally 'real' numerical distinctions (such as, for example, that between 'three' and 'more than three') do not. Nor does he mention cases which might cause problems for his type of explanation, such as Latin *turba* ('a crowd'). A crowd is not 'essentially' indivisible in the sense in which gold as a single metal is indivisible; but nor is it 'materially' indivisible in the sense in which one man cannot be further divided into several men. A 'real world' crowd may divide into smaller crowds, but the process of subdivision cannot go on to yield further crowds indefinitely. Nevertheless *turba* in Latin behaves grammatically exactly like *animal* and *homo*.

Thomas has a particularly hard time explaining Latin gender. He is forced to concede that masculine gender does not signify the male sex, (since both *vir* ('man') and *lapis* ('stone') are masculine), but claims that it signifies the property of acting upon something; as opposed to the feminine gender, which corresponds to the property of being acted upon. Thus for him the feminine counterparts of *vir* and *lapis* are *mulier* ('woman') and *petra* ('stone') respectively. When he comes to the neuter gender he has to say that this is the mode of signifying which is indeterminate with respect to the distinction between acting or being acted upon. His examples are the nouns *animal* ('animal') and *lignum* ('wood'). The trouble with these explanations, clearly, is that it is difficult to convince oneself that there is any semantic distinction between the words for 'stone' and 'wood' which could plausibly be construed in terms of acting and being acted upon; and that there is no contradiction involved in saying that a man was beaten by his wife, nor any grammatical impropriety in Latin in rendering this proposition with *vir* as the subject of a passive verb.

One of the most interesting examples of Thomas's indebtedness to Aristotle is to be seen in his treatment of syntax, where a four-way distinction between material, formal, efficient and final causes is adapted to the analysis of the sentence, along with the general philosophical distinction between 'substance' and its 'accidents' or 'properties'. For Aristotle the four causes constitute a general explanatory framework. (For instance, a painting may be 'explained' as having certain blobs of paint as its material cause; their arrangement on the canvas as its formal cause; the painter as its efficient cause; and the depiction of some object, scene or person as its final cause.) Thomas adapts this explanatory framework for purposes of syntax as follows.

There are four essential principles of constructing the sentence congruously and completely; i.e. material, formal, efficient and final.

Material. The material principle of constructing comprises constructibles; just as subject is to accident, so constructibles are to construction. The subject is the matter of the accident, for the accident cannot have matter extrinsically but only intrinsically; therefore constructibles are the matter of the construction. In any one construction, there are not several but as few as two constructibles, because, as we shall see, the construction is created from the dependence of one constructible on the other; but a dependence will be one of only two kinds, i.e. dependent or determinant. Therefore, there are only two principal constructibles in any one, i.e. dependent and terminant.

(*Grammatica Speculativa* XLV, 89)

Here Thomas is comparing the elements of a grammatical construction (for example *Fish swim*) to the substance or material of which an object is constituted. (*Fish* and *swim* would be the 'constructibles'.) His argument is that the constructibles are the 'material' basis: for without them there would be no construction. Furthermore, he argues, the basic construction is always binary, one of the two constructibles being dependent on the other. In analysing complex constructions, therefore, we must first reduce them to pairs of constructibles. *Socrates hit Plato*, for instance, cannot be a single construction, but must be a combination of binary constructions.

Formal. The formal principle of the construction is the union of the constructibles; this is the form of the thing by means of which the thing has essence. The construction has essence by means of the union of constructibles, therefore the union of the constructible is the form of the construction.

(*Grammatica Speculativa* XLV, 89)

This amounts to saying that the construction is more than the sum of its individual constructibles. In recognizing *Fish swim* as a construction we recognize that the two constructibles are united in a particular way (which is different, for example, from the union of the constructibles in *Swim fast*).

Efficient (*intrinsic, extrinsic*). The efficient principle of the construction is twofold, i.e. extrinsic and intrinsic. The intrinsic principle consists of the respective modes of signifying by reason of which one constructible is dependent on the other, or is the determinant of the dependence of the other; from these respective modes of signifying two general modes of signifying can be abstracted, i.e. in one constructible the mode of depending, and in the other constructible the mode of terminating the dependence.

These modes of signifying are said to 'effect' the construction, in short, because they prepare and dispose the constructibles for the actual union which is done by the mind . . . These modes of signifying are called the 'intrinsic' principle, because they remain, so to speak, between the constructibles.

(*Grammatica Speculativa* XLV, 89)

Thus, for example, *fish* and *swim* are two constructibles that have the potential for 'effecting' a construction, because one is a verb requiring ('depending' on) a subject, and the other is a noun which can supply the required subject, and thus 'terminate' (i.e. complete) the construction.

However, the extrinsic efficient principle of the mind is that which combines the constructibles arranged and prepared for the act by means of the modes of signifying in the construction as spoken. As for the constructibles, in whatever way they are maximally arranged for union by means of their modes of signifying, no one constructible, however, is at any time joined to another by its own act; this is done by means of the mind, as was stated. It is called the extrinsic principle of the mind because it remains, so to speak, outside the constructibles.

(Grammatica Speculativa XLV, 89)

In other words, although constructibles may have the potential for combining together in a construction (as *fish* and *swim* have), it nevertheless takes a separate mental act to combine them (thus producing *Fish swim*).

> *Final.* The final *(finale)* principle is the expression of a compound concept of the mind, because, as was stated in *V Metaph. Text 21*, the end *(finis)* is the means by which anything is completed. The construction of the parts of speech is made for the purpose of expressing a compound concept of the mind; therefore the expression of a compound concept of the mind is the goal *(finis)* of the construction. Hence, as said the philosopher *I Peri. Cap. 1*, the intrinsic aspects of expression, i.e. the significant expressions in the utterance, which are grammatical sentences, are the marks of movements of the soul, i.e. signs of a concept of the mind or soul. But the sign achieves its goal by virtue of its meaning. Therefore the construction or the sentence in grammar achieves its goal as a result of its expression of a concept of the mind.

(Grammatica Speculativa XLV, 89)

Here Thomas's two explicit references to the works of 'the philosopher' (i.e. Aristotle) underline his philosophical allegiance. The insistence that the ultimate goal ('final cause') of syntactically articulated constructions is the expression of ideas (as distinct from the communication of ideas to others) epitomizes the modistic version of surrogationalism.

What is perhaps the most interesting feature of the modistic approach to grammar is its underlying psychology, particularly in so far as this relates to the status of logic. Human reasoning is seen not as an independent capacity which merely uses language adventitiously for purposes of expression, but as a capacity which cannot be exercised at all without the systematization provided by grammar. For, on the one hand, in order to be a term (i.e. to be a constituent part of a proposition) an expression must first have a status as a sign; while on the other hand, what guarantees the validity of the syllogism requires no appeal other than to our analytic perception of reality. It is the constitution of reality which provides the ultimate backing both for the parts of speech and for our realization that if all men are mortal, and Socrates is a man, then Socrates must be mortal. Both grammar and logic are reflections of the way the universe is constructed, but the former is psychologically prior to the latter.

All Thomas's examples are taken from Latin. He does not consider the possibility that different languages might perhaps have different grammatical structures, or different modes of signifying. For this would mean, in effect, either a rejection of the Aristotelian assumption that the world as comprehended by human understanding is the same for all human observers; or else making an assumption for which there is no Biblical authority (namely, that God endowed different nations with different modes of perception). This theoretical straitjacket leaves him with no other option than to proceed as if one language will serve as a perfect exemplar for all the rest – an assumption that was long to outlive the heyday of modistic grammar, being overtly rejected in the nineteenth century, only to re-emerge in the twentieth.

Chapter seven

Caxton on dialects

And certaynly our langage now vsed varyeth ferre from that whiche was vsed and spoken whan I was borne. For we Englysshe men ben borne vnder the domynacyon of the mone, whiche is neuer stedfaste but euer wauerynge, wexynge one season, and waneth and dyscreaseth another season. And that comyn Englysshe that is spoken in one shyre varyeth from a nother. In so moche that in my dayes happened that certayn marchauntes were in a shippe in Tamyse, for to haue sayled ouer the see into Zelande, and for lacke of wynde thei taryed atte Forlond, and wente to lande for to refreshe them; And one of theym named Sheffelde, a mercer, cam in-to an hows and axed for mete; and specyally he axyd after eggys; And the goode wyf answerde, that she coude not speke no Frenshe. And the marchaunt was angry, for he also coude speke no Frenshe, but wolde haue hadde egges, and she vnderstode hym not. And thenne at laste a nother sayd that he wolde haue eyren: then the good wyf sayd that she vnderstod hym wel. Loo, what sholde a man in thyse dayes now wryte, egges or eyren. Certaynly it is harde to playse eueryman by cause of dyuersite and chaunge of langage.

(William Caxton, 1490)

The linguistic mentality of modern Europe is one in which English, French, German, Spanish, Portuguese, Italian, Dutch, etc. are all recognized as established national languages. Each has its own literature, history and grammar. Each is backed by the authority of an independent state. Each is the official medium of communication for all legal and constitutional purposes within certain political frontiers.

This state of affairs, which Europeans nowadays take for granted, and which leads them to treat languages as national badges of affiliation, came into being only at the Renaissance. Throughout the Middle Ages, linguistic thought in Europe had been moulded by the intellectual predominance of the two great languages of antiquity. Greek, although few could read it and even fewer speak it, was identified with the primary sources of European culture: it was the language of Homer, of Plato, of Aristotle, of Demosthenes. Latin, on the other hand, was the international working language of European education and administration: it was the language of law, of government, of the universities and of the Church. The eventual end of the long reign of Greek and Latin, together with the accompanying rise in status of the local European vernaculars, marked a most important watershed in the history of the Western linguistic tradition.

William Caxton (c.1422–1491), the first English printer, translated and published a number of French works, including the *Eneydos*, from his Prologue to which the above excerpt is taken. The fact that Latin is a moribund language and European culture no longer has a genuine *lingua franca* presents Caxton, as printer and publisher, with an opportunity but at the same time with a difficult linguistic choice.

For any writer of the 15th and 16th centuries, the only viable alternative to writing in Latin was to write in one or other of the current European vernaculars. But half a century after Caxton English writers were still apologizing for writing in English. For example, Roger Ascham, in his treatise on archery (1545), thinks it necessary to explain as follows.

And although to have written this boke either in latin or Greke
... had bene more easier and fit for mi trade in study, yet
neuertheless, I, supposinge it no point of honestie, that mi
commodite should stop and hinder ani parte either of the pleasure
or profit of manie, haue written this Englishe matter in the
Englishe tongue, for Englishe men ...

If any man woulde blame me, eyther for takynge such a matter
in hande, or els for writting it in the Englyshe tongue, this answere
I maye make hym, that whan the beste of the realme thinke it
honest for them to vse, I one of the meanest sorte, ought not to
suppose it vile for me to write. And though to haue written it in
an other tonge, had bene bothe more profitable for my study,
and also more honest for my name, yet I can think my labour wel

bestowed, yf with a little hynderaunce of my profyt and name, maye come any fourtheraunce, to the pleasure or commoditie, of the gentlemen and yeomen of Englande, for whose sake I tooke this matter in hande. And as for ye Latin or Greke tonge, euery thyng is so excellently done in them, that none can do better. In the Englysh tonge contrary, euery thinge in a maner so meanly, both for the matter and handelynge, that no man can do worse.

(*Toxophilus* Dedication)

The question of the 'inferiority' of the vernacular languages was a much laboured Renaissance debating point. But a much more mundane, practical problem was foremost in the mind of the first English printer. What most worried Caxton was the fact that English, unlike Latin, had no recognized common usage. It varied considerably from one part of the country to another, causing practical difficulties of everyday communication, as Caxton's anecdote about the merchant who wanted eggs illustrates. To put this problem in its historical perspective one must remember that when Chaucer, whose works were among those which Caxton printed, wrote *The Canterbury Tales* a hundred years earlier, the language of government in London was still officially French. Henry V, who defeated the French at Agincourt (1415), was the first English king since the Norman Conquest (1066) to use English in his official documents, and Caxton was probably born about the year of Henry's death. So the century in which Caxton set up the first printing press in Westminster (c.1476) was the first century in which the English language in England was no longer in competition with French.

Although Caxton specifically addresses the problem of linguistic variation in English, and offers the quaint explanation that the English are destined to linguistic vacillation because they are born under the sign of the moon, he would have been unobservant not to notice in the course of his long residence on the Continent that 15th-century French was no more uniform than 15th-century English. Every country in Europe was a linguistic patchwork of dialects, and would remain so for many generations after Caxton's death. But Caxton's observation is of historical significance because, for the first time, this is seen as a problem.

The lack of uniformity in English usage posed in fact more than one problem for Caxton. In a country where some people say *egges* but others say *eyren*, and those who say one do not understand those who say the other, it is a problem for any publisher who wishes to sell books to as many people as possible to know which among the conflicting dialects will be most widely understood. But even if that problem is soluble, there is a further question to be faced; namely, how to spell the dialect you have chosen to print, given that there is no accepted assignment of letters of the alphabet to the various competing dialectal pronunciations. These difficulties are further complicated if, as Caxton recognizes, the dialects themselves are caught up in a process of change. In the Prologue to *Eneydos*, Caxton recounts how he discovered for himself the rate at which English was evolving, when he was asked to update some documents for the Abbot of Westminster.

> And also my lorde abbot of Westmynster ded do shewe to me
> late certayn euydences wryton in olde Englysshe for to reduce it
> into our Englysshe now usid. And certaynly it was wreton in such
> wyse that it was more lyke to Dutche than Englysshe; I coude
> not reduce ne brynge it to be vnderstonden.

He then goes on to observe that English had undergone considerable modifications during his own lifetime. Perhaps his awareness of those changes was enhanced by the fact that he had spent much of his earlier career as a merchant and diplomat abroad and was struck by the disparity when he eventually returned to the country of his birth. Finally, it must be borne in mind that the problems relating to English usage which Caxton faced could not be solved by consulting dictionaries or grammars of the English language, because in Caxton's day English, unlike Latin, had no dictionaries or grammars.

The uncertainties of linguistic usage which Caxton found himself wrestling with were in certain respects by no means new. From antiquity onwards, scholars had recognized that vacillations might arise because of linguistic clashes between (i) different *dialects*, (ii) different *orthographies*, and (iii) different *generations*. The dialect problem, the orthographical problem, and the problem of linguistic change arise from conditions which are endemic in every literate society once it reaches a certain size and phase of development. What was novel about Caxton's dilemma (although not unique to Caxton's particular case) was that these old problems were brought into much sharper focus than ever before by the invention of printing. Printing was the technological foundation of the European Renaissance, and the most radical innovation in human communication since the invention of writing. Caxton is a man caught at the crossroads of history in more senses than one. He is trying to introduce and popularize a new technology which is destined to revolutionize the availability of information in civilized society. The political and educational consequences of this new technology will be profound. But this profoundly important initiative is being undertaken in the most linguistically adverse circumstances possible. For what has just broken down is the universal linguistic viability of Latin; and in England there is no comparably stable language to take its place. Printing is a communications technology which demands uniformity: and in Caxton's England, to say nothing of the rest of Europe, there was none.

Printing is the classic case of a technical innovation which necessitates rethinking basic assmptions about society; and in this particular instance about society's linguistic organization. Caxton's historical problem as England's first printer arose from the fact that he was committed to a technology which did not make it possible, as it had been when every readable document was laboriously hand-copied, to make individual alterations to individual copies. Printing means mass replication. It also means replication at great speed (relative to the speed of producing hand-written copies). These two factors – exact mechanical replication and speed of production – combine to afford unprecedented marketing possibilities for the product. They also combine to expand potential readership out of all (previous) recognition. But these possibilities are thwarted if the linguistic condition of society is such that linguistic fragmentation (for whatever reason) is valued above uniformity. One of the paradoxes of the Renaissance is that 'Caxton's problem' would never have arisen if printing had been invented two hundred years earlier. For then Latin would still have reigned unchallenged as the official language of Europe.

In Caxton's remarks we see no indication of a realization that he himself, and the technology he was introducing, were to play a key role in solving the problem of linguistic diversity which he so clearly perceived. By deciding, for better or for worse, to adopt the dialect of London and the South-East as the English for his books, Caxton took a decisive step forward in establishing that particular variety as 'the English language'. In retrospect, Caxton seems to have forged history's answer to his own question.

A rather different, but related problem was that faced by European writers educated to revere the Classics, but politically motivated to claim that their own vernacular was linguistically on a par with any other European language, including the great languages of Greece and Rome. This problem was bound to induce a kind of linguistic and cultural schizophrenia, of which du Bellay's *Deffence et Illustration de la Langue Francoyse* (1549) is a prime example. In the *Deffence*, du Bellay is driven to admit that the French of his day is lacking in the means of expression required to analyse, discuss and articulate all the ideas which civilized society needs. Nevertheless, he maintains that this is not the fault of 'the French language' as such. The French language may yet produce its Homers, Demosthenes, Virgils and Ciceros.

> And if our language be not so copious and rich as the Greek or Latin, that must not be imputed to it as a fault, as if of itself it could never be other than poor or sterile: but rather must one attribute it to the ignorance of our ancestors, who having (as someone says, speaking of the ancient Romans) in higher esteem well-doing than fair speaking, and liking to leave to posterity examples of virtue, rather than precepts, deprived themselves of the glory of their fine deeds, and us of the fruit of the imitation thereof: and by the same means have left our language so poor and bare that it has need of the ornaments and (so to speak) the plumes of other persons. But who would say that Greek and Latin were always in the state of excellence wherein they were seen in the time of Homer and of Demosthenes, of Virgil and of Cicero?
>
> (*Deffence* Chapter III)

Du Bellay's *Deffence* was written barely more than half a century after Caxton's Prologue to *Eneydos*. Its tone is apologetic: but the apologia in retrospect rings false. Du Bellay must have sensed that history was on his side; and on the side of the European vernaculars. There could be no nostalgic going back to a European linguistic mentality dominated by Latin and Greek. The interesting aspect of this linguistic attitude is its insistence that we – the linguistic community – constantly make, amend and improve our language: it is not our linguistic inheritance which determines the limits within which we may think and express ourselves. In this respect du Bellay marks an advance over Caxton. 'Caxton's problem' is still a problem of choice within the limits set by existing alternatives. 'Du Bellay's problem' is quite different: it opens up a linguistic horizon of endless possibilities. Learning from the past does not restrict us to the limitations of the past. To learn is already to transcend the limits of what was learned. The development of a language is not like a natural growth: it is an instrument human beings use, consciously, to advance into the future.

This typically Renaissance view of language as a communicational instrument which human beings are free to alter, adapt and embellish as they see fit marks a definitive rejection of medieval scholastic attitudes to language, and the triumph of conventionalism over naturalism. For it would hardly be possible, by our efforts, deliberately to mould the language of our own country in whatever ways we will, if the linguistic sign were not based on convention and human agreement, as Hermogenes argued in Plato's *Cratylus*. Du Bellay is not concerned, however, with academic arguments of the kind we find paraded in Plato's dialogue. For him, as for many Renaissance men of letters, it is as obvious that a language can be altered and improved by human design as that a nation can rise by its own efforts to heights of supremacy. Du Bellay's *Deffence* is a manifesto of patriotism more than a treatise of linguistic theory: but it is none the less significant for that.

A similar spirit of linguistic patriotism was beginning to emerge in other European countries. In the *Deffence*, in fact, du Bellay is merely copying and adapting to the needs of French a case which had recently been put forward by the Italian writer Speroni in his *Dialogo delle Lingue* (1542). Du Bellay's examples and even his phraseology in the *Deffence* are in many instances taken straight from Speroni. This fact itself highlights another paradoxical aspect of the Renaissance: willingness to learn from other countries, and in particular emulation of antiquity, went hand in hand with a preeminent insistence on establishing the claims of one's own culture as inferior to none.

In the formation of this new national consciousness, the role played by the languages of Europe was perhaps more important than any other, in part because the geography of Europe does not lend itself to setting up obvious administrative or military boundaries, as the Romans had discovered centuries earlier. For the first time it became essential to have a national language in order to secure proper recognition as a nation. A hotchpotch of regional dialects would no longer do. For the first time dictionaries and grammars of the vernacular languages begin to appear alongside dictionaries of Greek and Latin. Moreover these new dictionaries and grammars are not meant for foreigners. The task of the vernacular grammarians and lexicographers is seen as being 'to fix the language'; that is to eliminate vacillations and inconsistencies of the kind which perplexed Caxton, and impose linguistic uniformity. After centuries of linguistic fragmentation, Europe has at last awoken to a new sense of connection between linguistic identity and political identity.

The Port-Royal Grammar: Arnauld and Lancelot on the rational foundations of grammar

Grammar is the art of speaking.

Speaking is explaining one's thoughts by signs which men have invented for this purpose. [...]

Thus one can consider two things in regard to these signs. First, what they are by nature, that is to say, as sounds and characters.

Second, their signification, that is to say, the manner in which men utilize them for signifying their thoughts.

(*Grammar*: 41)

Until now we have only considered the material element of speech, and that which is common, at least as far as sound is concerned, to both men and parrots.

It remains for us to examine the spiritual element of speech which constitutes one of the greatest advantages which man has over all the other animals, and which is one of the greatest proofs of man's reason. This is the use which we make of it for signifying our thoughts, and this marvelous invention of composing from twenty-five or thirty sounds an infinite variety of words, which although not having any resemblance in themselves to that which passes through our minds, nevertheless do not fail to reveal to others all of the secrets of the mind, and to make intelligible to others who cannot penetrate into the mind all that we conceive and all of the diverse movements of our souls.

Thus words can be defined as distinct and articulate sounds which men have made into signs for signifying their thoughts.

This is why the different sorts of signification which are embodied in words cannot be clearly understood if what has gone on in our minds previously has not been clearly understood, since words were invented only in order to make these thoughts known.

All philosophers teach that there are three operations of our minds: *conceiving, judging,* and *reasoning.*

Conceiving is only the simple attention of the mind to things, either in a purely intellectual manner, as when I think of the notions of being, duration, thought, or God, or else accompanied by corporeal images, as when I imagine a square, a circle, a dog, or a horse.

Judging is the affirmation that a thing of which we conceive is such or is not such, as when, having conceived of what *the earth* is and what *roundness* is, I affirm of the earth that it is round.

Reasoning is the use of two judgments in order to make a third, as when, having judged that all virtue is laudable, and that patience is a virtue, I conclude that patience is laudable.

From whence it can be seen that the third operation of the mind is only an extension of the second. And thus it will suffice for our endeavor to consider only the first two operations or that part of the first which is contained in the second. For men scarcely speak simply to express what they conceive, but rather almost always in order to express the judgments which they make from the things which they conceive.

A judgment that we make about things, as when I say, *The earth is round*, is called a *proposition*, and thus every proposition necessarily embodies two terms: the first is called the *subject* and is that of which one predicates, as *earth* in the above example, and the second is called the *predicate* and is that which is predicated, as *round* in the above example. In addition to the terms, a proposition includes the connection between the two terms, the copula, *is*.

Now it is easy to see that the two terms properly belong to the first operation of the mind, because it is this which we conceive and which is the object of our thought, and that the connection belongs to the second operation, which could properly be termed the action of our minds, and the manner in which we think.

And thus the greatest distinction to be made about what occurs in our minds is to say that one can consider the object of our thought on the one hand, and the form or manner of our thought, the main form being judgment, on the other hand. But one must still relate to what occurs in our mind the conjunctions, disjunctions, and other similar operations of our minds, and all the other movements of our souls, such as desires, commands, questions, etc.

It follows from this that men, having had need of signs in order to mark everything that occurs in their minds, also found it necessary to draw a most general distinction among words into those that signify the objects of thoughts and those that signify the form and the manner or mode of our thoughts, although the latter often do not signify the manner alone, but only the manner in conjunction with the object, as we will show.

Words of the first kind are those which are called *nouns*, *articles*, *pronouns*, *participles*, *prepositions*, and *adverbs*. Those of the second kind are *verbs*, *conjunctions*, and *interjections*. These are all derived as a necessary consequence from the natural manner in which we express our thoughts. . . .

(*Grammar*: 65–8)

One of the most important texts in the history of linguistic thought was published in 1660 by two of the '*solitaires*' at the Port-Royal Abbey in France: the *General and Rational Grammar* by Antoine Arnauld and Claude Lancelot. Port-Royal also produced other works on language, including the important *Art of Thinking* (Arnauld and Nicole 1662: also known as 'The Port-Royal Logic') and a number of grammar manuals for the teaching of classical and vernacular languages. Among the latter the most important is the *New Method of Learning with Facility the Latin Tongue* (Lancelot 1644).

All of these works were intended as texts for the teaching of their subjects. For the Port-Royal Abbey was also one of the century's innovators in teaching methods. It hardly sounds innovative today, but the foundation of their radical pedagogy was the principle of inculcating new knowledge on the basis of knowledge already possessed by the pupil. For instance, it had been normal to instruct the beginning student of Latin entirely in Latin itself, even before he had learned a word of it. Nor did one learn to write Latin after having first learned how to write in one's own vernacular, for example French. Rather, from the very start, writing lessons were given in Latin. This traditional method of teaching thus involved a good deal of rote learning and memorization. For even the grammar rules the student was to memorize were in Latin (indeed, often in Latin verse).

However, Lancelot's new Latin grammar (1644), for instance, was written in French, giving its explanation of Latin paradigms and rules in a language already known to the student, instead of in the one he was attempting to learn. The overarching aim, then, was to make learning easier and faster.

> Since common sense teaches us that one must always begin with the easiest tasks and that what we already know should help to illuminate that which we do not yet know, it is apparent that we should use our native language as a means of entry into languages which are still strange and unknown to us. Any adult would think it a joke if, in order to learn Spanish, he were offered a grammar written in Spanish verse. If this is true for an adult, then how much more is it true for children, to whom even the clearest things appear obscure because of their unformed minds and youth.
>
> (Lancelot 1644: Preface: 2–3)

This method, going from the known to the unknown, from the easiest to the hardest, was followed in each of the grammars of vernacular and Classical languages written at Port-Royal. But what is perhaps most important, at least as far as our understanding of the *General and Rational Grammar* is concerned, is that the latter work is also an application of the same pedagogical principle.

If it was the aim of the Port-Royal grammars of particular languages to make the learning of each of those individual languages easier, the aim of the *General and Rational Grammar* (hereafter referred to simply as the *Grammar*) appears to have been to make the learning of any (and all) language(s) easier. (We might thus conceive of it as something like a 'master's guide' for the teaching of languages.) For the *Grammar* is an inquiry into the foundations of the art of speaking, providing an account of the nature of language. In this respect it is a 'general' (or 'universal') grammar: it is an explanation of the grammatical features shared by all languages. From the perspective of Port-Royal, learning a language is made easier if the student knows in advance, for example, what the difference between a noun and a verb is, what the functions of case endings are, what it means to say that there are different parts of speech, and why such categories and differences exist. The truth of this is easily seen by example. For instance, it is so much easier to teach students Latin, Greek, or Anglo-Saxon, if they already have a clear idea what declensions and conjugations are, or what it means to be a direct object, an indirect object, a subject, and so on. The Port-Royal *Grammar* has the purpose of just such an introduction to the nature of language. In this respect it is a continuation of the efforts of the Port-Royal grammarians, primarily Claude Lancelot, to simplify and 'illuminate' language-teaching methodology.

But the aim of the *Grammar* is not only to explain what a language is like, but also to support that explanation with a justification. That is, the *Grammar* says that languages have such-and-such characteristics because of the demands that are put on them. Here is perhaps the linchpin of Port-Royal linguistic thought: the primary function of speaking is said to be the communication of thoughts. And the only way that speech can successfully perform that task is by acting as a mirror of the structure of the thoughts being expressed. 'This is why the different sorts of signification which are embodied in words cannot be clearly understood if what has gone on in our minds previously has not been clearly understood, since words were invented only in order to make these thoughts known' (*Grammar* p. 66).

It is thought to be Antoine Arnauld, with his grounding in philosophy and logic, who is the source of the justification (or 'rationalization') of grammatical categories and rules contained in the *Grammar*. Influenced by, among others, Pascal, Descartes, Sanctius, and Augustine, Arnauld provided the *Grammar* with a theory of the mind, its operations and contents; and on this theory the Port-Royal explanation of the nature of language was founded. It is, for instance, his analysis of the component parts of a thought which justifies the distinction between noun and verb. A thought (or proposition) consists in two ideas which are joined by the mental operation of affirmation and judged to be similar or dissimilar. In a simple sentence, a subject noun stands for the first of these two ideas and the predicate noun (or attribute) for the second. The verb *to be* (or 'copula') stands for the operation of affirmation. Such an analysis thus not only explains what a noun and a verb are, but also why they exist and are different. It is in this way that the Port-Royal *Grammar* is not only general, but also rational. Its account of the general properties of language is based on a prior account of the general properties of human thought, the latter being taken as independent of both language and experience (*Art of thinking* pp. 30, 36). It is noteworthy that although the *Grammar* is not the first general grammar to be based on rational principles (medieval modistic grammars are not, in this respect at least, dissimilar), its influence was greater than any other in the seventeenth or eighteenth centuries. The principle (which we refer to as 'linguistic rationalism') that the structure of thought determines the structure of verbal expression is one of the guiding principles of European linguistic thought for many decades following the publication of the *Grammar*.

Port-Royal rationalism not only served to provide a justification for the general grammatical categories and rules identified in the *Grammar*, but also served to found its universalism: i.e. its claim to be an account of the grammatical features of *all* languages (not just French, Latin, Greek, and the other languages actually discussed in the *Grammar*). For Arnauld and Lancelot, grammar is the study of what they call 'the art of speaking'. Grammar in the Port-Royal sense (and in the sense of most linguistic discussion of the seventeenth and eighteenth centuries) is not conceived as a structure immanent in a language, nor as a set of rules which themselves constitute a language. Grammar studies the art of successful communication, of speaking in such a way that thought is fully and clearly expressed by the form of expression chosen. Grammar, therefore, is the study of an *activity*, not of a system (of rules, words, or sentences). And it consists in the elucidation and justification of the principles for the successful performance of and understanding of that activity. Thus, from the perspective of Port-Royal, those principles are the same, regardless of whether one is speaking French, Latin, English, or Hebrew; for the purpose of the art is always the same.

An analogy may be apposite here. Whether one is dressing in cotton, in silk, or in wool, the art of clothes design retains common principles: the clothes must be such as to allow the insertion of arms, legs, and head; they must permit free movement of the limbs when walking or sitting; they must protect the body from the elements, and so on. It is true that to design clothes in silk characteristics peculiar to that fabric must be taken into account, just as speaking in Latin requires that the speaker take into account a host of grammatical features that are peculiar to the Latin tongue. But, regardless of the fabric used, certain principles of the art of clothes design remain constant, and are so because of the common function of clothes: to cover and protect the human body. Similarly, regardless of the particular features of Latin, French and Hebrew, certain (grammatical) principles remain constant whichever of the languages one is speaking. And this is because of the common purpose of speech: the communication of thoughts. Thoughts, whether of a speaker of Latin, French or Hebrew, have the same properties, properties that are inherent to the rationality of the human mind. On these foundations the Port-Royal *Grammar* bases its claim to be both a general (i.e. universal) as well as a rational grammar.

The Port-Royal concept of how words signify is most fully discussed in the *Art of Thinking* by Arnauld and Nicole. Since speaking is described as incorporating a material side and a spiritual (or mental) side, the same may be said of the word. A word is produced in the form of articulate sounds. The idea formed upon hearing these sounds evokes another idea, which is that of a particular thing. This latter idea is the meaning of the word. So there are four terms involved: two material (the sounds and the thing) and two spiritual (the idea of the sounds and the idea of the thing, the former evoking the latter).

It is interesting that although the Port-Royal grammarians take there to be only a conventional connection between a word and the idea for which it stands, their picture of the connection between a sentence and the thought which it represents is not so avowedly conventionalist. That is, words are held to be inherently categorized into classes, according to the type of idea or operation they signify. These 'parts of speech' are combinable only in certain ways. The manner in which ideas and operations themselves are combined in a thought determines how the words which stand for them may be combined in a sentence. Thus, the general principle which we have called 'rationalism' is akin to the naturalism of classical and medieval linguistic thought with the difference that it is intended to be applied only to the explanation of the connection between whole thoughts and their verbal expression in sentences, and not to the connection between individual ideas (or things) and words.

> And thus the greatest distinction to be made about what occurs in our minds, is to say that one can consider the object of our thought on the one hand, and the form or manner of our thought, the main form being judgment, on the other hand. [...] It follows from this that men, having had need of signs in order to mark everything that occurs in their minds, also found it necessary to draw a most general distinction among words into those that signify the objects of thoughts and those that signify the form and the manner or mode of our thoughts...
>
> (*Grammar*: 67–8)

From the fact that there are two types of mental phenomena (ideas and operations) which it is the business of speech to signify, Arnauld and Lancelot draw the conclusion that there are therefore two types of words: those that stand for ideas (the 'objects' of thought) and those that stand for operations (the 'form or manner' of our thoughts). Thus the structure of a thought, consisting in the joining of two ideas in a judgement, is *isomorphic* with the structure of a simple sentence: the subject noun and predicate noun each stand for one of the ideas, and the verb 'to be' (or 'copula') stands for the mental operation of judgement. The *Grammar* accepts nine parts of speech, the first six of which (nouns, articles, pronouns, participles, prepositions, and adverbs) are all concerned with signifying the objects of our thoughts (ideas), with the remaining three having the role of signifying mental operations, judgement in particular.

Now, it may not be obvious how, say, a preposition or an adverb could be construed as standing for an idea. This problem is only partly clarified by the assertion that although standing for objects or operations in the mind is the primary function of words, they are also subject to additional demands. For one, there is the desire of speakers to abbreviate their speech. But it is this which has led, for instance, to the creation of adverbs from the abbreviation of 'preposition plus noun' constructions.

> The desire which men have to abbreviate discourse is what has made a place for adverbs, for the majority of these particles are used only for signifying in a single word what could only be otherwise indicated by a preposition and a noun: as for example *sapienter* ('wisely') in Latin for *cum sapientia* ('with wisdom'), or as another example *hodie* ('today') in Latin for *in hoc die* ('on this day').
>
> (*Grammar*:121)

A preposition, on the other hand, has the same role as that of case endings on nouns: indicating how the relationship that two things have to each other is incorporated in the conception of them. Presumably, this also is the result of man's desire to abbreviate discourse, since that relationship itself could be stated explicitly in a judgement of its own. Most of the Port-Royal *Grammar* consists of accounts of the different parts of speech and their specific functions in the general task of a sentence: viz. to express thought.

The treatment of the verb given in the *Grammar* is noteworthy. The only true verb is said to be the third person singular present indicative of the verb 'to be': that is, *is*. Only this form, known as 'the copula', directly signifies the mental operation of judgement, which it is the task of the verb to perform. Other words which are ordinarily classified as verbs are in fact combinations of the copula and some other part of speech having the function of a noun. So, in a sentence such as *John walks*, the verb *walks* is really to be understood as *is walking* with the participle *walking* acting as a noun standing for the idea of 'walking'.

> ... one can say that the verb in itself ought to have no other use save to mark the connection that we make in our minds between the two terms of a proposition, but it is only the verb *to be* ... which remained in this simple state... For, as men naturally proceed to shorten their expressions, they have almost always joined to the affirmation some other signification in the same word.
>
> (*Grammar*:123)

Not only do many verbs incorporate the predicate noun, such as is the case with *walks*, but verbs in some languages, such as Latin, may also incorporate the subject noun or pronoun. '... when one says in Latin *sum homo* ('I am a man'), ... *sum* not only signifies the affirmation, but also includes the signification of the pronoun *ego* ('I'), which is the subject of this proposition' (*Grammar*:124).

> The diversity of these significations joined in the same word is that which prevented many otherwise very astute people from properly understanding the nature of the verb, because they did not consider it according to what is essential to it, namely affirmation, but rather according to ... relationships which are accidental to it *qua* verb.
>
> (*Grammar*:124)

It is the aim of the Port-Royal *Grammar* to explain what is *essential* to the rules, categories, and distinctions which are involved in grammar: what is essential to a verb, what is essential to the sentence, and so on. For it is these essential properties which, coming from the nature of thought, speech must express and which therefore merit the attention of a 'general' grammar.

A clear example of the consequence of treating the structure of language as isomorphic with the structure of thought may be seen in the account Arnauld and Lancelot give of the distinction between nouns and adjectives (which they call 'substantive and adjectival nouns').

The objects of our thoughts are either things, like the earth, the sun, water, wood, what is ordinarily called *substance*, or else are the manner or modification of things, like being round, being red, being hard, being learned, what is called *accident*.

There is this difference between things or substances and the manner of things or accidents: substances exist by themselves, whereas accidents depend for their existence on substances.

It is this which has engendered the principal difference among the words which signify the objects of thought. For those words which signify *substances* have been called *substantive nouns*, and those which signify accidents, in marking the subjects in which these accidents inhere, have been called *adjectival nouns*.

This then is the first origin of substantive and adjectival nouns. But the matter went beyond this consideration, and we find that it was not so much signification itself that was dwelt upon as the manner of signification. For since substance is that which exists by itself, people came to call all those words which exist by themselves in discourse without requiring another noun *substantive* nouns, even though they in fact signified accidents. And on the contrary, those words which signified substances came to be called adjectives when, by their manner of signifying, they needed to be joined to other nouns in discourse.

(*Grammar*: 69–71)

In other words, substantives and adjectives are distinguished as parts of speech because the ideas for which they stand are themselves distinct: substantives standing for ideas of things which have material substance (as do trees, people, animals, etc.) and adjectives standing for ideas of accidental qualities (for example red, cowardly, honourable). Furthermore, in the same way that accidental qualities themselves conform to the substances in which they inhere, adjectives (which stand for accidental qualities) conform to the substantive nouns (standing for the things in question): for instance, by agreeing in number, gender, and case in some languages. Adjectives depend on substantive nouns in a parallel fashion to the dependence of accidents on substances.

Thus the guiding principle of the *General and Rational Grammar* is a simple one: the foundations of the art of speaking are best understood if one has a firm grasp of the structure of thoughts which it is the purpose of speech to convey. Knowledge of the structure of thoughts will help to elucidate the basic, universal categories, distinctions, and rules of the particular grammars of all languages. In the appeal to the isomorphism of language and thought lies the answer to such general grammatical questions as 'What is a verb?', 'What are cases?', and 'Why must an adjective agree with its substantive noun?'

Nevertheless, this approach can only carry the grammarian so far. For there are countless differences between individual languages. If the grammarian were to attempt to explain and justify all the grammatical facts of every language, or even of just one language, in terms of the isomorphism of language and thought, the amount of conflicting detail would be overwhelming and he would soon find that he had to contradict himself. For instance, in Latin, the number, case, and gender of the adjective must accord with those of the substantive noun, but this is not the case in English (nor, indeed, in many other languages). In English, the distinction between singular and plural nouns is marked by the adding of an -*s* to the end of the singular form: for example *cat*, *cats*; *hat*, *hats*. But many English nouns do not obey this rule: for example *sheep*, *sheep*; *mouse*, *mice*; *child*, *children*; etc. These so-called 'irregularities' of language obviously pose a problem for a rationalist grammar such as that of Port-Royal. One of the notable advances of the Port-Royal *Grammar* over the modistic grammars of the Middle Ages is that it implicitly acknowledges that rational principles in grammar form only the essential foundations of a language and do not extend (and cannot be extended) to the myriad details of the conventional and often arbitrary structures which particular languages build on top of these foundations. It is arguable that this acknowledgement of the limits of general grammar is a consequence of the view that the vernacular languages of Europe were not just poor imitations of the Classical languages, but were in fact their linguistic equals (cf. Chapter 7).

One strategy adopted by Arnauld and Lancelot for dealing with the limitations of the appeal to rational principles is based on the distinction between reason and usage (or custom). The goal of the Port-Royal *Grammar* is to identify the rational (and thus universal) principles underlying the art of speaking, not to explain or justify those categories and structures of individual languages which are not based on, or even deviate from, rational principles. That is to say, the Port-Royal grammarians distinguish in the grammatical patterns of a language between that which is determined by the rational structure of thought and that which is not so determined but rather is the result of human agreement. It is only the former which the *Grammar* aims to account for. Usage, they point out, can vary unpredictably from language to language, and its full description is thus properly the subject of grammar books written particularly for each of those languages: for instance the Port-Royal grammars of Latin, Greek, Spanish, and Italian. The idiosyncrasies in the usage conventions of an individual language cannot be explained by reference to rational principles of thought. Nor, one might say analogously, can an appeal to general or rational principles be used to explain the differences between the conventions of dress in Paris as opposed to those in Peking or Jeddah. It is simply a matter of custom that people dress differently in those cities. The individual customs of Jeddah are not explicable by reference to the general purpose of dress, i.e. to cover and protect the human body. In the same way, it is simply a matter of custom that people speak differently in Peking and Paris. Those customs are not justifiable by reference to the purpose of speech, viz. to express thought. The customs simply have to be learned by rote and are not reducible, as are general grammatical principles, to principles of the formation of thought. Usage patterns, regardless of their rationality, must be conformed to; yet, on the other hand, their idiosyncrasies should not form the analogical basis of future grammatical innovations.

> It is a maxim that those who work on a living language must always keep sight of the fact that those modes of speech which are authorized by a general and uncontested usage ought to pass as legitimate, even if they are contrary to the rules and internal analogy of the language. On the other hand, one ought not to adduce them in order to cast doubt upon the rules and disturb the analogy of languages, nor should they be used to authorize as consequences of themselves other modes of speech which usage has not authorized. Otherwise, he who will linger only on these aberrations of usage, without observing the foregoing maxim, will cause a language to remain forever uncertain, and lacking any principles, it will never be able to be determined.
>
> (*Grammar*:113–14)

Whereas differences between the conventional usage of one language and that of another are explained by reference to the distinction between reason and usage, this distinction is supplemented when 'irregularities' within a language are at issue, i.e. when usage seems to run counter to reason. Here the Port-Royal grammarians refer to the difference between 'natural' and 'figurative' constructions. For instance, in referring to rules of agreement, they write

> If one encounters something apparently contrary to these rules, it is by figure of speech, that is to say, by some word being understood, or else by considering the thoughts [that the words stand for] rather than the words themselves.
>
> (*Grammar*:170–1)

> ... because men often follow the meaning of their thoughts rather than the words which are used to express them, and because often, in order to abbreviate, they omit something from discouse, or even because, considering elegance of style, they allow some word which seems superfluous, or they reverse the natural order of words – for all these reasons it has come about that four modes of speaking called *figurative* were introduced, which are like so many irregularities in grammar, although they are sometimes perfections and beautifications of a language.
>
> (*Grammar*:173)

In his Latin grammar, Lancelot claims that one of the principle aims of grammar is 'to bring [such] figurative construction(s) into line with the laws governing the simple one [i.e. the simple, non-figurative construction], and to demonstrate that such expressions repose upon the ordinary and essential principles of linguistic construction'. For the figurative expressions of ordinary speech do not transparently reveal their construction on foundations of general and rational principles. In order to clarify the nature of grammar and to make it easier for students to learn the grammars of particular languages it is essential to reveal not only what those general and rational principles are but also to demonstrate how they may be related to the diverse (and often misleadingly arbitrary) constructions of the ordinary usage of particular languages. In this respect, the Port-Royal *Grammar* expands the province of grammar not only to include much of what others have seen as belonging to logic (for example the discussion of the structure of thought and of the nature of meaning) but also to include the interest of rhetoric in figures of speech. For the Port-Royal grammarians realized full well that there are other factors besides reason influencing the expression of thought in speech, factors that a full account of a language could not ignore. They mention, for instance, the desire to circumvent 'bothersome repetition', to avoid 'bad taste', to abbreviate speech for the purpose of expediency, and more. But how individual languages respond to such demands is a concern not of a general and rational grammar but of the grammars of those individual languages.

Another way of putting this is to say that the aim of a general grammar is to explain and justify what every sentence must do, regardless of the language in which it is expressed; while it is the task of a particular grammar to describe the customary ways that those essential requirements are accomplished in the simple, as well as the figurative, constructions of particular languages. It is this which accounts for the fact that Arnauld and Lancelot have very little to say about syntax in the *Grammar*. Much of what they do say about syntax concerns figurative constructions. For apart from the 'natural' subject-verb-predicate order, other features of syntactic construction are peculiar to the usage of individual languages.

Arnauld and Lancelot's *General and Rational Grammar* was best known by philosophers and linguists of the seventeenth and eighteenth centuries for its attempt to give rationalist foundations to general grammar. This also is the basis of its renown in contemporary linguistic discussion, even though its pedagogical motives have been largely misunderstood or ignored in modern attempts to picture it as a precursor of modern generative theory. But what has also been misunderstood is the influence of its distinction between reason and usage. For, in spite of its avowed rationalism, the Port-Royal *Grammar* was explicitly dependent on the principle that much of the structure of speech – its usage patterns, its figures of speech, its rules of word order and syntax – does *not* in fact have its source in inherent principles of the human mind. It is as if Arnauld and Lancelot say: 'If the student bears these rational principles in mind, the task of learning any language will be easier. But this is not all there is to language, nor to learning a given language. However, the rest is not within the reach of rational explanation and must be approached from a different perspective entirely.' It is this lesson which was learned by the empiricist linguists of the eighteenth century and which, later on, gave inspiration to the growing belief in the autonomy of language and of its study.

Chapter nine

Locke on the imperfection of words

Man, though he have great variety of Thoughts, and such, from which others, as well as himself, might receive Profit and Delight; yet they are all within his own Breast, invisible, and hidden from others, nor can of themselves be made appear. The Comfort, and Advantage of Society, not being to be had without Communication of Thoughts, it was necessary, that Man should find out some external sensible Signs, whereby those invisible *Ideas*, which his thoughts are made up of, might be made known to others. For this purpose, nothing was so fit, either for Plenty or Quickness, as those articulate Sounds, which with so much Ease and Variety, he found himself able to make. Thus we may conceive how *Words*, which were by Nature so well adapted to that purpose, come to be made use of by Men, as *the Signs of* their *Ideas*; not by any natural connexion, that there is between particular articulate Sounds and certain *Ideas*, for then there would be but one Language amongst all Men; but by a voluntary Imposition, whereby such a Word is made arbitrarily the Mark of such an *Idea*. The use then of Words, is to be sensible Marks of *Ideas*; and the *Ideas* they stand for, are their proper and immediate Signification.

The use Men have of these Marks, being either to record their own Thoughts for the Assistance of their own Memory; or as it were, to bring out their *Ideas*, and lay them before the view of others: *Words in their primary or immediate Signification, stand for nothing, but the Ideas in the Mind of him that uses them*, how imperfectly soever, or carelessly those *Ideas* are collected from the Things, which they are supposed to represent. When a Man speaks to another, it is, that he may be understood; and the end of Speech is, that those Sounds, as Marks, may make known his

Ideas to the Hearer. That then which Words are the Marks of, are the *Ideas* of the Speaker: Nor can any one apply them, as Marks, immediately to anything else, but the *Ideas*, that he himself hath: For this would be to make them Signs of his own Conceptions, and yet apply them to other *Ideas*; which would be to make them Signs, and not Signs of his *Ideas* at the same time; and so in effect, to have no Signification at all. Words being voluntary Signs, they cannot be voluntary Signs imposed by him on Things he knows not.

(Essay Book III, Chapter 2, Sections 1–2)

To make Words serviceable to the end of Communication, it is necessary, (as has been said) that they excite, in the Hearer, exactly the same *Idea*, they stand for in the Mind of the Speaker. Without this, Men fill one another's Heads with noise and sounds; but convey not thereby their Thoughts, and lay not before one another their *Ideas*, which is the end of Discourse and Language. But when a word stands for a very complex *Idea*, that is compounded and decompounded, it is not easy for Men to form and retain that *Idea* so exactly, as to make the Name in common use, stand for the same precise *Idea*, without any the least variation. Hence it comes to pass, that Men's Names, of very compound *Ideas*, such as for the most part are moral Words, have seldom, in two different Men, the same precise signification; since one Man's complex *Idea* seldom agrees with another's, and often differs from his own, from that which he had yesterday, or will have to morrow.

(Essay Book III, Chapter 9, Section 6)

This Inconvenience, in an ill use of Words, Men suffer in their own private Meditations: but much more manifest are the Disorders which follow from it, in Conversation, Discourse, and Arguings with others. For Language being the great Conduit, whereby Men convey their Discoveries, Reasonings and Knowledge, from one to another, he that makes an ill use of it, though he does not corrupt the Fountains of Knowledge, which are in Things themselves; yet he does, as much as in him lies, break or stop the Pipes, whereby it is distributed to the publick use and advantage of Mankind.

(Essay Book III, Chapter 11, Section 5)

John Locke (1632–1704), the son of a small landowner from Somerset in the west of England, came to hold an important position in government during the reign of William and Mary. As might be expected, many of his writings were on political topics, for instance his *Letter on Toleration* and the *Two Treatises of Government*. But, above all, he has gained a place in history for his *Essay Concerning Human Understanding*, first published in 1689. It is from Book III of Locke's *Essay* that the extracts chosen in this chapter are taken.

Locke's *Essay* is primarily a treatise on epistemology, dealing with the nature of knowledge, how we acquire knowledge, and the obstacles to the acquisition of knowledge. It is because Locke sees language not only as the sole means of communicating knowledge but also as a potentially dangerous obstacle to the acquisition and growth of knowledge that he devotes Book III to the topic 'Of Words'. And yet he confesses that when he began writing the *Essay* he had not foreseen the need to discuss the properties of communication and language.

> But upon a nearer approach, I find, that there is so close a connexion between *Ideas* and Words; [...] that it is impossible to speak clearly and distinctly of our Knowledge, which all consists in Propositions, without considering, first, the Nature, Use, and Signification of Language.
>
> (*Essay* Book II, Chapter 33, Section 19)

Why did Locke attribute so much importance to language in his theory of knowledge? It will help to begin with a brief sketch of the foundations of that theory. The *Essay* argues that all human knowledge consists of ideas. The human mind is pictured as a repository of ideas, and thinking as the mental manipulation of stored ideas. Verbal communication, in turn, consists in telementation: that is, in the conveyance of ideas from the mind of one individual to that of another. Language is the vehicle, 'the great Conduit', by which telementation takes place. In Book I of the *Essay*, Locke argues against the assumption, held by many in the 17th century, that we are innately endowed with some, or even all, of our ideas (the position supported, for example, by Descartes). Rather, as he argues at length in Book II, our ideas are derived from experience. The mind at birth is a *tabula rasa*, a clean slate, on which the story of experience is subsequently inscribed. Experience provides us with ideas by two distinct routes. On the one hand, by means of our five senses, we form what Locke calls 'simple ideas of sensation', such as the ideas of sweetness, of smoothness, of green, etc. On the other hand, we acquire 'simple ideas of reflection' by experiencing the operations of our own mind. (Locke did not deny that we are innately equipped with the capacity to perform certain mental operations.) By this latter means, we acquire such ideas as those of perception, reflection, will, desire, etc. On the basis of these two types of simple ideas, derived directly from experiences, we are able to construct further ideas, by combining simple ideas into complexes. So, says Locke, the idea of 'gold' is a complex idea resulting in the combination of the simple ideas of 'heaviness', 'yellowness', 'fusibility', 'malleableness', and 'fixity'. Likewise, the idea of 'glory' is extremely complex; but in the end it is the result of multiple combinations of simple ideas of both sensation and reflection. Thus all ideas have their ultimate source in experience (both internal and external) and in innate abilities of the mind to act upon and combine the simple ideas derived from experience.

Two of the kinds of complex ideas identified by Locke are of particular interest: namely, those he calls 'mixed modes' and 'ideas of substances'. An idea of a substance, although a complex idea, is an idea of something that does in fact have a real existence, such as gold. 'Sugar' is another idea of a substance, formed by combining the simple ideas of 'sweetness' and 'whiteness'. But sugar, like gold, is also a real thing. Justice, a mixed mode formed by the combination of a number of simple ideas (Locke never tells us just which), exists only as an idea. Unlike sugar and gold, justice is not a thing which we can locate in the world. It has only a mental, not a real, existence; although the simple ideas from which it is formed do in fact ultimately derive from the experience of real objects. But, argues Locke, it is only due to the power of the human mind that these simple ideas are grouped together into a mixed mode and given the single name *justice*: the real objects from which its component simple ideas are derived do not themselves exist together in reality as a single complex entity.

As Locke argues in our first extract, it is only by means of words, of language, that an individual may make his thoughts and their component ideas known to others. Otherwise, they remain 'within his own Breast, invisible, and hidden from others'. Indeed, one of the two main functions of language is to convey ideas from one mind to another, the other function being to enable us to record our thoughts for future consultation.

In order to make our ideas accessible to one another – that is, to communicate them – we must use words. Locke does not speak of language as a stable, autonomous system, but rather as an act, the act of expressing one's ideas with words. Uttering a word consists in producing an articulate sound as a sign of one of the speaker's invisible ideas. The hearer interprets the perceived sound as a sign of one of his own ideas. If the speaker's and the hearer's idea are the same, the communicational act is a success. By the utterance of a (properly structured) string of such words, then, a speaker may convey his otherwise private ideas to others. In this way, language may serve as 'the great Conduit, whereby Men convey their Discoveries, Reasonings, and Knowledge, from one to another'.

Just as Locke takes words to be signs of ideas, he takes ideas to be signs of things, with the exception of those ideas, such as mixed modes, for which there exist no correlates in reality.

> For since the Things, the Mind contemplates, are none of them, besides it self, present to the Understanding, 'tis necessary that something else, as a sign or Representation of the thing it considers, should be present to it: And these are *Ideas*.
>
> (*Essay* Book IV, Chapter 21, Section 4)

So a word is a vocal sign of an idea, and an idea is a mental sign of a thing. It is thus only by an indirect connection that, in speaking, an individual may be said to be speaking *about* objects in the real world. It is a mistake, as Locke argues in the second paragraph of our first extract, to conceive of words as standing for things. This is shown by the fact that if a speaker has no idea of a given object, no word that the speaker utters can signify that object. Words can only serve to express the speaker's ideas; they 'cannot be voluntary Signs imposed by him on Things he knows not'.

Locke did not believe that the function of all words is to stand for ideas. Some words, for instance those he calls 'particles', serve to express the relations between the different ideas in a complete thought. By 'particles' Locke was referring primarily to those types of words we call prepositions and conjunctions. This interpretation was, even in Locke's time, traditional. Particles had long been seen as having not a designative but a relational function.

On these fundamental principles Locke constructed his idealized conception of language and communication. As such, they were not, even in 1689, completely original. Both Francis Bacon and Thomas

Hobbes, among others, took words to stand for ideas, as opposed to things, and conceived of communication as the conveyance of ideas from the mind of one individual to that of another. Indeed, it could be said that this telementational conception of communication and its attendant mentalist concept of meaning derive originally from Aristotle. But Locke did not write on language in his *Essay* in order to promote these relatively uncontroversial views on the nature of language and communication. Indeed, if he had thought that language did actually conform to this idealized conception, he would not have felt any need to include a discussion of language in a treatise on epistemology. What draws Locke to language is what he calls its 'imperfections'. For it was Locke's view that language does *not*, in fact, ordinarily conform to the idealized mentalist conception presented above. And, in particular, it is because of its imperfections that language can be an obstacle to understanding and to the acquisition, progress, and spread of knowledge. Unfortunately (from Locke's point of view), these imperfections are part of the very essence of language and of the link between words and ideas. Locke's account of this link may be summarized as follows.

First, a word is an *arbitrary* sign of the idea it stands for. That is, there is no general principle which determines the appropriate sign for any given idea. Thus there is no necessity that the colour of grass should be called *green* or the colour of blood *red*.

Second, the act of uttering a word as the vocal sign of a given idea is an act of the individual speaker's will. This is what is meant by saying that words are *voluntary* signs of ideas. They are imposed by the will of the individual speaker. His act of using a given word as the sign of a given idea is not determined by anything other than his own free will. Even if, in choosing a word to stand for a given idea, he attempts to conform his choice to what he takes to be common usage, he does so voluntarily.

This is connected to the third characteristic attributed by Locke to the connection between word and idea: it is a connection effected by an *individual*. It is not communities of speakers who choose to make a given word the sign of a given idea. (How indeed could a community make such a choice: by majority vote?) Uttering a word as a vocal correlate of an idea is an act, and it is the voluntary act of an individual. For only the individual speaker knows the idea to be conveyed; so the speaker alone is able to choose a sound to stand as a sign of that idea.

The fourth characteristic of the connection between words and ideas we have already touched upon: *privacy*. Since the ideas which a speaker wants to convey are, according to Locke, unobservable ('invisible') to anyone except the speaker, no one else can know what any word uttered signifies. The connection between the speaker's words and his ideas is known only to him. Consequently, as Locke claims in the second paragraph of our first extract, a word may stand for only an idea in the mind of the speaker who produces that word. A word produced by me stands for an idea in my mind; but you cannot know what idea I intend it to stand for because the connection between word and idea, effected by me, is unobservable to you. In sum, because meaning is a voluntary act, arbitrarily performed by an individual in mental privacy, producing words is (at best) an imperfect way of making ideas known to others. Against his idealized view of what language *should* enable, namely the conveyance of knowledge from one mind to another, Locke lays this disturbing picture of the insufficiency of language as a vehicle of thought.

> And every Man has so inviolable a Liberty, to make Words stand for what *Ideas* he pleases, that no one hath the Power to make others have the same *Ideas* in their Minds, that he has, when they use the same Words, that he does.
>
> (*Essay* Book III, Chapter 2, Section 8)

Thus is language potentially dangerous to the acquisition and spread of knowledge. For, at first glance, it appears to have the characteristics of a perfect vehicle for the telementational conveyance of ideas from the privacy of one individual's mind to that of another. But upon closer reflection, language in fact may be seen to be subject to what Locke calls 'imperfections', structural faults which, if ignored, will confound the trust we intuitively place in language as 'the great Conduit'. The aim of Book III of the *Essay* is first of all to point out these imperfections to all those who seek knowledge and who are thus unavoidably dependent on language, and second to offer a remedy for these imperfections.

Locke discusses another threat to the use of language as a tele-mentational vehicle, although this threat cannot strictly be deemed an imperfection of *language*. Not only is the link between words and ideas arbitrary, voluntary, individual and private; it is also the case that many ideas are themselves formed as the result of arbitrary, voluntary, individual and private mental operations. Here the type of idea Locke calls the 'mixed mode' is vulnerable. Simple ideas are taken directly from our experience of objective reality and from our experience of innate mental operations. They are thus, as Locke sees it, the same for all men. Simple ideas are 'perfectly taken from the existence of things, and are not arbitrary at all' (Book III, Chapter 4, Section 17). In this respect, then, their privacy is not a problem, for they will be the same in all individuals. Complex ideas, however, are formed by the voluntary and, in some cases, arbitrary act of the individual's mind. Ideas of substances pose less of a problem than those of mixed modes. For every idea of substance refers to a real object that exists in nature; and, Locke suggests, individuals naturally attempt to conform their ideas of a substance to the pattern of the real object to which it refers. But there are no real objects to be correlated with mixed modes. My mixed-mode idea of 'truth' does not refer to and so cannot conform to any objectively available thing existing in nature. There is no pattern for us all to copy in forming our idea of 'truth'. Instead, these complex ideas are formed arbitrarily, by a private act of the individual will. Consequently, 'one Man's complex *Idea* seldom agrees with another's, and often differs from his own, from that which he had yesterday, or will have to morrow' (Book III, Chapter 9, Section 6).

So, not only does a hearer not ordinarily know what ideas a speaker's words stand for, but the hearer also cannot be sure that the speaker's ideas of mixed modes are the same as any of the hearer's own ideas. It is not just the link between word and idea which is obscure, but also the structure of the ideas themselves. How, given what we might call 'the double imperfection' of words and of ideas, can one individual hope to communicate ideas to others by means of language? How can speakers avoid having their utterances do no more than 'fill one another's Heads with noise and sounds; but convey not thereby their Thoughts'?

It is interesting that Locke never discusses the question of the ordinary use of language. He admits that, in spite of its imperfections, common use 'regulates the meaning of Words pretty well for common Conversation', although it is not sufficient for scientific and philosophical discourse (Book III, Chapter 9, Section 8). And yet although in everyday conversation we would appear, from Locke's account, to be doing little more than filling each other's heads 'with noise and sounds', he never explains how language none the less succeeds in fulfilling the purposes of ordinary discourse. How is it that language, in spite of its 'imperfections', makes any communicational events

MECHANICS' INSTITUTE LIBRARY
57 Post Street
San Francisco, CA 94104
(415) 421-1750

possible? How do the meanings of words come to be well (enough) regulated for the conduct of daily affairs?

These are not questions which hold any vital interest for Locke, although, as will become evident in subsequent chapters, they are part of a puzzle which greatly concerned those who were influenced by Locke's views on language. Rather, having pointed out what he saw as the imperfections of language, and thus the threat they posed to the acquisition and spread of knowledge, Locke turns instead to the proposal of remedies to those imperfections in order that language may be safely used for the purposes of science and philosophy.

Locke's remedy to the imperfections of language hinges on his notion of definition. As long as the name of a complex idea – either a mixed mode or an idea of a substance – is defined in terms of the simple ideas from which that complex idea is composed, then the speaker who uses that name may be sure that hearers will interpret it as the sign of the same complex idea. For according to Locke there is little danger that names for simple ideas will be understood differently by different individuals. Simple ideas are directly derived from our experience of natural objects. My notion of 'redness' is derived directly from my experience of red objects. Your idea of 'redness' is derived by the same means. To determine if we mean the same thing by the word *red*, I need only point to what seems to me a red object and say 'This is red'. If our simple ideas of 'redness' differ or if we use *red* as a sign for different simple ideas, this would immediately become apparent. We may thus be sufficiently certain not only that we share the same simple ideas but also that in using names for simple ideas our hearers will take them as signs of the same simple ideas as we do.

Now every complex idea is a structure of simple ideas. So if we analyse every complex idea we name in terms of its component simple ideas, we should be able to provide a definition for each such complex name. And this definition should allow our hearers to determine exactly the complex idea for which we want that name to be taken as a sign. Thus, the analysis of ideas and the definition of words together allow us to bridge the gap between the minds of individuals, a gap which, due to its imperfections, ordinary language is of itself unable to bridge.

It is for this reason that Locke claimed that 'Morality is capable of Demonstration, as well as Mathematicks' (Book III, Chapter 11, Section 16). All moral terms are names of mixed modes. So, by the process of definition just described, we may give exact demonstrations of our ideas of 'goodness', 'evil', 'right', 'wrong', etc., a process Locke evidently felt to be similar to the demonstration by proof of a mathematical conclusion. However, Locke's remedy for the imperfections of language is obviously of little use for ordinary conversational uses of language. (Are we to stop every time we produce a name for a complex idea and give it a definition in terms of simple ideas?) Nevertheless, he appears to have thought it sufficient for the use of language in scientific and philosophical discourse. It is at least in part due to the influence of Locke's notion of definition that the 18th century was a period in which many English dictionaries (such as that of Samuel Johnson) were printed and in which linguistic prescriptivism in general reached its zenith. Locke was taken to have shown that, in spite of its obvious imperfections, if a language were given the meticulous attention of educated authorities, it could be perfected.

There is one often noted gap in Locke's account of definition as a remedy for the imperfections of language. He does not explain whether or how we may be certain that someone else signifies the same idea as we do by the name for a simple idea of reflection: for example, *belief* or *knowledge*. It is perhaps plausible that we should be able to tell if someone else signifies the same idea as we do by the name for a simple idea of sensation, like *red*; but how can we tell if they signify the same as we do by *opinion*, or *perception*, or *will*? If these words signify simple ideas of reflection and if simple ideas are acquired by (private) internal observation of innate mental operations, how can I tell if the idea you signify by *opinion* is not in fact the idea I signify by *belief*? There are no external samples for us to test ourselves on, as there are in the case of simple ideas of sensation. And yet it is presumably the case that mixed modes, the ideas which pose the greatest threat to the commonality of understanding, include among their component simple ideas such simple ideas of reflection.

Locke's awareness of this problem and perhaps a suggested solution to it are indicated in the following extract:

> It may also lead us a little towards the Original of all our Notions
> and Knowledge, if we remark, how great a dependence our
> *Words* have on common sensible *Ideas*; and how those, which are
> made use of to stand for Actions and Notions quite removed
> from sense, have their rise from thence, and from obvious sensible
> *Ideas* are transferred to more abstruse significations, and made
> to stand for *Ideas* that come not under the cognizance of our

senses; v.g. to Imagine, Apprehend, Comprehend, Adhere, Conceive, Instill, Disgust, Disturbance, Tranquillity, etc. are all Words taken from the Operations of sensible Things, and applied to certain Modes of Thinking. *Spirit*, in its primary signification, is Breath; *Angel*, a Messenger: And I doubt not, but if we could trace them to their sources, we should find, in all Languages, the names which stand for Things that fall not under our Senses, to have had their first rise from sensible *Ideas*. By which we may give some kind of guess, what kind of Notions they were, and whence derived, which filled their Minds, who were the first Beginners of Languages; and how Nature, even in naming of Things, unawares suggested to Men the Originals and Principles of all their Knowledge: whilst, to give Names, that might make known to others any Operations they felt in themselves, or any other *Ideas*, that came not under their Senses, they were fain to borrow Words from ordinary known *Ideas* of Sensation, by that means to make others the more easily to conceive those Operations they experimented in themselves, which made no outward sensible appearances; and then when they had got known and agreed Names, to signify those internal Operations of their own Minds, they were sufficiently furnished to make known by Words, all their other *Ideas*; since they could consist of nothing, but either of outward sensible Perceptions, or of the inward Operations of their Minds about them.

(Essay Book III, Chapter 1, Section 5)

What is the point of this passage? Locke seems to be suggesting that names for simple ideas of reflection (and for other ideas that 'come not under the cognizance of our senses') are in fact metaphors, originally borrowed from their literal use as names for ideas of sensation. This certainly is what many of his 18th-century followers took him to mean. As a result, this passage is one of those most frequently quoted from Book III in the 18th century. For, taken literally, it seems to imply that the vast majority of words are metaphorical in origin (given that only a small minority of words could be taken as names for simple ideas of sensation). This in turn suggested to many that, with the help of etymology, we should in principle be able to work out the original meaning (for some, such as Horne Tooke, the 'true' meaning) of those words not standing for simple ideas of sensation. The structure of our vocabulary (and so of the ideas for which the vocabulary items stand) could thus be exposed in terms of a step-by-step metaphorical expansion from an original core vocabulary of names for simple ideas of sensation. The strong renewal of interest in metaphor and other tropes in the 18th century is in part a reflection of this interpretation of the passage quoted, although in truth there is very little evidence elsewhere in the *Essay* to suggest that this was how Locke intended his remarks to be interpreted.

Many 18th-century followers found even more in this passage. For instance, it seems to suggest that the historical expansion of a vocabulary, from a core of names for simple ideas of sensation, goes hand in hand with the expansion of the mind's store of ideas: that is, that the development of language and the development of knowledge are interdependent processes. Thus, by the etymological study of how a language developed and expanded its vocabulary, one could gain insight at the same time into the development and expansion of the ideas of the people who spoke that language. Paradoxical as it may sound, and perhaps through a misinterpretation by his 18th-century followers, one of the seeds of 19th-century Romanticism may thus be found in these 17th-century Lockean remarks: in particular the Romantic notion that the language spoken by a community somehow reflects, even determines, the way that the members of that community think.

Locke's influence on 18th-century thought is immeasurable. To linguistic thought he bequeathed not only a more detailed and explicit version of the mentalist conception of language that had originated with Aristotle, but also serious, explicitly reasoned worries about the capacity of language to serve as an adequate vehicle for the telementational communication of ideas. As a remedy to language's imperfections, Locke offered the techniques of analysis and definition. Yet, ironically, Locke's immediate influence on the linguistic thought of his own followers in the 18th century was more the legacy of the final extract quoted above. For it was from this legacy that came, to a large degree, the 18th-century interest in metaphor, in etymology, in the origin of language, and in the interrelation of language and the mind.

Chapter ten

Condillac on the origin of language and thought

... we cannot recall a thing to mind, unless it be in some manner connected with something else which is in our power. Now a man who has only accidental and natural signs, has none at all at his command. [...] Hence we may conclude that brutes have no memory; and that they have only an imagination which they cannot command as they please. They represent to themselves an absent object, only because the image of it in their brain is closely connected with the object present. It is not their memory that directs them to a place, where the day before they met with nourishment: but it is because the sensation of hunger is so strongly connected with the ideas of that place and of the road leading to it, that these ideas are revived, as soon as they feel the sensation. [...]

But as soon as a man comes to connect ideas with signs of his own choosing, we find his memory is formed. When this is done, he begins of himself to dispose of his imagination, and to give it a new habit. For by means of the signs which he is able to recall at pleasure, he revives, or at least is often capable of reviving the ideas which are connected with them. [...]

(*Essai* I, 2, 4)

If a thought is not linear in the mind, it has a linear order in discourse, where it is analysed into as many parts as it includes component ideas. By this means we may observe and even understand what we do when thinking; consequently we may learn to control our reflections. Thinking thus becomes an art, and it is the art of speaking. [...]

Languages are therefore more or less perfect relative to their adequacy for analysis. The more they facilitate analysis, the more they give assistance to the mind. In effect, we judge and reason

with words, just as we calculate with numerals; and languages
are for ordinary people what algebra is for geometricians.

(*Grammaire*: 286–7)

The eighteenth century in Europe was a period of great interest in
the theory of language. Much of this interest may be traced to the
influence of Locke's *Essay*. However, as we saw in the last chapter,
Locke did not explicitly propose a theory of language. Instead, he
offered several vague suggestions which it was the work of his followers to expand into explicit accounts of the nature of language.

More than anyone it was Etienne Bonnot, Abbé de Condillac,
who was responsible for taking up Locke's hints and suggestions
and making language theory a central topic within philosophical
empiricism. Indeed, when Nugent's 1756 English translation of Condillac's *Essai sur l'origine des connoissances humaines* (*Essay on the
Origin of Human Understanding*) was published, it was given the
subtitle of 'A Supplement to Mr Locke's Essay on the Human
Understanding'. There is no evidence that Condillac objected to this
description. On the contrary, throughout the *Essai* there are glowing
comments about Locke and his *Essay*.

Nevertheless, even in the *Essai*, Condillac's earliest major work,
he objects to Locke's account of language and understanding for a
variety of reasons. Of most importance is Condillac's argument that
in order to grasp the fundamental principles of language, and indeed
of the mind, we must inquire into their origins and subsequent
development. And by 'origins' Condillac meant historical origins:
i.e. how primitive man took his first linguistic steps and first made
progress in the development of his mental abilities. Only by discovering how a given ability originated in 'the state of nature' could
one come to know its fundamental principles, even those underlying
its present state of sophistication.

At the same time Condillac rejected Locke's argument that the
imperfections of language could be remedied by giving definitions to
all potentially misleading terms (for example, names of mixed
modes). Rather, Condillac argues, in order to understand the true
meaning of names for complex ideas we must 'reduce the ideas to
the simple ideas from which they were composed and then follow
the successive steps of their generation' (*De l'art de penser*:118). It is
the second step which is unique to Condillac, the insistence on

121

tracing the history of the meaning of a word in order to come to an understanding of its present signification. We return to this point later in the chapter.

Nearly all of Condillac's works, unlike those of Locke, deal with language. His best known work, the *Essai sur l'origine des connoissances humaines* (1746), was only the first publication of many in which Condillac attempted to explain the nature of language, its origin and development, its proper use in reasoning, and its mutually dependent relationship with the mind. Much of his multi-volume *Cours pour le prince de Parme* (published in 1782, although completed much earlier and circulated in manuscript form) deals with language: including treatises on universal grammar, reasoning, style, and the art of thinking. Published just before or after his death were a *Logique* (1780: the 1982 English translation is cited here) and a treatise comparing the language of arithmetic with natural languages, *La langue des calculs* (1798). All of these deal primarily or at least to a large extent with the theory of language.

However, without a doubt it is Condillac's 1746 *Essai* which had the greatest influence on 18th-century linguistic ideas. Even so, the *Essai* does not constitute a fully developed formulation of Condillac's linguistic thought. Some of the cornerstones of his later thought are only hinted at in the *Essai*; others are not even mentioned. Furthermore, one important aspect of his early thought, the claim that the signs of ordinary languages are arbitrary, is explicitly rejected on numerous occasions in his more mature publications. Nevertheless, it is possible to view Condillac's linguistic thought as forming a coherent whole, from the early *Essai* to the later *Logique* and *Langue des calculs*. New themes are added in the later works, terminology is changed, and some concepts are altogether replaced; but Condillac never strays far from his fundamental principles. As it is these principles which we aim here to present, we will focus on the unity of Condillac's ideas, rather than on differences and development. It should not be forgotten, however, that these principles are never explicitly formulated as a coherent whole anywhere in Condillac's works, early or late. One consequence of our strategy will be that the extracts chosen are from three different works: the 1746 *Essai*, the *Grammaire*, and the *Logique*.

As with Locke's ideas on language, an exposition of Condillac's linguistic ideas must begin with an account of his ideas about the nature and component operations of the human mind. Although he is not always clear on this point in the *Essai*, by his later works

Condillac is explicit: all the faculties of the mind are derived from the faculty of sensation. For instance, what Condillac calls the faculty of attention is supposed to consist simply in focusing on one component of a complex sensation to the exclusion of all others. The faculty of comparison is no more than that of attending to two sensations at the same time. Memory is the comparison of a present sensation with an absent one. Judgement is 'to perceive resemblances or differences' between sensations, and thus consists in 'nothing more than sensations' (*Logic*: 368). The faculty of reflection 'is only a series of judgements made through a series of comparisons; and since these comparisons and judgements contain only sensations, thus there are only sensations in reflection' (*Logic*: 368–9). Indeed, all faculties and operations of the mind are held to be similarly reducible to sensation.

Reflection is perhaps the most important of mental faculties to Condillac's account of the relations between language and the mind, and in particular to his claim that it is only by the use of language that man has voluntary control of the operations of his mind.

> If I want to know, for example, how two trees differ, I successively observe the form, the trunk, the branches, the leaves, the fruit, and so forth. I successively compare all these things. I form a series of judgments. And because my attention reflects, as it were, from one object to another, I say that I reflected.
>
> (*Logic*: 368)

Condillac makes a fundamental distinction between voluntary and involuntary actions. This distinction also applies to operations of the mind. I may connect ideas together, forming a particular train of thought, either under the direction of my will or involuntarily. An involuntary connection, like an involuntary action, may occur either because it is the result of my bodily makeup or because it is determined by the situational circumstances. For instance, I cannot help but blink when I sneeze; this is the result of what we might call physiological determination. On the other hand, seeing the face of a young girl may automatically bring that of her mother to mind. This reaction is not a voluntary act, nor is it physiologically determined (since it will not happen to everyone); rather, it is determined by the circumstantial stimulus of seeing the daughter's face.

Perhaps the most crucial step in Condillac's argument, and certainly one which distinguishes him from Locke, is the claim that without the use of a language man does not have voluntary control of the faculty of reflection, nor indeed of the other faculties of the mind. Condillac argues that the mind of prelinguistic man is subject to physiological determination and to environmental stimuli. A given sensation, produced by some chance event, might *cause* such a man to remember another past sensation and even to judge of those two sensations that they are similar; but before he has language man cannot *of his own will* remember a past sensation, compare two sensations, or guide the direction of his mental reflection. Man is at birth endowed with natural desires and with a variety of mental faculties, but not until he has some mastery of a language can he make purposeful use of his mental faculties to accomplish one of his desires. It is thus the acquisition of language which is the crucial step in Condillac's story of the progress of human understanding; for language gives man the voluntary use of his natural mental endowment.

In the *Essai* Condillac distinguishes between three kinds of signs: accidental, natural, and institutional (later called 'artificial'). An accidental sign is an object which particular circumstances have connected with one of our ideas: a given lake reminds us of antelope, for we have often seen them drinking there. Natural signs include the cries and gestural expressions which nature makes us produce as involuntary responses to certain sensations, desires, passions, and so on. So, a cry of pain is a natural, physiologically determined sign of that pain. The child's distinctive fretting sounds are natural signs of its desire for some object. However, artificial signs are voluntary creations: we choose to call a certain object a *pillow*; this name is not determined by circumstance nor by our physiological makeup. In the *Essai* Condillac says that artificial signs 'bear only an arbitrary relation to our ideas' (*Essai* I, 2, 4). Later, however, he repeatedly denies the arbitrariness of artificial signs. We will consider this reversal later in this chapter. For the moment it is important only to focus on what is always for Condillac the distinguishing characteristic of artificial signs: they are chosen by an act of free will and thus remain under the voluntary control of man. This threeway distinction between signs helps elucidate the importance of language to man's development of the power to control the operations of his mind.

Condillac takes it for granted in our first extract that, because artificial signs are creations of man's own choosing they remain under the voluntary control of man. He can recall them at will. Artificial signs, because they are voluntary creations, thus give man voluntary control of the mental contents signified by them.

Although this is only hinted at in the *Essai*, in his later works Condillac develops an account of another means by which the acquisition of language gives man control over the operations of his mind (see our second extract). A language, Condillac argues in the *Grammaire* and elsewhere, is an analytic method. Without language man cannot analyse his thoughts: by this is meant that he cannot break down complex thoughts into their component parts (i.e. ideas) and in turn recompose them in order to understand their structure and manipulate them at will. The more detailed and the more analogically structured a language is, the more precise and efficient it is as a method of analysing thought. But natural language (i.e. the physiologically determined language of gestures and emotive cries) does not analyse thought into component parts. Rather a natural gesture conveys a complex thought holistically; it does not break down a complex perception into its component parts but instead conveys them all simultaneously. This is more natural, Condillac argues, because thought itself is like a picture. Thought does not consist in the linear scrolling of individual ideas but rather in the simultaneous perception of a complex bundle of individual sensations. With artificial language, because of the linear structure of its sentences, we are forced to analyse our thoughts in order to present their component parts one after the other.

So not only does the acquisition of language give man voluntary control over the operations and contents of the mind, it also puts within his power the ability to analyse thoughts into component ideas and to manipulate those ideas in order to form new thoughts at will. Thus thinking becomes a creative act, instead of one determined by external circumstances. In this case it is understandable why Condillac saw the acquisition and progress of language as the key to the progress of the human mind. But a question remains. If primitive man required language in order to gain creative control over the operations and analytical powers of the mind, how was he ever able to perform the complicated mental task of creating an artificial language? Primitive man may have been endowed with a natural language of gestures and emotive cries, but this natural language was not under his voluntary control.

Condillac was well aware of the problem this dilemma posed for his theory and faced it squarely in the *Essai*.

It seems that we could never make use of instituted signs, unless we were previously capable of sufficient reflection to choose those signs, and to affix ideas to them: what is the reason then, some perhaps will object, that the habit of reflection is to be acquired only by the use of these signs?

My answer is that I shall solve this difficulty when I come to treat of the history of language.

(*Essai*: I, 2, 4–5)

In fact Condillac provided two sorts of answers to this genetic question, one in Part II of the *Essai*, and the other, dealing more specifically with the genesis of analysis, in the *Grammaire* and in the *Logique*. We will deal with them in that order.

At the beginning of Part II of the *Essai* Condillac speculates about the origin of language. He begins by imagining two children living alone in a pre-linguistic state of nature. Their mental faculties include attention, comparison, judgement, reminiscence, and imagination; but they have no control over them. Their operation is at the mercy of contextual stimuli. 'Thus the habit of the imagination was not in their power; it was no more than the effect of the circumstances in which they were placed' (*Essai*, II, I, i, 1). At this stage of development, the only signs produced were natural signs, those emotional cries and gestures which they produced as involuntary responses to emotional stimuli: for example, a cry of fear, a squeal of delight, a howl of pain.

However, by living together they acquire a different view of these natural signs. For when one child hears the other produce a cry of pain, he connects that cry with the emotion that produced it. That is, because he himself uttered a similar cry when in pain, hearing someone else produce that cry causes him to think of the emotion that stimulated it.

It is important to see that at this stage the production of natural signs, and indeed the interpretation of such signs, are *involuntary* acts. It is not by an act of individual will that the child produces a cry of fear upon the sight of an approaching lion or that his partner recognizes it as a cry of fear. Such acts are instead involuntary responses to emotional stimuli; and these emotions are in turn involuntary responses to contextual stimuli. At this stage of development, just as man still has no control over the operations of his mind, he also has no control over his production and interpretation of signs. In this crucial respect, that is in the lack of free will with regard to the operations of his own mind, he is no different from other animals. It is artificial language which will give him free will, the characteristic distinguishing man from beast (*Traité des Animaux*: 529).

In the genesis of language the crucial threshold is reached when for the first time the children make voluntary use of their natural signs. Condillac imagines this event as follows:

> For example, he who saw a place in which he had been frightened, mimicked these cries and movements which were the signs of fear, in order to warn the other not to expose himself to the same danger.
>
> (*Essai* II, 1, i, 3)

But how was it that they suddenly were able to make voluntary use of natural signs which previously they only produced involuntarily? This is an important step in the logic of Condillac's genetic narrative; for once man does have voluntary control of some signs (even natural signs), he simultaneously acquires at least some voluntary control over the operations of his mind. And once he has some control over the powers of reflection, he is then in a position to invent new signs. This enlarged list of signs will give him even greater control of his mind, enabling him in turn to create new signs, and so on. The mutually assisted progress of language and mind has begun. As Condillac points out in the first part of the *Essai*, given (a) that the development of man's reflective powers depends on the development of his language-using abilities, and (b) that the development of the latter in turn depends on the development of the former, the most crucial step in the interdependent genesis of language and mind must have come when man somehow gained voluntary control of one of them. In the *Essai* it is voluntary control of language that man first acquires. Thus Condillac's narrative hangs on his explanation of this point.

Unfortunately, Condillac is not very clear on how this crucial feat is accomplished.

> And yet the same circumstances could not be frequently repeated, but they must have accustomed themselves at length to connect with the cries of the passions and with the different motions of the body, those perceptions which were expressed in so sensible a manner. The more they grew familiar with those signs, the more they were in a capacity of reviving them at pleasure. Their memory began to acquire some sort of habit, they were able to command their imagination as they pleased, and insensibly they

learned to do by reflection what they had hitherto done merely by instinct.

(*Essai* II, 1, i, 3)

All that Condillac appears to be saying here is that once the involuntary connection of sign and emotion had become a habit, man was able for the first time to make voluntary use of the sign. Indeed, Condillac has argued earlier in the *Essai* (I, 2, i–ii) that man does in fact have the voluntary ability to recall to mind certain habitual perceptions, including sounds, with which he is very familiar. Thus if he is very familiar with certain emotional cries, the natural signs of given sensations, he should be able to recall, as well as produce, those signs at will. And this is the distinguishing characteristic of artificial signs: they are under man's voluntary control. Consequently, it is man's growing familiarity with natural signs which eventually enables him to produce them voluntarily. These voluntarily controlled natural signs thus become the first artificial signs and so begin the progress of language.

Even if we accept this as the means by which man acquires voluntary control of signs and of the operations of his mind, we are left with the second question. If it is by the use of sentences with a linear structure that man learns to analyse the operations and contents of his mind, how, *before* acquiring a language composed of such linear structures, can he accomplish the analytical task of inventing one? In other words, even if the *Essai* is taken to offer a solution to the dilemma of the origin of artificial signs, it leaves unsolved the parallel dilemma of the origin of sentential structures. And yet Condillac maintains that the progress of the human mind depends on the powers of analysis given to us by an artificial language with linear structures. In the following passage from the *Logique* Condillac offers an explanation of the stages of development from a natural language of holistic signs (called here 'the language of gestures') to an artificial language of linear expression.

Although everything in the [natural language of gesture] is confused, it still contains everything they [i.e. its speakers] feel. It includes everything that they will distinguish when they know how to analyse their thoughts, that is, their desires, fears, judgments, reasoning – in short, all the operations the mind is capable of. For finally, if all these were not there, analysis could not find them. Let us see how these men learn from nature to analyse all these things. [...]

First, they obey nature. And without a plan, as we have just remarked, they say at the same time everything that they feel, because it is natural to their movements to do so. However, he who listens with his eyes will not hear if he does not decompose these gestures in order to observe the successive movements. But it is natural for him to decompose it, and consequently he does so before having planned to. For if he sees all the movements at once still, at a first glance, he looks only at those that strike him the most forcibly; in a second glance, he looks at others; in a third, still others. He thus observes them successively, and analysis is performed.

Thus, each of these men will sooner or later notice that he never understands others better than when he has decomposed their gestures. Consequently he can notice that, to make himself understood, he needs to decompose his own gestures. Then he will gradually develop the habit of repeating, one after another, the movements that nature causes him to make all at once. For him, the language of gesture naturally becomes an analytic method. I say *method* because the succession of movements will not be made arbitrarily and without rules. For since gesture is the effect of one's needs and circumstances, it is natural to decompose it in the order given by these needs and circumstances. Although this order can and does vary, it can never be arbitrary. [...]

Since the whole pattern of gesture is the picture of the whole thought, partial gestures are so many pictures of ideas that make up a part of this whole. Thus, if this man decomposes these partial gestures, he will likewise decompose the partial ideas they are signs of, and he will continually construct new and distinct ideas.

This means of analysing his thought, the only one he has, he can elaborate it down to the smallest details. For, given the first signs of a language, we have only to consult analogy, which will give us all the others.

There will be thus no ideas that the language of gesture cannot express. And it will express them with all the more clarity and precision as analogy appears more perceptibly in the series of signs chosen. Perfectly arbitrary signs will not be understood because, since they are not analagous, the meaning of a known sign would not lead to the meaning of an unknown sign. It is analogy that makes up the whole art of languages.

(*Logic* pp. 389–90)

Thus it is by breaking down the holistic gestural signs into parts that man begins to analyse. Indeed he is led by nature to do this, because it is more natural for him, as an interpreter of another's gestural sign, to focus first on one part of it, then another, then another, and so on. In other words, the attempt to understand leads man naturally to convert the holistic perception of a gestural sign into parts perceived one after the other, in linear succession. And then the natural drive to make his own signs understood leads him in turn to break down those signs into component parts, producing them one after another in a linear sequence. But what is most important is that this decomposition of holistic gestures is effected with a concurrent decomposition of the complex thought for which that gesture is the natural sign. These two analyses are analogical: the decomposition of the gesture is isomorphic with the decomposition of the thought it conveys. It is that analogical relation which Condillac sees as the shared foundation of the arts of speaking (grammar) and reasoning (logic).

Imagine, for instance, that nature causes me to produce a given complex gesture when I am hungry and within sight of potential food. I want to convey that desire to you, and I have learned that signs are best understood when they are decomposed into component parts which are produced in sequence. Consequently, I break the gesture down into three component parts and produce them one after the other. But what is important is that simultaneously, and *by analogy*, I also break down that complex desire into three parts, i.e. into component ideas. Hand in hand with my analysis of the sign into parts I perform a parallel analysis of the desire or thought which I had previously registered only as a whole. This analysis of my thought is analogous to the analysis of my gesture.

One crucial point remains. These analyses are not produced arbitrarily: they are (or ought to be) guided by nature. If my thought is naturally composed of three parts, then I will analyse it into three parts. For example, if my desire for food is composed of an idea of desire, an idea of food, and an idea of myself, then if I follow natural principles of analogy I will decompose the complex gesture into three component parts, each of which will stand for one of the component ideas of the signified desire. In other words, we are led by nature to analyse a thought 'at the joints', so to speak. In so far as they follow such natural analogies, languages will break down complex signs according to the parallel of the decomposition of thoughts.

To the extent that a given language does follow analogy, it will be an effective vehicle for communicating thoughts. The natural language of gestures was such a perfect means of communication; for any artificial language also to be a perfect communicational vehicle, its words and grammatical structures must maintain a clear analogical relation to that original language. But to the extent that the formation of a language, or an individual sentence, is not analogical, but arbitrary, it will be an obstacle to the conveyance of thoughts. Only by following natural principles in the formation of languages may we develop complex artificial languages that, like the innate language of gesture, remain effective vehicles for the transmission of thought.

In addition to denying a role for arbitrariness in the development of analytical structure in language, Condillac also explicitly denies the arbitrariness of individual signs. Signs could not be arbitrary because they would not be understood. In a number of other places in his later work Condillac gives the same reason for claiming that signs in instituted languages like our own could not be arbitrary. For those signs to have been understood when they were first invented, they must have been analogous to other signs already in existence, which leads to the conclusion that all signs, in all languages, must be able to be linked by a chain of natural analogies to the original natural gestural and vocal signs.

At first glance it may seen surprising that Condillac repeatedly denies the arbitrariness of signs when in the *Essai* he appears to have made arbitrariness a primary characteristic of artificial signs. This apparent contradiction can be resolved, however, if one reads further in the *Essai*. For it becomes clear that what Condillac really means in the *Essai* by calling institutional signs arbitrary is that they are the voluntary creations of man's will. Voluntariness remains a characteristic of institutional signs in all of Condillac's later work. Thus it appears that both in the *Essai* and in his later work Condillac is arguing that, as compared to natural signs, artificial, institutional signs are the creations of man's will: i.e. they are not given by nature or by God. But they are not, and indeed could not be, arbitrary in the sense of their choice being totally without motivation.

> It is a mistake to think that in the first creation of languages men
> could choose indifferently and arbitrarily which words were to
> be the signs of which ideas. If this had been the case, how could
> they have understood one another?
>
> (*Grammaire*: 365–6)

In the *Grammaire* Condillac speculates further on the origin and
development of vocal signs. The first vocal signs would simply have
been component parts of the original gestural signs: for example, the
complex sign produced in the presence of food would have included,
say, a grunt. But these would only be signs of emotion and desires,
such as hunger. For a concrete object that made some noise, such as
an animal, this noise was imitated and made to stand for the object
itself. For objects which made no noise, such as a stone, the vocal
sound would be used which was naturally analogous to the colour,
smell, taste, or feel of the object. In other words, synaesthesic metaphors provided the means for expanding the vocabulary from purely
imitative sounds. For ideas that did not affect the senses, Condillac
suggested, like Locke, that words which did designate sensible objects
were borrowed as metaphorical designations of non-sensible objects.
Finally, to designate a new object, two existent words could be
blended to form a new creation. So, in naming an edible grass of a
whitish colour, one might combine *white* and *eat* to produce *wheat*.

> Should one have wanted to indicate an object in which he noticed
> a number of sensible qualities, a number of words would be
> combined, each of which expressed one of these qualities. In this
> way the first words became the elements with which new ones
> were composed. [...] Now is it chance which guides the creation
> of such combinations? Certainly not. It is analogy which,
> although you may not be aware of it, determines your choice.
> Analogy also guided men in the formation of languages.
>
> (*Grammaire*: 367)

Condillac's picture of the origin and development of languages
thus relies heavily on the image of natural creation and growth. His
is a naturalist theory of language, one which, like Locke's theory,
views arbitrariness as an obstacle to understanding, as an imperfection. The difference is that Locke had viewed arbitrariness as an
essential feature of signs. For Condillac, it is natural analogy which
is the first principle of signs, and arbitrariness only intervenes as an

occasional flaw. By returning to the origins of language, Condillac hoped to solve Locke's puzzle about the possibility of linguistic communication.

The result is a picture of a language as a system genetically derived on the basis of natural analogical principles. This applies both to the grammatical structure of sentences as well as to lexical relations in the vocabulary. Indeed any language, to the extent that it was an effective vehicle of communication, could be seen as a system analogically derived from the first language of natural gestures. Furthermore this picture leads to the conclusion that the only way of coming to a true understanding of a language and its words is to trace its analogical development from the first language of natural signs. Condillac himself encouraged this suggestion.

> Finally, we shall know how to use words when analysis has enabled us to acquire the habit of looking for the chief meaning in their first use, and all the others in analogy.
>
> (*Logic*: 399)

Still, Condillac does not deny the existence of arbitrariness in languages. Indeed it is arbitrariness and differing analogical choices which explain why there are so many languages in the world, rather than a single one derived from the original. All languages are descendants of the original language of gesture, but in its development one language will have incorporated arbitrary choices and will have drawn certain analogies where another did not. Consequently, some languages will have better grammars and more transparent vocabularies than others, depending on the extent to which their development was based on natural analogies.

> Since languages, which take form in proportion as we analyse them, became so many analytical methods, it is understandable that we find it natural to think according to the habits that they caused us to acquire. We think with them. Rulers of our judgment, they determine our knowledge, opinions, and prejudices. In short, they do in this domain everything good or bad. Such is their influence, and it could not have happened differently. [...]
> In conjecture, the first ordinary languages were the most appropriate for reasoning. For nature, which was in charge of their construction, had at least made a good beginning. The

development of ideas and of the faculties of the mind had to be perceptible in these languages where the original meaning of a word was understood and where analogy provided all the others. In the names of ideas that eluded the senses one found the names of the sensible ideas they came from. And, instead of being seen as the proper names of these ideas, they were seen as figurative expressions that revealed their origin. Then, for example, it was not asked if the word *substance* meant anything other than *what lies beneath*. If the word *think* meant anything than *to weigh, balance, compare*. In short, no one imagined formulating the questions that metaphysicians pose today. Languages, which answered all questions beforehand, did not allow them to be posed ...

A language would be indeed superior if the people who made it cultivated the arts and sciences without borrowing from any other community, for in this language, analogy would perceptibly show the progress of knowledge, and we would not need to look elsewhere for its history. This would be a truly learned language, and it would be unique. But when a language is a collection of several unrelated languages, everything is confounded: Analogy can no longer make clear in the different meanings of words, the origin and the development of knowledge: we no longer know how to make our speech precise.

(*Logic*: 396)

Linguistic thought of the latter half of the 18th century was dominated by the ideas of Condillac. The remarkable surge of interest in the origin and development of language is a certain testimony to Condillac's influence. Many of the great philosophers of the period offered their own speculative accounts of the origin of language, and most of these were only trivially different from Condillac's own account. There were in the next fifty years accounts published by the Scots economist Adam Smith, by Jean-Jacques Rousseau, by James Burnett (Lord Monboddo), by the German Romantic philosopher Herder, by the French philosophers Diderot and Maupertuis, and many others.

By means of his language-origins theory Condillac also legitimized the naturalist solution to Locke's puzzle about the intersubjectivity of communication. As long as language is analogically derived from the original language of nature it will be a perfect vehicle of communication. This position also provided a source for the politically sensitive etymological metaphysics of John Horne Tooke and others (see Chapter 11). For in so far as a word was analogically derived from one or more original signs of the language of nature, the 'true meaning' of that word could be discovered by working back, by means of etymology, through the word's history of analogical transformations to that original sign. Consequently, Condillac's ideas seemed to offer a means of finding out the true, original signification of such ideologically and politically powerful words as *rights*, *justice*, *law*, and *truth*.

Finally, there is in Condillac's work a suggestion that the language a person speaks influences the way that person thinks. For Condillac argues at length that some languages are better than others, according to the analysis they impose on thoughts. This suggestion is taken up and more fully developed in the works of Herder and von Humboldt (see Chapter 12). By the end it constitutes a complete reversal from the semantic rationalism of Port-Royal, i.e. from the view that innate structure of thought determines the grammatical structure of linguistic expression. The subsequent development of this new position will eventually lead to the abandonment of the mentalist foundations which had dominated linguistic thought since Aristotle.

Chapter eleven

Horne Tooke on etymological metaphysics

H. And do you, with me, pity the ignorance and folly of those regular governments who . . . do not see that a claim of RIGHTS by their people, so far from treason or sedition, is the strongest avowal they can make of their subjection: and that nothing can more evidently show the natural disposition of mankind to rational obedience, than their invariable use of this word RIGHT, and their perpetual application of it to all which they desire, and to every thing which they deem excellent.

F. I see the wickedness more plainly than the folly; the consequence staring one in the face: for, certainly, if men can claim no RIGHTS, they cannot justly complain of any WRONGS.

H. Most assuredly. But your last is almost an identical proposition; and you are not accustomed to make such. What do you mean by the words RIGHT and WRONG?

F. What do I mean by those words? What every other person means by them.

H. And what is that?

F. Nay, you know that as well as I do.

H. Yes. But not better: and therefore not at all.

F. Must we always be seeking after the meaning of words?

H. Of important words we must, if we wish to avoid important error. The meaning of these words especially is of the greatest consequence to mankind; and seems to have been strangely neglected by those who have made the most use of them.

F. [. . .] RIGHT itself is an abstract idea: and, not referring to any sensible objects, the terms which are the representatives of abstract ideas are sometimes very difficult to define or explain.

H. Oh! Then you are for returning again to your convenient abstract ideas; and so getting rid of the question.

F. No. I think it worth consideration. Let us see how Johnson handles it. [...] He gives no explanation: except of RIGHT hand ... – 'Not the Left.'

H. You must look then for LEFT hand. What says he there?

F. He says – LEFT 'sinistrous, Not right.'

H. Aye. So he tells us again that RIGHT is – 'Not wrong' and WRONG is – 'Not right.'

But seek no further for intelligence in that quarter; where nothing but fraud, and cant, and folly is to be found – misleading, mischievous folly; because it has a sham appearance of labour, learning, and piety.

RIGHT is no other than RECT-um (*Regitum*), the past participle of the Latin verb *Regere*. Whence in Italian you have RITTO; and from *Diregere*, DIRITTO, DRITTO: whence the French have their antient DROICT, and their modern DROIT. The Italian DRITTO and the French DROIT being no other than the past participle *Direct-um*.

In the same manner our English word JUST is the past participle of the verb *Judere*.

DECREE, EDICT, STATUTE, INSTITUTE, MANDATE, PRECEPT, are all past participles.

F. What then is LAW?

H. It is merely the past tense and past participle *Law* or *Laew*, of the Gothic and Anglo-Saxon verb *Lagjan* ... and it means (something or any thing ...) laid down – as a rule of conduct.

Thus when a man demands his RIGHT; he asks only that which it is ordered he shall have.

A RIGHT conduct is that which is ordered.

A RIGHT reckoning is that which is ordered.

A RIGHT line is that which is ordered or directed (not a random extension, but) the shortest between two points.

The RIGHT road is that ordered or directed to be pursued, (for the object you have in view).

To do RIGHT is to do that which is ordered to be done.

To be in the RIGHT is to be in such situation or circumstances as are ordered.

To have RIGHT or LAW on one's side is to have in one's favour that which is ordered or laid down.

A RIGHT and JUST action is such a one as is ordered and commanded.

A JUST man is such as he is commanded to be – *qui leges*

juraque servat – who observes and obeys the things laid down and commanded.

The RIGHT hand is that which custom and those who have brought us up have ordered or directed us to use in preference, when one hand only is employed: and the LEFT hand is that which is leaved, leav'd, left; or which we are taught to leave out of use on such an occasion. So that LEFT, you see, is also a past participle. [...]

F. Well, but Mr Locke uses the word in a manner hardly to be reconciled with your account of it. He says – 'God has a RIGHT to do it, we are his creatures.'

H. It appears to me highly improper to say that God has a RIGHT: as it is also to say that God is JUST. For nothing is ordered, directed, or commanded concerning God. The expressions are inapplicable to the Deity; though they are common and those who use them have the best intentions, they are applicable only to men; to whom alone language belongs, and who are by nature the subjects of orders and commands, and whose chief merit is obedience.

F. Everything then that is ordered and commanded is RIGHT and JUST!

H. Surely. For that is only affirming that what is ordered and commanded is – ordered and commanded.

F. Now what becomes of your vaunted RIGHTS of man? According to you, the chief merit of men is obedience: and whatever is ordered and commanded is RIGHT and JUST! This is pretty well for a Democrat! And have these always been your sentiments?

H. Always. And these sentiments confirm my democracy.

F. These sentiments do not appear to have made you very conspicuous for obedience. There are not a few passages, I believe, in your life, where you have opposed what was ordered and commanded. Upon your own principles, was that RIGHT?

H. Perfectly.

F. How now? Was it ordered and commanded that you should oppose what was ordered and commanded? Can the same thing be at the same time both RIGHT and WRONG?

H. [...] A thing may be at the same time both RIGHT and WRONG, as well as RIGHT and LEFT. It may be commanded to be done, and commanded not to be done. The LAW ... i.e. that which is laid down, may be different by different authorities.

I have always been most obedient when most taxed with dis-
obedience. [...] The RIGHT I revere is not the RIGHT adored
by the sycophants; the *Jus vagum*, the capricious command of
princes or ministers. I follow the LAW of God (what is laid
down by him for the rule of my conduct) when I follow the
LAWS of human nature; which, without any human testimony,
we know must proceed from God: and upon these are founded
the RIGHTS of man, or what is ordered for man. I revere the
Constitution and constitutional LAWS of England; because
they are in conformity with the LAWS of God and nature: and
upon these are founded the rational RIGHTS of Englishmen.
If princes or ministers, or the corrupted sham representatives
of a people, order, command, or lay down any thing contrary
to that which is ordered, commanded, or laid down by God,
human nature, or the constitution of this government; I will still
hold fast by the higher authorities. If the meaner authorities are
offended, they can only destroy the body of the individual; but
can never affect the RIGHT, or that which is ordered by their
superiors.

(*Diversions of Purley*: 302–11)

The writings of John Horne Tooke occupy a pivotal place in the
history of linguistic ideas. His *Letter to Mr Dunning* (1778) and *The
Diversions of Purley* (two volumes, 1786 and 1805) were perhaps the
most widely discussed linguistic works in Britain at the end of the
eighteenth and the beginning of the nineteenth century. However,
they did not meet with uniform approval. Tooke was well known
for his radical political ideas, and these were not kept out of his
linguistic writings. Far from it. Both the *Letter to Mr Dunning*
and *The Diversions of Purley* had strong undercurrents of political
polemic. The reception of Tooke's linguistic ideas was to some degree
influenced by the reaction to his politics.

Tooke was known by his peers not only for his radical politics,
but also for the radical position he espoused in philosophical and
linguistic discussions. Furthermore, he argued that only through a
clear conception of the nature and function of language could a
correct understanding of more general philosophical and political
topics be attained. For, like Locke, he believed that linguistic con-

fusion was often the primary source of political, scientific, moral, religious, and philosophical confusion.

> ... I very early found it, or thought I found it, impossible to make many steps in the search after truth and the nature of human understanding, of good and evil, of right and wrong, without well considering the nature of language, which appeared to me to be inseparably connected with them. I own therefore I long since formed to myself a kind of system, which seemed to me of singular use in the very small extent of my younger studies, to keep my mind from confusion and the imposition of words.
>
> (*Diversions of Purley*: 7)

> I think Grammar difficult, but I am very far from looking upon it as foolish: indeed so far, that I consider it as absolutely necessary in the search after philosophical truth; which, if not the most useful, perhaps, is at least the most pleasing employment of the human mind. And I think it no less necessary in the most important questions concerning religion and civil society.
>
> (*Diversions of Purley*: 13)

In his most extensive linguistic work, *The Diversions of Purley*, Tooke chooses a dialogue format for the presentation of his radical theory of language. Participating in the dialogue are John Horne Tooke himself (H), Sir Francis Burdett (F), Richard Beadon (B), and William Tooke (T), the owner of the estate where the dialogue takes place and the benefactor from whom John Horne respectfully took his name in 1783. (Following custom, when we refer to the author, John Horne Tooke, we will simply use his adopted surname *Tooke*.) The book may be roughly divided into two parts of unequal length. In the opening pages, Tooke presents his theory of language and the mind, a theory which he claims to have deduced from *a priori* principles. But the bulk of the two volumes is devoted to the presentation of the empirical proof of his theory, a proof presented in the form of an etymological analysis of over two thousand (primarily English) words.

> ... it was general reasoning *a priori* that led me to the particular instances; not particular instances to the general reasoning. This etymology, against whose fascination you would have me guard myself, did not occur to me till many years after my system was

settled: and it occurred to me suddenly, in this manner: – 'If my reasoning ... is well founded, there must then be in the original language from which the English (and so of all other languages) is derived, literally such and such words bearing precisely such and such significations.' – [...] The experiment presented to me a mean, either of disabusing myself from error (which I greatly feared); or of obtaining a confirmation sufficiently strong to encourage me to believe ... that I had really made a discovery. [...] The event was beyond my expectation: for I instantly found, upon trial, all my predictions verified. This has made me presumptuous enough to assert it universally.

(*Diversions of Purley*: 67–9)

Tooke may thus be seen as attempting to transform the study of language from a speculative discipline, dependent on philosophy and based on *a priori* reasoning, into an empirical (etymological) science. To a large degree, it was by appearing to give language study solid empirical foundations that Tooke's writings acquired such influence in philosophical and philological circles, in spite of his political radicalism.

Tooke's empirical study of language is based on a materialist theory of mind. Like Condillac (with whose work he was familiar), Tooke sees himself as going further than Locke in taking the mind to be an entirely passive instrument, capable only of receiving sense-impressions. What others have called the operations of the mind are in fact only the operations of language. Tooke argues that for too long our picture of the mind has been distorted by projecting into the mind a similarly distorted picture of language. Where we observed complex terms, we imagined there to be corresponding complex ideas: the meanings of these terms. Where we noted different classes of words, we imagined there to be different classes of ideas, one for each of the different parts of speech. These are illusions fostered by the rationalist myth that the structure of language is determined by, and thus is a mirror of, the structure of the mind. This myth can only be exploded by means of a strictly empirical study of language.

The business of the mind, as far as it concerns language, appears to me to be very simple. It extends no further than to receive impressions, that is, to have sensations or feelings. What are called its operations, are merely operations of language. A consideration of ideas, or of the mind, or of things (relative to the parts of speech) will lead us no further than to nouns; i.e. the signs of those impressions, or names of ideas.

(Diversions of Purley: 25)

One of the chapters of the *Diversions* is devoted to 'Some consideration of Mr Locke's Essay'. Tooke argues that Locke was on the right track in his study of human understanding but made too many concessions to rationalism, such as admitting the existence of mental operations. Furthermore, even where Locke was right, he did not realize that most of the statements he made about the mind and about ideas were only correct if they were reconstrued as, respectively, statements about language and words.

I only desire you to read the Essay over again with attention, and see whether all that its immortal author has justly concluded will not hold equally true and clear, if you substitute the composition, etc., of *terms*, wherever he has supposed a composition, etc., of ideas.

(Diversions of Purley: 19)

Like Locke and Condillac, Tooke argues that the purpose of language is the communication of thoughts from speaker to hearer. And, like Locke, he does not believe that the use of language for communicational purposes is ordinarily successful. Instead we often 'gabble like things most brutish', not knowing even the meaning of what we say. But, unlike Locke, he is not worried by imperfections of language, for in his view it is not language that is imperfect.

It is important to see the originality of Tooke's position within a framework which is nevertheless quite Lockean. For Locke, communicational intersubjectivity is threatened because language, with its characteristics of arbitrariness, voluntariness, individuality, and privacy, cannot be a reliable vehicle for communicating thoughts. Condillac's answer to this threat is to deny that language is arbitrary; its natural origins and principled analogical development mean that the linguistic vehicle is shared and thus adequate for the task of conveying thoughts. But Tooke is not interested in the origin of language, natural or conventional. Speculation about origins is of interest only to curiosity (*Diversions*: 8). Rather, Tooke is saying that language itself is perfect; it is our understanding of the nature of language which is defective. We think language is something which it is not. We think that given words mean something quite different from what in fact they do mean. Because of our beliefs about language, we are led to equally miguided philosophical and psychological views. And these in turn lead us to further misconceptions about the nature of language and meaning. Unlike that of Locke, Tooke's critique is directed at the *study* of language, not at language itself. It is linguistics which is imperfect, not language. Indeed, it is 'the perfections of language, not properly understood, (which) have been one of the chief causes of the imperfections of our philosophy' (*Diversions*: 19). But what are the roots of our misunderstanding of the perfections of language?

H. The purpose of language is to communicate our thoughts –

B. You do not mention this, I hope, as something new, or wherein you differ from others?

H. You are too hasty with me. No. But I mention it as that principle, which, being kept *singly* in contemplation, has misled all those who have reasoned on this subject.

B. Is it not true, then?

H. I think it is. And that on which the whole matter rests.

B. And yet the confining themselves to this true principle, upon which the whole matter rests, has misled them!

H. Indeed I think so.

B. This is curious!
    [...]

H. I imagine that it is, in some measure, with the vehicle of our thoughts as with the vehicles for our bodies. Necessity produced both. The first carriage for men was no doubt invented to transport the bodies of those who from infirmity, or otherwise, could not move themselves: But should any one, desirous of understanding the purpose and meaning of all the parts of our modern elegant carriages, attempt to explain them upon this one principle alone, viz. that they were necessary for conveyance, he would find himself woefully puzzled to account for the wheels, the seats, the springs, the blinds, the glasses, the lining, etc. Not to mention the mere ornamental parts of gilding, varnish, etc. Abbreviations are the wheels of language, the wings of Mercury. And though we might be dragged along without them, it would be with much difficulty, very heavily and tediously.
    [...]

B. I think I begin to comprehend you. You mean to say that the errors of grammarians have arisen from supposing all words to be *immediately* either the signs of things or the signs of ideas; whereas in fact many words are merely *abbreviations* employed for despatch, and are the signs of other words. And that these are the artificial wings of Mercury, by means of which the Argus eyes of philosophy have been cheated.

H. It is my meaning. [...] The first aim of language was to *communicate* our thoughts; the second to do it with *despatch*. [...] The difficulties and disputes concerning language have arisen almost entirely from neglecting the consideration of the latter purpose of speech: which, though subordinate to the former, is almost as necessary in the commerce of mankind, and has a much greater share in accounting for the different sorts of words. Words have been called *winged*; and they well deserve that name, when their abbreviations are compared with the progress which speech could make without these inventions; but compared with the rapidity of thought, they have not the smallest claim to that title. Philosophers have calculated the difference of velocity between sound and light: but who will attempt to calculate the difference between speech and thought! What wonder, then, that the invention of all ages should have been upon the stretch to add such wings to their conversation as might enable it, if possible, to keep pace in some measure with their minds. Hence chiefly the variety of words.

Abbreviations are employed in language three ways:
1. In terms.
2. In sorts of words.
3. In construction.

Mr Locke's Essay is the best guide to the first; and numberless are the authors who have given particular explanations of the last. The second only I take for my province at present; because I believe it has hitherto escaped the proper notice of all.

(*Diversions of Purley*: 9–15)

The extract above contains the core of Tooke's argument. The first principle of language is that its purpose is the conveyance of thoughts. But this is not the only principle of language. Language must also perform this task efficiently. And this means that it must allow for the conveyance of thoughts at or near the speed at which those thoughts are produced. If, as that first principle suggests, each word in a language were to stand immediately for a simple idea in the mind (and Tooke believes that the mind contains only such simple ideas), then in order to convey even an ordinary thought a speaker would require a sentence of impossibly great length. As Tooke points out, this was realized by Locke. Furthermore, thought moves at a much faster rate than that at which a speaker could produce such long sentences. Consequently, a language which only respected what we have called the first principle of language would be so cumbersome that speech could not proceed at anything like the rate at which speakers think. It would be like trying to carry on a conversation with signal flags, where each flag stood for a single letter. With such a vehicle of communication, conveying a sentence even as long as the last would require a tediously long performance.

The key to the perfection of language as a communicational vehicle (and the principle the ignorance of which had misled philosophers for centuries) is that many of its words do not in fact stand for ideas, but act as substitutes for other words. These are what Tooke calls 'abbreviations'. One such abbreviation might stand for a number of other words. So the utterance of that abbreviation would substitute for the much more cumbersome sequential utterance of all of those words for which it is an abbreviation. Analogously, we might imagine one signal flag which stood not for a single letter but for a sequence of letters often joined together: for example, a single flag for the sequence *a-t-i-o-n*.

If grammarians and philosophers had realized the role of abbreviation in language, they would not have been led to make so many errors in metaphysics, in mental philosophy, and in grammar. For, paying attention only to the first principle, they took each word in a language to stand for an idea (or, in the case of a realist semantics, for a thing). This then meant that there had to be an individual idea for each of the words in a language to signify. In the case of abstract and complex terms, this meant postulating the existence of abstract and complex ideas in the mind; and this in turn raised the problem of how such ideas could be acquired. In this way Locke was led to populate the mind with complex ideas, abstract ideas, mixed modes, ideas of substances, and the like. At the same time it led philosophers like Locke to wonder what words other than nouns might be signs of. Locke spoke of conjunctions and prepositions as standing for mental operations. Others spoke of them as standing for abstract relations between ideas. Recognition of a greater variety of parts of speech thus led philosophers to admit a greater variety of ideas in the mind (and metaphysicians a greater variety of things in the world).

Tooke's solution to this confusion is to let words stand for simple ideas (i.e. simple sense impressions). There are no other entities or operations in the mind for words to signify. But this solution only holds for a small subset of words. Most words are abbreviations: they stand as subtitutes for one or more already existing words. Thus, directly or indirectly (i.e. by means of abbreviation), every word stands for a simple idea. This is its meaning. Tooke distinguishes between a word's 'force of signification' (the idea for which it stands) and its 'manner of signification' (whether it stands for an idea directly or by means of abbreviation, i.e. substituting for one or more other words which themselves stand for simple ideas).

At the same time, Tooke distinguishes between those parts of speech which are necessary to communication (the noun and verb) and those which are abbreviations of these and which are added to language solely for the purpose of 'despatch'. These are the abbreviations in sorts of words, for the discovery of which Tooke claims the honour.

B.   But you have not all this while informed me how many parts of speech you mean to lay down.

H.   That shall be as you please. Either two, or twenty, or more. [. . .] I am inclined to allow that rank only to the necessary words: and to include all the others (which are not necessary to speech, but merely substitutes of the first sort) under the title of Abbreviations.

B.   Merely substitutes! You do not mean that you can discourse as well without as with them?

H.   Not as well. A sledge cannot be drawn along as smoothly, and easily, and swiftly as a carriage with wheels; but it may be dragged.

B.   Do you mean then that, without using any other sort of word whatever, and merely by the means of the noun and verb alone, you can relate or communicate any thing that I can relate or communicate with the help of all the others?

H.   Yes. It is the great proof of all I have advanced. And upon trial you will find that you may do the same. But, after the long habit and familiar use of abbreviations, your first attempts to do without them will seem very awkward to you; and you will stumble as often as a horse, long used to be shod, that has newly cast his shoes. Though indeed (even with those who have not the habit to struggle against) without abbreviations, language can get on but lamely: and therefore they have been introduced, in different plenty, and more or less happily, in all languages. And upon these two points – abbreviation of terms, and abbreviation in the manner of signification of words – depends the respective excellence of every language. All their other comparative advantages are trifling.

(*Diversions of Purley*: 24–5)

From this extract it may be seen that Tooke is a universalist. All languages are held to share a common 'underlying' structure: namely, a structure consisting of names for simple sensations (nouns and verbs). But the speed of thought makes man incorporate abbreviations into his languages and thus add different parts of speech, which are in fact only abbreviations of already existing nouns and verbs. How one community will do this may differ from another. The obvious, 'superficial' differences between the grammars of languages stem from different uses of the methods of abbreviation. Such a simple explanation, both of the essence of universal structure and of the 'surface' differences between languages, made Tooke's universalism much more accessible than that proposed by earlier universal grammarians such as Arnault, Lancelot, and Condillac; at the same time it brought the comparison of different grammars under a more rigorous method: the method of etymology.

H.   I take the word FROM (preposition, if you choose to call it so) to have as clear, as precise, and at all times as uniform and unequivocal a meaning, as any word in the language. FROM means merely BEGINNING, and nothing else. It is simply the Anglo-Saxon and Gothic noun *Frum*, ... Beginning, Origin, Source, Fountain, Author. [...].
Figs came FROM Turkey.
Lamp falls FROM ceiling.
Lamp hangs FROM ceiling.
[...]
Have we occasion to communicate or mention the commencement or beginning of these motions and of this attachment; and the place where these motions and this attachment commence or begin? It is impossible to have complex terms for each occasion of this sort. What more natural, then, or more simple, than to add the signs of those ideas, viz. the word

BEGINNING (which will remain always the same) and the name of the place (which will perpetually vary)?

Thus,

Figs came – BEGINNING Turkey.

Lamp falls – BEGINNING ceiling.

Lamp hangs – BEGINNING ceiling.

That is,

Turkey the place of BEGINNING to come.

Ceiling the place of BEGINNING to fall.

Ceiling the place of BEGINNING to hang.

(*Diversions of Purley*: 184–5)

The result of Tooke's argument is that there is no need to postulate any other mental (or metaphysical) entities for 'minor' parts of speech or for complex or abstract nouns to stand for. Consequently, Tooke's picture of the mind is much simpler than that of philosophers who people it with complex and abstract ideas and relations. Furthermore, there is no reason to worry about the perfection of language as a communicational vehicle. For, in the final analysis, the meaning of every word, regardless of its part of speech, is given by the simple idea(s) for which it stands, directly or through abbreviation. Indeed, Tooke believed that the thesis that every word stands, directly or indirectly, for a simple idea may be proven by means of etymological research. Thus Locke's worries about the understanding of complex and abstract terms disappear, for their manner of signification is to stand as substitutes for simple terms, the common understanding of which Locke never doubted.

It is essential to Tooke's theory that abbreviation not be thought of as an operation performed voluntarily by individual speakers. It is the result of an historical process operating within the language itself, conceived of as independent of the speaker's will. Analogously, it is not an individual signalman who decides to make a single flag stand for *a-t-i-o-n*; it is the signal code itself which determines that abbreviation. The same goes for a single word acting as an abbreviation for other words. Consequently, the meaning which a word has in a language may be a subject of empirical research, through etymology. Any word which does not stand directly for a simple idea should in principle be traceable to one or more other words which do. The etymological discussion which makes up the bulk of the *Diversions* thus acts as an empirical confirmation of Tooke's *a priori* theory of the nature of language, mind, and meaning. At the same time, its etymologies provide an account of what many English words 'really mean'.

For instance, Tooke shows how the English preposition *through* in face derives its meaning from its origin as a noun.

B.   But of what real object is THROUGH the name?

H.   Of a very common one indeed. For as the French peculiar preposition CHEZ is no other than the Italian substantive CASA or CA, so is the English preposition THOR-OUGH, thourough, thorow, through, or thro', no other than the Gothic substantive *dauro*, or the Teutonic substantive *thuruh*: and, like them, means door, gate, passage. [...] I am persuaded that Door and Through have one and the same Gothic origin *dauro*, mean one and the same thing; and are in fact one and the same word.

(Diversions of Purley: 180–3)

Here the (purported) fact that *through* really means 'door' is a fact of the language, not of some individual speaker's use of the terms.

For Tooke a language is a system – of word-to-word relations, of relations of abbreviation and substitution, of ellipsis and sub-audition, etc. – a system that is essentially independent of the mind and its categories and operations (because those categories and operations are essentially properties of language). It is furthermore an etymological system: knowledge of a language requires knowledge of its history. To know what a given word really means you must know the etymon from which it has, by processes of abbreviation and corruption, been derived. A speaker who does not know that *from* is derived from a word meaning 'beginning' or *through* from a word meaning 'door' does not know what those words mean. Hence, when that speaker uses *through* and *from*, he is not fully aware of what he is in fact saying. If the hearer is in the same position, then it is easy to see why they might be thought of as 'gabbling like things most brutish'. Again, our language is perfect; it is our understanding of it, misled by centuries of philosophical mystification, which is imperfect and which leads us to use it ignorantly and inaccurately, thus threatening communicational success.

Another important feature of Tooke's linguistic thought, then, is its firm distinction between the structure of a language and how that language is used by its speakers. For Tooke, most speakers do not know what many of the words they use really mean: i.e. they do not know the meanings assigned to those words by their language. They have been fooled by philosophers and others in the educated classes into thinking that those words meant something else. And by being led into confusion about the meanings of their words they have also been led into conceptual confusion. With Tooke's great discovery, the instrument of etymological analysis, they may investigate the true meanings of the words they use, and so disabuse themselves of centuries of speculation and mystification, by which the ordinary man has been deprived of his language, of its true meanings, and of the most important concepts of religious, moral, and civic life. Tooke's empirical linguistics was intended to end the control which the established authorities had long exercised over language, its concepts, and, through these, the human mind. It is no wonder that Tooke's contemporaries had difficulty separating his political from his linguistic and philosophical ideas.

And yet, at the same time, this was also one of the main reasons for Tooke's dominating influence in the English-speaking world at the end of the eighteenth and the beginning of the nineteenth century. With Tooke it all seemed to fall into place: the eighteenth-century ideas that language is a mirror of the mind, that in the history of a language lay its explanation, and that, according to the empiricist strain in philosophy, the mind acquires its contents by means of sensory experience. Uniting these ideas into a coherent theory, Tooke also offered for the first time to move the study of language (and thus of mind) from the realm of the speculative into that of empirical science. Like chemistry, a science which made great strides in the eighteenth century, the study of language could be guided by scientific principles.

> Mr Tooke ... treated words as the chemists do substances; he separated those which are compounded from those which are not decompoundable. He did not explain the obscure by the more obscure, but the difficult by the plain, the complex by the simple. This alone is proceeding upon the true principles of science: the rest is pedantry and *petitmaitreship*.
>
> (Hazlitt, 1825, quoted in Aarsleff 1983: 71)

Chapter twelve

Humboldt on linguistic and mental diversity

Now in language, insofar as it actually appears in man, two
constitutive principles may be distinguished: the *inner linguistic
sense* (by which I understand, not a special power, but the entire
mental capacity, as related to the formation and use of language,
and thus merely a tendency); and *sound*, insofar as it depends on
the constitution of the organs, and is based on what has been
handed down already. The inner linguistic sense is the principle
which dominates language from within outwards, and
everywhere supplies the guiding impulse. Sound, in and for itself,
would resemble the passive matter which receives form. But since
permeation by the linguistic sense transforms it into *articulate*
sound, containing both intellectual and sensuous power,
inseparably united and in constant mutual interaction, it becomes,
in its perpetual symbolizing activity, the actual *creative principle*
in language, and seemingly even an independent one. Just as it is
a general law of man's existence in the world, that he can project
nothing from himself that does not at once become a thing that
reacts upon him and conditions his further creation, so sound
also modifies in its turn the outlook and procedure of the inner
linguistic sense. Thus every subsequent creation does not
maintain the simple direction of the original force, but is subject
to a composite influence, made up of this and the force supplied
by the product created earlier. Since the *natural disposition* to
language is universal in man, and everyone must possess the key
to the understanding of all languages, it follows automatically
that the *form* of all languages must be essentially the *same*, and
always achieve the universal purpose. The *difference* can lie only
in the means, and only within the limits permitted by attainment
of the goal. It is multifariously present in languages, however,

and not in the mere *sounds* alone, so that the same things are just differently designated; it also occurs in the *use* which the linguistic sense makes of sounds, with a view to the form of language, and even in its own conception of this form. Through it alone, indeed, so far as languages are purely formal, should mere *uniformity* be able to arise in them. For it must demand in all of them the *correct* and *regular* structure, which can only be one and the same. But in reality matters are not like this, partly owing to the *retroactive effect of sound*, partly because of the *individuality* of the inner sense, as manifested in appearance. It is a matter, that is, of the *energy* of the force whereby it acts upon the sound, and transforms the latter in every nuance, even the finest, into a living expression of thought. But this energy cannot everywhere be the same, cannot everywhere display a like intensity, vivacity and regularity. Nor is it always supported by a similar inclination to treat the thought symbolically, or a similar aesthetic pleasure in sonic abundance and euphony. [...] In all of this, taken together, lie the grounds for the necessary *diversity of structure in the languages of man*. Languages cannot contain it in themselves, since the nations who speak them are different, and have an existence governed by different circumstances.

In consideration of *language as such*, a form must be disclosed, which of all those imaginable *coincides the most* with the *aims of language*, and we must be able to judge the merits and defects of existing languages by the *degree* to which they approximate to this one form. [...] We have everywhere set out at first from the *structure* of languages alone, and in forming a judgement about it have also confined ourselves solely to this. Now that this structure is better in one than another, is more excellent in Sanscrit than in Chinese, and in Greek than in Arabic, could hardly be disputed by any impartial scholar. However we might try to weigh off their respective virtues, we should always have to admit that one of these languages is animated by a *more fruitful principle of mental development* than the other. But now we should inevitably have misconstrued all the mutual relations of *mind* and *language*, if we were unwilling to extend the various consequences thereof to the *reverse action* of these languages, and to the *intellectuality* of the peoples who created them (so far as this lies within human capacity at all). So from this point of view our proposed approach is perfectly justified.

(*On language*: 214–17)

If we enter, however, as we cannot refrain from doing, into the nature of this *diversity* in the particular form of language-structure, we can no longer seek to apply to the details of language an investigation of mental individuality, first undertaken separately for its own sake. In the early epochs to which the present considerations transport us, we know the nations, as such, only by their languages, nor do we ever know exactly which people, even, we are to think of, by descent and affinity, in connection with each language. [...] Among all manifestations whereby spirit and character can be recognized, language, however, is also the only one suited to exhibit both, even to their inmost windings and recesses. If we look upon *languages*, therefore, as a basis for explaining successive *mental development*, we must indeed regard them as having arisen through intellectual individuality, but must seek the nature of this individuality in every case in its *structure*.

(*On language*: 46–7)

On language: the diversity of human language-structure and its influence on the mental development of mankind was first published in 1836, one year after the death of its author, Wilhelm von Humboldt. It has proven to be one of the most important texts in the history of European linguistic ideas, bridging the transition between the philosophical orientation of linguistic study in the 17th and 18th centuries and the newly emerging interest in an autonomous science of language characteristic of much of the 19th and 20th century.

Humboldt was a member of the Prussian aristocracy and served in a variety of administrative and diplomatic positions, travelling widely in Europe, until he retired in 1819 in order to devote the rest of his life to the study of language. *On language*, which was written during this period, was conceived as the introduction to a much longer work *On the Kawi language on the island of Java*. The latter, published from 1836 to 1839 in three volumes, is a study of the old sacred language of the (now Indonesian) island of Java, a language of interest to Humboldt because of its mixing of Sanskrit vocabulary and Malayan grammatical structure. *On language* was to serve as a philosophical introduction to the longer work and to provide a theoretical foundation for the interpretation of the empirical data on the Kawi language.

We may take Humboldt's general position in the history of linguistic thought to be that of relating the findings of the new field of comparative-historical linguistics both to the philosophical ideas on language characteristic of the 18th century as well as to the philosophy of anthropology which was an integral part of German Romanticism. More specifically, his aim could be said to be that of raising and attempting to answer the philosophical questions suggested by the recent linguistic discoveries about the relatedness and diversity in the structural patterns adopted by human languages. In this light, we may take him to be asking questions such as the following. Why do the languages of different peoples manifest such regularly different structures? What determines the evolutionary path a language takes? Why is a language with one sort of structure spoken by, say, the Delaware Indians, while a language with a very different sort of structure is spoken by the Chinese? And what effect do these differing linguistic structures have on the ideas of the peoples who speak them? Apparently Humboldt felt that, although comparative-historical linguistics was an important new science, its purview was too restricted to the exclusively formal study of the 'sound-form' of languages, that is to their sound patterns and grammatical organization. For he felt that it was in the 'hidden' mental side of language, in what he calls in the first extract above the 'inner linguistic sense', that the causes of formal linguistic relationship and differentiation could be found and, at the same time, their effects revealed.

The answers that Humboldt provides to these questions have their foundation in 17th- and 18th-century linguistic thought, particularly in the writings of Condillac and Diderot. At the same time, they are strongly influenced by the incorporation of the viewpoints and prejudices of German Romanticism, especially the Romantic theory of aesthetics as well as what might be called a Romantic theory of anthropology (a theory which looks to us today very much like a theory of racial difference). It is to this influence that we may attribute Humboldt's aim not only to explain the source and effects of the differences between different language families but also to establish criteria for placing language structures on a scale ranging from 'perfect' to 'most imperfect'.

Humboldt's theory of language is founded on an opposition between what he identifies in the first extract as the two constitutive principles of language: inner linguistic sense and sound. With regard to the former, he argues, language is an activity (*energeia*) not a product (*ergon*): it is 'the ever-repeated mental labour of making the articulated sound capable of expressing thought; ... language proper lies in the act of its real production' (*On language* p. 49). Yet at the same time, Humboldt argues, because the sound-form of a language 'is based on what has been handed down already', 'the mental activity which as earlier explained produces the expression of thought, is always directed at once upon something given; it is not a purely creative, but a reshaping activity' (*On language* p. 50). That is (we might say), language is always encountered as *ergon*, a product already 'in place'. But how can both of these statements be true?

On the one hand, Humboldt sees language as a creative act, as a doing, rather than a something done. Furthermore, he takes there to have been a moment in time (now so distant that we can have no historical knowledge of it) when the ancestors of today's languages were created, each the result of a spontaneous, collective outburst of the inner linguistic sense of what Humboldt will call variously a nation, a people, or a race. This is a purely creative act, based on nothing other than the 'mental force' shared by all the people of that nation. It is an expression of the inner freedom and energy of the people, but expressed in a voice which they all share and which is characteristic of them all as a nation.

> Words well up freely from the breast, without necessity or intent, and there may well have been no wandering horde in any desert that did not already have its own songs. For man, as a species, is a singing creature, though the notes, in his case, are also coupled with thought.
>
> (*On language*: 60)

In other words, language is originally something that comes 'from the inside'. And the particular form of singing that comes from the inside of one nation, one race, will depend on the mental characteristics of that nation, that is, on their inner linguistic sense. In the same way that one species of bird will spontaneously emit one variety of song, or warble, or quack, or coo, and another another kind, also in man different races will spontaneously express themselves in fundamentally different ways. Furthermore, the differentiating mental characteristic of the race will also reveal itself in other social and cultural practices, although it will be best revealed in language. Humboldt's theory of language is, then, at the very outset and in its foundational principles, a fundamentally racialist theory. According to Humboldt, there is something mental, something spiritual, something organically different about different nations (peoples, races) which makes them creatively express themselves in the way they originally do and, within limits, continue to do throughout their history. Humboldt's theory is also in this respect a form of racial determinism.

> ... every nation, quite apart from its external situation, can and must be regarded as a human individuality, which pursues an inner spiritual path of its own.
>
> (*On language*: 41)

> Language and intellectual endowment, in their constant interaction, admit of no separation, and even historical destinies may not be so independent of the inner nature of peoples and individuals, for all that the connection is far from being evident to us on every point.
>
> (*On language*: 183)

Yet the spontaneously creative aspect of language is not to be regarded as confined to the origin of language; it is present in every act of speech. Language is *always* 'an act, a truly creative performance of the mind', and an act performed by an individual with freedom of the will. The difference is that in a given linguistic act performed today (i.e. as opposed to the original act in the formation of a language), the individual speaker finds himself in a historical contingency, a contingency characterized in part by the existence of a given language belonging to the nation of which he is a member. And this language comes already provided with a sound-form, that is, with a grammar and a phonology. Thus the individual cannot, in fact, in any given act of speech behave entirely creatively and with complete freedom. He must to some extent conform to the rules of his language. Here Humboldt speaks of the 'ascendancy of the sound-form', the power of the already-created over the new act of creation, of the *ergon* over the *energeia*, the product over the producing.

Analogously we might consider the purely creative act of a poet, an act which is a free expression of his individual personality. And yet a poet always writes, always produces poetry within a particular historical context, a context which in part will be characterized by particular conventions of poetic form. In this case his otherwise purely free, spontaneously creative act must pour itself into a pre-existing mould determined by the conventions of the day, conventions which are themselves the legacy of earlier creative acts of poem-making. These conventions, then, constitute the rules of the game in which and as a part of which any new act is to occur. Nevertheless, this does not mean that the conventions are fixed for all time or that poetic form is not subject to evolution. For every creative act of poem-making is always an outburst of 'inner' mental energy, that is, the expression of what by analogy we might call 'inner poetic sense'. And in so far as that creative act is individual and determined by the character of the poet himself, it will stretch the formal limits imposed by poetic convention. Thus every truly poetic act will to some greater or lesser degree alter established poetic form and will push the established conventions towards change. In the same way every new act of speech will contribute to the evolution of the sound-form of the language. Consequently, the shared inner linguistic sense of a people, through its spontaneous expression in every act of speech, will cause the language inch-by-inch, step-by-step to change in a regular, uniform way. From this perspective, then, linguistic evolution is the continuous outcome of this dialectic between inner linguistic sense and sound-form; that is, between *energeia* and *ergon*.

> ... the goal, therefore, of mankind's developing progress is always the fusion of what is produced independently from within with what is given from without, ...
>
> (*On language*: 30)

It should now be clear that language undergoes shaping from two different directions. On the one hand, it is imbued with a spirit, a character which is particular to the individual speaker, although its essential characteristics will be shared by all the individuals in his nation/race. So what a speaker says is to this extent determined from within, by his individual (national) character (which itself can be reflected in the degree of his mental power). On the other hand, what he says is also determined from without, by the rules and patterns of the language which he speaks, the sediment of past individual linguistic acts performed by the members of his nation/race.

Related to this central dialectic between *energeia* and *ergon* are Humboldt's views on the relation between language and thought. Like Condillac, Humboldt argued that it is only because man has a language that he is able to control the operations of his mind.

Language enables self-consciousness and the articulation and analysis of the otherwise formless thought stream.

> Language is the formative organ of thought. Intellectual activity, entirely mental, entirely internal, and to some extent passing without trace, becomes, through sound, externalized in speech and perceptible to the senses. Thought and language are therefore one and inseparable from each other. But the former is also intrinsically bound to the necessity of entering into a union with the verbal sound; thought cannot otherwise achieve clarity, nor the idea become a concept.
> [...]
> Subjective activity fashions an object in thought. For no class of presentations can be regarded as a purely receptive contemplation of a thing already present. [...] But language is indispensable for this. For in that the mental striving breaks out through the lips in language, the product of that striving returns back to the speaker's ear. Thus the presentation becomes transformed into real objectivity, without being deprived of subjectivity on that account. Only language can do this; and without this transformation ... all true thinking is impossible.
>
> (*On language*: 54–6)

So language is necessary for 'true thinking', as well as for the communication of thoughts. Without language, as Condillac, and to some extent also Locke, argued, the mind cannot bind individual sensory inputs into manipulable concepts (and so it cannot truly 'know' what it passively experiences). Nor can it analyse complex experiences into comprehensible parts.

'True thinking' consists in separating and combining (*On language*: 110) – i.e. in analysing – as opposed to the more primitive, formless mental activity which, without language, often 'passes without a trace'. And the efficacy of a language, particularly its sound-form, is that it is a mechanism which enables man to separate and combine otherwise formless mental activity into true thought. It is because the sound-form of a language is articulated that it can be used in turn to articulate thought. And only in this way can the passive reception of experience be fused with the subjective phenomenon of 'inner mental activity'. Consequently, how we make sense of our experiences and 'view' the world around us is dependent upon the articulating structure that our language makes available to us. Language is thus the medium by which man synthesizes objective experience with subjective mentality. It is because we have language that, unlike the animals, we can control the operations of the mind, attain self-consciousness, and understand our experiences.

However, the way that a people analyse their experiences, construct concepts, and combine concepts in the formation of thought is itself a reflection of and is itself determined by (albeit indirectly) their national/racial character. This results in the double bind which Humboldt describes in the following:

> The true synthesis springs from the inspiration known only to
> high and energetic power. In the imperfect one, this inspiration
> has been lacking; and a language so engendered likewise exerts a
> less inspiring power in its use. [...] The smaller mental power of
> the nation, which carries the blame for this deficiency, then evokes
> the same again, through the influence of a more imperfect
> language, in subsequent generations...
>
> (*On language*: 89)

National mental individuality determines the sort of language a people have; that language in turn determines the way they think, perceive and understand reality. In this way, the individual's membership of a particular nation – possessing its inner linguistic sense – would have a determining effect on the structure of the language he spoke and, therefore, also on his thinking. Language is thus the instrument not only for the synthesizing of subject and object, but also for moulding national identity.

Because of this argument Humboldt has often been said to be a linguistic relativist. In opposition to linguistic rationalists (for example the Port-Royal grammarians) who take the structure of thought to determine the structure of language, the relativist takes the structure (or articulation) of language to determine the structure of the language-user's thoughts. Although this characterization of Humboldt's views has some merit, at least in opposing Humboldt to the rationalist, at a less superficial level it is quite wrong: and wrong in two ways. For, like the Port-Royal grammarians, Humboldt did argue that all languages shared a universal form, a form determined by the nature of their purpose: i.e. the expression of thoughts. Furthermore, far from taking a relativist stance on the nature of the connection of language to thought, Humboldt's position would be more accurately characterized as a form of linguistic absolutism, an absolutism which is strangely reminiscent of the prescriptivism of the rationalist linguists of the 18th century.

That Humboldt believed that all languages share certain universal properties is clear from the first extract quoted at the beginning of this chapter.

> Since the natural disposition to language is universal in man, and everyone must possess the key to the understanding of all languages, it follows automatically that the form of all languages must be essentially the same, and always achieve the universal purpose. The difference can lie only in the means, and only within the limits permitted by attainment of the goal.
>
> *(On language*: 215)

In an earlier work, the *Grundzüge des allgemeinen Sprachtypus* (1824–6), Humboldt argues that what is common to all languages has its source in universal laws of thought.

> The similarity of the laws of thought produces what is shared by the grammar of all languages, by means of which each can be related to the universal grammar and to each other. Every grammatical form may, in some way or another, be pointed out in every language, ...
>
> *(Grundzüge* V: 453 in Manchester 1986: 74)

Apparently, Humboldt believed that all languages somehow had to indicate such universal grammatical features as the parts of speech, case relations, active and passive voice, and verbal mood. And if a given language did not explicitly indicate one of these features, then – as many universal grammarians argued before as well as after Humboldt – they would have to be 'added in thought'. Again in the *Grundzüge* he says

> When a grammatical form possesses no designation in a language, it is nevertheless still present as a guiding principle of the understanding of those who speak the language...
>
> *(Grundzüge* V: 469 in Manchester 1986: 77)

So it would be inaccurate to describe Humboldt's position as a form of relativism in which the thought of a people is solely determined by the language they speak. Rather he argued that there are some universal principles of thought which determine the grammatical functions which every language must perform. What varies from language to language is the means by which these grammatical functions are realized. For instance, every language must somehow indicate the case relations that hold between the different component parts of a thought (or at the very least add them in thought). But how this task is accomplished in different languages will vary. Latin shows these relations by means of inflections. Chinese shows them by word order. But in both cases the same task is achieved. 'The difference can lie only in the means, and only within the limits permitted by attainment of the goal' (*On language*: 215).

One aspect of linguistic variation with which Humboldt was expressly concerned is that of grammatical typology. Humboldt identifies four basic types of language: isolating, agglutinating, inflecting, and incorporating. These four types of languages differ in the grammatical means adopted for identifying the constituent parts of a sentence and for uniting those parts into a coherent whole reflecting the structure of the thought expressed. The isolating language relies almost exclusively on word order and grammatical words such as prepositions and conjunctions to accomplish this task. Humboldt used Chinese as his example of an isolating language, although as he pointed out every language is in fact a mixture of different types. Languages that are agglutinating (for example Turkish) or inflecting (for example Latin or Sanskrit) rely on word formation to accomplish the same task that the isolating language achieves by word order and grammatical words. Whereas an agglutinating language adds an affix onto a word for each of the grammatical relations indicated, the inflecting language signals its grammatical relationships by a single affix attached at the end or incorporated directly into the root. Incorporating languages (such as Delaware) are distinguished by their method of incorporating most of the significant parts of the sentence into a single word, with the verb morpheme as the unifying root. Humboldt argued that the grammatical type adopted by any language was determined by the inner linguistic sense of its speakers. Certain nations were more mentally disposed towards agglutinating languages, others towards isolating languages, and so on.

The final stage in Humboldt's argument and the source of his linguistic absolutism is the claim that although every language must perform the universal grammatical functions such as signalling the parts of a thought, indicating the construction of a concept, and signalling the relationships of each of the parts of the sentence to the others, nevertheless the means by which one language might achieve these universal grammatical tasks could be better or worse than those adopted by another language. Which method is adopted by a given language (or language family) depends on the mental individuality of its nation of speakers. Yet, according to Humboldt, one of these methods will indisputably be better than the others. Consequently, because the speakers must make use of their language to articulate their thoughts and control their mental operations, the less grammatically efficient form will hamper the intellectual operations of its users. So the inferior creative impulse which led them to adopt a less efficacious method of signalling grammatical relations has a permanent effect which cannot be transcended.

Humboldt believed in the notion of what might be called an ideal language, a language which perfectly accomplished the universal grammatical tasks.

> ... a form must be disclosed, which of all those imaginable coincides the most with the aims of language, and we must be able to judge the merits and defects of existing languages by the degree to which they approximate to this one form.
>
> (*On language*: 217)

In principle, all languages could be placed on a scale reflecting their nearness to the ideal language. Humboldt found the inflecting language Sanskrit to be the closest to this ideal and Chinese, as an isolating language, to be the furthest from it. But why are inflecting languages closest to the ideal?

> Grammatical formation arises from the laws of thinking in language, and rests on the congruence of sound-forms with the latter. Such a congruence must in some way be present in every language; the difference lies only in degree, and the blame for defective development may attach to an insufficiently plain emergence of these laws in the soul, or to an inadequate malleability of the sound-system. But deficiency on the one point always reacts back at once upon the other. The perfecting of language demands that every word be stamped as a specific part of speech, and carry within it those properties that a philosophical analysis of language perceives therein. It thus itself presupposes inflection.
>
> (*On language*: 140)

Essentially Humboldt's favouring of inflectional languages is based on his conviction that they most efficaciously accomplish the grammatical tasks which are required of a language. He argued that ideally in designating a concept a word should indicate and distinguish between two different functions. It must not only pick out the relevant concept, it must also indicate

> ... the special operation of the mind which transposes that concept into a particular category of thought or speech; and the word's full meaning is the simultaneous outcome of that conceptual expression and this modifying hint.
>
> (*On language*: 145)

What is ideal about an inflecting language is that it accomplishes this within the same word, fusing each of the functions of the word within the same form. This mirrors the way in which the concept is itself a fusion of the passive representation of an object of experience and the subjective categorizing of that representation in the logic of thought. Thus the ideal language for Humboldt is one which mirrors the dialectical opposition of subject and object, *energeia* and *ergon*, both synthesized in the simultaneous formation of language and thought.

> If I have succeeded in depicting the method of inflection in all its completeness, how it alone imparts true inner fixity to the word for both mind and ear, and likewise separates with certainty the parts of the sentence, in keeping with the necessary ordering of thought, then there can be no doubt but that it harbours exclusively the sure principle of language-structure. In that it takes every element of speech in its two-fold significance, its objective meaning and subjective relation to thought and language, and designates this duality in its relative weight by sound-forms appropriate thereto, it elevates the most primary essence of language, viz. articulation and symbolization to their highest degree.
>
> (*On language*: 145)

Thus Humboldt's ideal language is one in which word formation mirrors concept formation, the latter being thought of as a fusing of the passive experience of an object and the active subjective articulation of that concept in thought.

On the other hand an isolating language like Chinese was seen by Humboldt to be most imperfect, precisely because it does not indicate grammatical relations by way of affixes, but almost exclusively by means of word order and grammatical words like prepositions. (According to these criteria, English, with many more isolating characteristics than inflectional, would be a most imperfect language. Yet Humboldt excepts English from this condemnation – and the Romance languages and German as well – because although they no longer now appear to be inflecting, they once were and that inner – i.e. hidden – form remains).

It is only in an inflectional language that the system of word formation approaches the ideal of what Humboldt calls 'explicability within itself'.

> The essential basis of sound-connection among words is that a moderate number of root-sounds, underlying the whole vocabulary, is applied, by additions and changes, to concepts increasingly definite and compounded. The recurrence of the same ancestral sound, or even the possibility of recognizing it by specific rules, and the regular significance of the modifying affixes or inner changes, thereupon determine that explicability of the language from itself which may be termed a mechanical or technical one.

> (*On language*: 94)

Chapter thirteen

Müller on linguistic evolution

Even Epicurus, who is reported to have said that in the first
formation of language men acted unconsciously, moved by
nature, as in coughing, sneezing, lowing, barking, or sighing,
admitted that this would account only for one-half of language,
and that some agreement must have taken place before language
really began, before people could know what each person meant
by these uncouth utterances. In this Epicurus shows a more
correct appreciation of the nature of language than many who
profess to hold his theories at present. He met the objection that
words, if suggested by nature, ought to be the same in all
countries, by a remark in which he anticipated Humboldt, viz.
that human nature is affected differently in different countries,
that different views are formed of things, and that these different
affections and views influence the formation of words peculiar
to each nation. He saw that the sounds of nature would never
have grown into articulate language without passing through a
second stage, which he represents as an agreement or an
understanding to use a certain sound for a certain conception.
Let us substitute for this Epicurean idea of a conventional
agreement an idea which did not exist in his time, and the full
elaboration of which in our own time we owe to the genius of
Darwin; – let us place instead of agreement, *Natural Selection*,
or, as I called it in my former Lectures, *Natural Elimination*, and
we shall then arrive, I believe, at an understanding with Epicurus,
and even with some of his modern followers. As a number of
sensuous impressions, received by man, produce a mental image
or a *perception*, and secondly, as a number of such perceptions
produce a general notion or *conception*, we may understand that
a number of sensuous impressions may cause a corresponding

vocal expression, a cry, an interjection, or some imitation of the sound that happens to form part of the sensuous impressions; and secondly, that a number of such vocal expressions may be merged into one general expression, and leave behind the root as the sign belonging to a general notion. But as there is in man a faculty of reason which guides and governs the formation of sensuous impressions into perceptions and perceptions into general notions, the gradual formation of roots out of mere natural cries or imitations takes place under the same rational control. General notions are not formed at random, but according to law, that law being our reason within corresponding to the reason without – to the reason, if I may so call it, of nature. Natural selection, if we could but always see it, is invariably rational selection. It is not any accidental variety that survives and perpetuates itself; it is the individual which comes nearest to the original intention of its creator, or what is best calculated to accomplish the ends for which the type or species to which it belongs was called into being, that conquers in the great struggle for life. So it is in thought and language.

(F. Max Müller, *Lectures on the science of language*)

The greatest single influence on linguistic thought in the nineteenth century was exercised not by a linguist but by a biologist: Charles Darwin. Of revolutionary impact in so many fields, Darwin's *The origin of species* (1859) was a work which could hardly have failed to polarize opinion among scholars engaged in the comparative and historical study of the Indo-European languages. The arrival of Darwinism on the linguistic scene was announced by the publication in 1863 of August Schleicher's *Die Darwinische Theorie*, in which sound change is held to take place in accordance with fixed laws, which are assimilated to natural laws. The extent and rapidity of the incursion of Darwinian ideas in linguistics is attested in the passage quoted above from the writings of one of the best known Indo-Europeanists of the day, Friedrich Max Müller. Müller's lecture was published in 1864, only five years after *The origin of species* itself. Why was the intellectual penetration of this biological theory into linguistics so immediate and so profound?

What Darwin actually says about languages in *The origin of species* does not, at first sight, seem to amount to very much; for linguistic communication is a topic far removed from the main theme of the work. But Darwin invokes the study of languages in a crucially important theoretical passage, where he wishes to justify his contention that there is a 'Natural System' of classification. This system, he claims, is based on 'descent with modification'. The point is vital for his thesis, which is otherwise open to the objection that he has erected an arbitrarily chosen schema of classification into a historical explanation. Looking for a non-biological example to support his argument, Darwin finds one in the analysis of linguistic affiliation.

> It may be worth while to illustrate this view of classification by taking the case of languages. If we possessed a perfect pedigree of mankind, a genealogical arrangement of the races of man would afford the best classification of the various languages now spoken throughout the world; and if all extinct languages, and all intermediate and slowly changing dialects, were to be included, such an arrangement would be the only possible one. Yet it might be that some ancient languages had altered very little and had given rise to few new languages, whilst others had altered much owing to the spreading, isolation, and state of civilisation of the several co-descended races, and had thus given rise to many new dialects and languages. The various degrees of difference between the languages of the same stock would have to be expressed by groups subordinate to groups; but the proper or even the only possible arrangement would still be genealogical; and this would be strictly natural, as it would connect together all languages, extinct and recent, by the closest affinities, and would give the filiation and origin of each tongue
>
> (*The origin of species*, Chapter 14)

The significance of this single paragraph for a linguistics still striving to establish its own scientific credentials in the academic world of the 19th century cannot be overestimated. In effect, Darwin says that linguistics, as practised by the leading exponents of comparative Indo-European philology, offers *the* paradigm of scientific method. It has moved from mere comparison to *historical* comparison; and historical comparison is nothing other than genealogy. The same judgement was to be endorsed for a later generation of linguists by Saussure, who was born two years before the publication of *The origin of species*. The first chapter of Saussure's *Cours de linguistique générale*, although it does not mention Darwin by name, restates Darwin's point. Classification which is based on comparison alone is not enough: linguistics reached maturity when linguists began to realize that comparison between languages is meaningless until placed in a developmental context. For Saussure, this intellectual breakthrough was the work of the German school of linguists known as the Neogrammarians (*Junggrammatiker*). Their six leaders Saussure names as Brugmann, Osthoff, Braune, Sievers, Paul and Leskien. 'The achievement of the Neogramarians was to place all the results of comparative philology in a historical perspective, so that linguistic facts were connected in their natural sequence' (Saussure 1922:18). It is the phrase 'natural sequence' (*ordre naturel*) which marks the link between Darwin's concept of a natural system of classification and Saussure's view of the history of linguistics.

The new intellectual alliance between biology and linguistics was, understandably, welcomed more warmly by linguists than by biologists. Max Müller, a German Sanskrit scholar who had been appointed to Oxford's first Chair of Comparative Philology, was particularly anxious to establish the claims of his subject to be regarded as a 'science'. He was a brilliant popularizer, whose gift for explaining philological technicalities to a general audience has probably never been surpassed. In 1861 he gave the first of a series of *Lectures on the science of language* in London; and their success established his reputation. By a 'science' Müller meant one of the natural sciences. He claimed:

> the language which we speak, and the languages that are and that have been spoken in every part of our globe since the first dawn of human life and human thought, supply materials capable of scientific treatment. We can collect them, we can classify them, we can reduce them to their constituent elements, and deduce from them some of the laws that determine their origin, govern their growth, necessitate their decay; we can treat them, in fact, in exactly the same spirit in which the geologist treats his stones and petrifactions, – nay, in some respects, in the same spirit in which the astronomer treats the stars of heaven or the botanist the flowers of the field. There *is* a Science of Language as there is a science of the earth, its flowers and its stars.
>
> (*Lectures on the science of language*, vol. 2: 1)

The academic honeymoon was prolonged when Darwin responded in kind in *The descent of man* (1871).

Languages, like organic beings, can be classed in groups under groups; and they can be classed either naturally according to descent, or artificially by other characters. Dominant languages and dialects spread widely, and lead to the gradual extinction of other tongues. A language, like a species, when once extinct, never, as Sir C. Lyell remarks, reappears. The same language never has two birth-places. Distinct languages may be crossed or blended together. We see variability in every tongue, and new words are continually cropping up; but as there is a limit to the powers of the memory, single words, like whole languages, gradually become extinct. As Max Müller has well remarked:– 'A struggle for life is constantly going on amongst the words and grammatical forms in each language. The better, the shorter, the easier forms are constantly gaining the upper hand, and they owe their success to their own inherent virtue.' To these more important causes of the survival of certain words, mere novelty and fashion may be added; for there is in the mind of man a strong love for slight changes in all things. The survival or preservation of certain favoured words in the struggle for existence is natural selection.

(*The descent of man*: 138–9)

Quite apart from the fact that Darwin had provided a validation of the methodology evolved in 19th-century linguistics, he had also provided a glib answer to the question which most vexed those linguists who still wondered how the apparently inexorable processes of linguistic change were to be explained. A teleological explanation seemed totally unacceptable once linguistics had parted company with contemporary theology and the Bible. 'Natural selection' appeared on the horizon like a supply convoy to a beleaguered garrison. Languages changed because the mechanisms of natural selection so determined.

*   *   *

The acuteness of the explanatory dilemma which was posed by historical linguistics, and to which 'natural selection' appeared to supply an answer, cannot be appreciated without a brief excursus to examine the theoretical position the Neogrammarians adopted.

Already in 1822 Jacob Grimm, in the second edition of his *Deutsche Grammatik*, had introduced the notion of systematic sound change (*Lautverschiebung*) and set out a famous example which came to be known as 'Grimm's Law' (although the facts on which it is based had first been noticed by the Danish scholar Rasmus Rask and published by him in 1818). Grimm's Law attempts to demonstrate a systematic correspondence between Greek, Gothic and Old High German in respect of the consonants occurring in etymologically related sets of words. According to Grimm's formula, where Greek has *p*, Gothic has *f*, and Old High German has *b*; where Greek has *b*, Gothic has *p* and Old High German *f*; etc. The whole set of correspondences may be tabulated as:

Greek	p	b	f	t	d	th	k	g	ch
Gothic	f	p	b	th	t	d	h	k	g
O.H.G.	b(v)	f	p	d	z	t	g	ch	k

and summarized as:

Greek	T	M	A
Gothic	A	T	M
O.H.G.	M	A	T

Here T stands for *tenues* ('voiceless consonants': k, t, p), M stands for *mediae* ('voiced consonants': g, d, b), and A stands for *aspirates* ('breathed consonants': kh, th, h, f, z). The formula claims that there is a regular rotational pattern of phonetic development as between Greek, Gothic and Old High German, whereby tenues 'become' aspirates, which 'become' mediae; while mediae 'become' tenues, which 'become' aspirates; and aspirates 'become' mediae, which 'become' tenues. (As systematized by Grimm, the 'Law' does not in fact hold, a snag which later scholars pointed out; but this inadequacy is less important for our present purposes than the idealization which Grimm's Law captures.)

Indo-European scholars were encouraged by the discovery of Grimm's Law to look for similar patterns of phonetic correspondence between the Indo-European languages, and thus to work out a coherent theory of sound changes which would 'explain' the relationships obtaining between them, on the assumption that they were descended from a common ancestral language. To this extent, Indo-European comparative philology was already Darwinian in spirit before Darwin. However, Grimm had not himself claimed that such a pattern as his *Lautverschiebung* had the status of a 'law': he was content to describe it simply as a general tendency, not invariably followed in every case. The Neogrammarians, a generation later, were not satisfied with this. In their view, if linguistics was to become a science it must discover linguistic *laws*, just as the natural sciences discovered natural laws: and a law in this more rigorous sense was not just a general tendency, which might or might not be followed in particular instances. Accordingly, they championed the view that linguists must devote their efforts to the search for changes to which there were no exceptions at all: indeed, this they proposed as their *definition* of a sound change. The text which is generally regarded as the manifesto of the Neogrammarian view of language is the Preface to the *Morphologische Untersuchungen* by Hermann Osthoff and Karl Brugmann, published in 1878. There it is claimed that 'Every change of sound, in so far as it is a mechanical process, takes place according to *laws which admit of no exception*.' The reason for adopting this definition, however, had been stated more clearly two years earlier by Leskien in his book *Die Declination im Slavisch-Litauischen und Germanischen*. According to Leskien, 'To admit haphazard deviations, impossible to coordinate, is to assert in reality that the object of our science, language, is inaccessible to science.'

*   *   *

Sound change, for the Neogrammarians, was a gradual, unconscious, cumulative process, explicable by reference to the physiology of the human speech organs. Minimal shifts of articulation built up over generations to a point where, in the retrospective view of the historian, a change of pronunciation could be seen to have taken place. This was constantly going on, but so slowly that it escaped contemporary observation, in the same way that the gradual erosion of stone by weathering remains 'invisible', or, as in Darwin's theory, the gradual evolution of new species remains hidden because it takes longer than the lifetime of any observer.

The Neogrammarians were perfectly well aware, nevertheless, that if the operation of exceptionless sound laws had been solely responsible for linguistic change, it should have produced a far closer and more regular pattern of correspondences between the various Indo-European languages than was actually attested. Therefore they were forced to admit the existence of a second factor operative in the processes of linguistic change. This second factor was analogy. Analogy was to account for all cases of the preservation or creation of forms due to the recognition of similarities. (*Shoes* replaced the older form *shoen* as the plural of *shoe*, because of the analogy with other noun plurals ending in -*s*.) By combining sound change with analogy, the Neogrammarians arrived at a very simple theory which recognized just two forces constantly shaping the languages of the world: one physical or mechanical and the other psychological. This duality had in its favour an immediately recognizable parallel with the traditional distinction between body and mind. Human language was constantly evolving, according to this theory, because of the endless cumulative interplay between physiological and psychological processes in speech activity.

The Neogrammarian theory of language was from one point of view simply a more rigorous, systematic statement of certain assumptions about linguistic variation which many linguists of the 19th century had often in practice accepted. But once articulated in the form of an explicit theory, these assumptions immediately generated a problem. If *that* was how language changed, why wasn't the result simply ever-increasing chaos? Why did certain words, forms, pronunciations survive and come regularly to replace earlier words, forms and pronunciations? Why did not language just go on accumulating the verbal detritus of a thousand generations of speakers, without jettisoning any of it? This was the problem to which Darwinism now seemed to supply an answer: the principle of 'natural selection', or 'survival of the fittest'. If that principle held good generally in Nature, there was no reason why it should not apply to language too. Darwin had offered 19th-century linguistics the key concept which could suddenly make everything fit into place.

Or could it? That depended rather crucially on just how far linguistics was prepared to take Darwinism. Two possibilities emerged. It was possible to invoke Darwinistic explanations simply in order to account for the particular facts of evolution within a given language. On the other hand, it was also possible to give a more ambitious, all-embracing Darwinistic explanation for the evolution of language itself.

The former strategy is exemplified in the following passage from Hermann Paul's *Principien der Sprachgeschichte* (*Principles of the history of language*).

> Suppose that we now endeavour to answer the question, What is the real cause of the change of usage in language? Changes produced by the conscious intention of single individuals are not absolutely excluded [*cf.* the history of the words *gas*, etc.].

Grammarians have endeavoured to reduce written languages to regularity. The terminology of sciences, arts, and trades is settled and enriched by teachers, investigators, and discoverers. Under a despotism, it may happen that the caprice of the monarch has in a single point prevailed. But it has not in most cases aimed at an absolutely new creation, but only at the settlement of some point on which usage had not yet decided; and the significance of such capricious decisions is as nothing compared with the slow, involuntary and unconscious changes to which the usage of language is perpetually exposed. The real reason for the variability of usage is to be sought only in regular linguistic activity. From this all voluntary influence on usage is excluded. No other purpose operates in this, save that which is directed to the immediate need of the moment – the intention of rendering one's wishes and thoughts intelligible to others. For the rest, purpose plays in the development of language no other part than that assigned to it by Darwin in the development of organic nature, – the greater or lesser fitness of the forms which arise is decisive for their survival or disappearance.

(Principles of the history of language: 12–13)

Paul clearly sees the main advantage of the doctrine of natural selection as being that it overcomes what would otherwise be an insuperable obstacle in the progress of regular sound change. That is to say, if individual speakers do not reproduce exactly the sounds they hear (from a previous generation of speakers) but alter them unconsciously and imperceptibly in attempting to reproduce them, why do not such minute variations in the long run cancel one another out and thus leave the language unchanged? The answer must be that certain of these phonetic variants had a natural advantage over others. (Otherwise Grimm's Law could not have come into operation: an original sound p would have remained p and never become f.)

Unfortunately, at first sight the solution is even more puzzling than the original problem. Why should the pronunciation f be more fit for survival than the pronunciation p? Paul's attempt to smooth out the difficulty is very instructive, and demonstrates quite clearly the limits of this level of Darwinian theorizing in historical linguistics. What Paul claims is that 'fitness' in language means fitness to serve as a standard for the linguistic community as a whole at any one time. Standardization, however, is in turn determined by the practice of the majority. An individual who does not conform to majority usage becomes an isolated eccentric. Linguistic eccentricities will not survive, because the only purpose of speech is communication, and a linguistic eccentric will stand less chance of communicating successfully to the majority of his or her co-speakers.

> Precisely the same causes which prevent the minority from departing too far from the common movement, forbid also that it should lag much behind the advance of the majority. For the superior frequency of any pronunciation is the only measure for its correctness and fitness to serve as a standard.
>
> (*Principles of the history of language*: 53)

What Paul does not appear to notice is that the account has now come full circle. The fittest pronunciations survive because they are those of the majority, and the majority has selected the fittest pronunciations. It is not a Darwinian explanation but a Darwinian historical snowball.

*   *   *

More interesting in many ways – and certainly more controversial – was the possibility of adopting a Darwinian strategy to explain humanity's linguistic development as a whole. In this, as in other fields, Darwinism encountered opposition because it was seen as conflicting head-on with Christian accounts of the origin of language (and of *homo sapiens*). The passage from Müller quoted at the beginning of this chapter is of some significance because it represents an ingenious attempt to forge a compromise between Darwinian evolutionism and the Bible's account of language. Although Müller saw the advantages to be gained by adopting Darwinian explanations in linguistics, he could not bring himself to accept that Darwin had explained how language itself had originated. He rejected the idea that there was a smooth evolutionary progression linking the calls of wild animals to the words of the human being. 'No process of natural selection,' Müller proclaimed intransigently in 1861, 'will ever distill significant words out of the notes of birds or the cries of beasts' (*Lectures on the science of language*, vol.1: 340).

A couple of years later he had changed his tune. In the interim he had doubtless felt which way the wind was blowing in linguistics. By 1864 he acknowledges 'the genius of Darwin'. His compromise with Darwinism reverts to the ancient Greek notion of *logos*. Müller now admits that there is no good case for distinguishing between the way the senses of animals operate and the way the senses of human beings operate. So on that level there is no ground for denying to animals the capacity to recognize and reproduce similarities in sound patterns (granted the physiological equipment required). A parrot, after all, as both Locke and Descartes had acknowledged, can imitate human speech. Müller's originality lies in his attempt to graft a Darwinian concept of evolution on to a Cartesian linguistic stock. He invokes the 'faculty of reason' (*logos*), unique to *homo sapiens*, as the explanation for how human beings (unlike parrots) were able to make the unprecedented evolutionary leap from calls to words, from spontaneous chatter to deliberate language. The triumph of *homo sapiens* as a species in the 'great struggle for life' was due to the naturally endowed capacity for harnessing sound-production to serve the purposes of *logos*. Hence, where language is concerned, 'natural selection, if we could but always see it, is invariably rational selection'. Here at last Darwin, Comparative Philology and Victorian theology were finally reconciled.

Chapter fourteen

Saussure on language and thought

In itself, thought is like a swirling cloud, where no shape is intrinsically determinate. No ideas are established in advance, and nothing is distinct, before the introduction of linguistic structure.

But do sounds, which lie outside this nebulous world of thought, in themselves constitute entities established in advance? No more than ideas do. The substance of sound is no more fixed or rigid than that of thought. It does not offer a ready-made mould, with shapes that thought must inevitably conform to. It is a malleable material which can be fashioned into separate parts in order to supply the signals which thought has need of. So we can envisage the linguistic phenomenon in its entirety – the language, that is – as a series of adjoining subdivisions simultaneously imprinted both on the plane of vague, amorphous thought, and on the equally featureless plane of sound....

Just as it is impossible to take a pair of scissors and cut one side of paper without at the same time cutting the other, so it is impossible in a language to isolate sound from thought, or thought from sound. To separate the two for theoretical purposes takes us into either pure psychology or pure phonetics, not linguistics.

Linguistics, then, operates along this margin, where sound and thought meet. *The contact between them gives rise to a form, not a substance.*

(*Cours de linguistique générale*: 155–7)

This striking metaphor from Saussure's posthumously published

Cours de linguistique générale ushers in what was subsequently described as a 'Copernican revolution' in Western linguistic thought. The term 'Copernican' is apt. For just as Copernicus had claimed that the Earth rotated about the Sun, instead of the Sun rotating about the Earth, Saussure claims something analogous in the case of language. His thesis was that languages are the instruments which enable human beings to achieve a rational comprehension of the world in which they live. Instead of seeing words as mere adjuncts to our grasp of reality, Saussure saw our understanding of reality as depending essentially upon our social use of the verbal signs which constitute the language we use. Words are not peripheral but, on the contrary, central to human life. Human existence is, by definition, a linguistically articulated existence.

Saussure's claim goes far beyond the traditional view of language as the universal mode of human communication. It also goes beyond Locke's view of words as signs which stand for ideas. Many philosophers had agreed that without language human reason would be deprived of its principal instrument of expression. But Saussure's thesis goes further and deeper. The impossibility of cutting a sheet of paper without simultaneously cutting recto and verso symbolizes for Saussure the *intrinsic* inseparability of the phonetic and conceptual facets of language. What Saussure is saying about the nature of language may from one point of view be regarded as a resurrection or modern restatement of the primitive Greek concept of *logos*, although Saussure does not put it in that way. What *logos* and Saussure's notion have in common, however, is the idea of a *single* organizational structure which accounts simultaneously for both human speech and human reason. This structure he called *langue*, and he proposed the study of *langue* as the primary task of linguistics.

Linguistics thus conceived was for Saussure only one branch of a more general science of signs, which he proposed to call 'semiology' (*sémiologie*). Each branch of semiology would need a theory of the signs it dealt with. Accordingly, linguistics would need a theory of the linguistic sign, the basic unit of *langue*. Such a theory Saussure proceeds to offer. As his paper-cutting analogy illustrates, he treats the linguistic sign as a unit defined purely by its form, which has two exactly complementary facets, or 'opposite sides'. The Saussurean technical terms for these two facets of the sign are *signifiant* and *signifié* (the 'signifying' plane and the 'signified' plane). Every *langue* is a complete semiological system of bi-planar signs, each of which has its *signifiant* and its *signifié*. Although each plane may, for convenience, be studied separately, no linguistic sign can be defined without reference to both planes, neither of which is more important than the other. It is by mastering a semiological system of this type that human beings are able both to communicate linguistically with others who share the same system and also to think analytically about the world in which they live.

Saussure did not arrive at his revolutionary concept of *langue* by studying what the Greeks had written on the subject of *logos*. He reached it – according to his own account – by reflecting on the theoretical shortcomings and inconsistencies of language studies in the 19th century. Born in 1857, Saussure had a distinguished academic career as an Indo-European philologist before embarking upon the mature work in linguistic theory which occupied his later years. He gave only three courses of lectures on general linguistics, at the University of Geneva in the years 1907–11. It was the lecture notes taken by his students at these lectures, subsequently compiled and synthesized by his colleagues, which formed the basis of the work published in 1916 under the title *Cours de linguistique générale* ('Course in general linguistics').

To what extent the published text of the *Cours* faithfully reflects Saussure's thinking about language is a matter of some controversy. That controversy, however, is irrelevant to the subsequent chapter in the history of ideas which opens with the *Cours*. For, whether Saussure would have 'authorized' it or not, the text as published became the cornerstone of modern linguistic theory, as well as the manifesto of a more general intellectual movement of the 20th century, which has influenced such diverse disciplines as psychology, social anthropology and literary criticism. That broader intellectual movement is nowadays known as 'structuralism'.

Although *structuralism* was not a term Saussure himself invented or ever used, one of Saussure's central tenets may nevertheless be stated as follows: in order to make any serious study of linguistic phenomena we must give priority to the concept that *langue* is a structure, and that its essential – indeed sole – properties are structural properties. Everything else about language is marginal and accidental: even the fact that sound is the medium universally used for the linguistic activity of speech. For speech (*parole*), according to Saussure, is not to be confused with *langue*. *Parole*, although a reflection of *langue*, is merely its external manifestation. What was fundamentally wrong with 19th-century language studies, in Saussure's view, was its complete failure to distinguish between *langue* and *parole*. Furthermore, the same failure must, if Saussure is right, flaw the traditional Western concept of words as 'significant sounds' (Aristotle's *phonē semantikē*); for sounds belong to *parole* not to the structure which is *langue*.

Saussure's notion of *langue* as a structure immediately raises two questions. The first is: 'A structure in what sense?' As a first approximation, one might answer: 'A structure in much the same sense as when we say a building is a structure.' Maybe if we take away one brick or one joist, the whole edifice will not fall down straight away. But, by taking something away, we have none the less made a structural alteration. As a result of taking something away, eventually cracks will start to appear; because bricks need other bricks to support them. In this sense, every building is unique, and no two buildings have the same structure. A structural alteration to one building affects just that building and no other. This Saussure also held to be true in the case of *langue*. (The French linguistic sign *arbre* belongs to a quite different structural system from the English linguistic sign *tree*, even though dictionaries tell us that both words 'mean the same thing'.)

The comparison with a building, however, offers what is in one respect a misleading approximation to the Saussurean notion of linguistic structure (or *système*, to use the term he most frequently employed). It is misleading because we normally think of a building as a structure composed out of pre-existing units: bricks, joists, planks, and other materials. But a crucial feature of Saussurean structuralism is the idea that the structure itself creates the units and their relations to one another. So to think of a house built by cementing one brick to the next gives us the wrong idea of structure for Saussure. Linguistic structure is not an assemblage: it is not built up piecemeal. It exists only as a whole. This is a very important and in some respects a very difficult idea. Again, it involves a claim which distinguishes Saussure's view of language quite radically from those of his contemporaries and immediate predecessors in the field of linguistic studies. Saussure's theory of *langue* emerges as being rather like a theory of architecture according to which individual bricks only come into existence once the whole building is in place.

This idea seems less paradoxical if we think of another analogy which Saussure was fond of using, that of games. Playing chess is not an activity which has somehow evolved out of the prior independent use of pawns, bishops, knights and the other chess pieces. Chess is a game complete in itself, and it is this completeness which confers on the individual pieces their separate but interdependent roles. Without pawns, or without bishops, or without any of its other constituent elements, chess would be a different game. But, more importantly, without the game a pawn or a bishop would be simply an ornamental carved figure of a certain shape: it would not be a chessman. Chessmen as such do not exist outside the context of the game. Similarly, for Saussure there is no linguistic sign outside the context of its *langue*. Saussure's concept of *langue* is thus essentially holistic: the constituent parts do not exist independently of the whole.

The other question which the Saussurean notion of linguistic structure raises is this: 'If our *langue* is a structure, then a structure *of what* exactly?' Saussure's answer to this is also a difficult one. He envisaged *langue* as being simultaneously a structure of the mental operations of the individuals who use it, and also a structure of the communicational processes by means of which a community functions as a cultural entity. So *langue* is ultimately supra-individual in the sense that it is vested in society and depends for its existence on external social relations; yet it presupposes in each individual the mastery of an internally represented system of linguistic signs. More precisely, each individual member of the linguistic community must be in possession of a system which approximates to that of the community as a whole: for *langue*, Saussure insists, 'is never complete in any single individual, but exists perfectly only in the collectivity' (*Cours*: 30).

Saussurean structuralism is thus doubly holistic; or holistic in two senses at once. There is a social dimension of holism, which denies to the individual any separate linguistic existence: the individual is allowed no linguistic role other than that of utilizing in *parole* the collective system of *langue*. At the same time there is a systemic dimension of holism, which denies to linguistic units any separate existence: they are constituted solely and simply by relations internal to the *langue* as a whole. Saussurean structuralism, in short, is both 'internally' and 'externally' holistic.

It is interesting to note that in Saussure's day holistic theories were beginning to come into fashion in other fields than linguistics. Durkheimian sociology is 'externally' holistic, in so far as it claims to be dealing with an order of facts which are the property of collectivities, and cannot be reduced to sets of facts about individuals, even though activity by individuals is essential to the life of the collectivity. (E. Durkheim, *Les règles de la méthode sociologique*, 1895.) This idea in turn may be seen as an extension of the view developed by Spencer, under Darwinian influence, that societies may be viewed as organisms, whose parts cannot function independently of the whole. 'Internally' holistic theories were becoming prominent in psychology, notably in the work of the Gestalt school. In 1890 von Ehrenfels argued that a holistic theory of perception was necessary in order to account for our recognition of melody in music. In 1912 Max Wertheimer published his classic paper on the visual perception of movement, which argued along the same lines. What the Gestalt psychologists were reacting against was the immediately preceding psychological tradition, principally established by Wundt (1832–1920), which assumed that perception was to be explained atomistically, as a construction out of individually perceived elements, which the mind then assembled into a whole. In contrast to this, the Gestalt psychologists thought they had found evidence in favour of a view of perceptual organization in which the whole comes first, and the parts are identified in relation to it.

To what extent Saussure himself was directly influenced by the holistic theorizing current in other academic fields than his own is debatable. Nevertheless, it is difficult not to see Saussurean structuralism in retrospect as the natural culmination of a growing trend towards holistic explanation in the human sciences, from which the study of language could not in the end remain isolated.

*   *   *

It was not so much Saussure's view of language which caused a revolution in linguistics as the consequences which are spelled out in the *Cours de linguistique générale*. If these were accepted, linguistic studies could no longer proceed on the assumptions which the comparative and historical philologists had implicitly treated as valid. For in their view there had been no problem about tracing the 'evolution' of consonants and vowels from primitive Indo-European down to more recent times. Thus, for example, as Grimm's Law had claimed, an original *b* might eventually 'become' *p* (see Chapter 13). Or the Latin word *causa* might, over the course of centuries, eventually 'become' the French word *chose*. Such examples of linguistic 'evolution' were the stock-in-trade of all the 19th-century philological manuals.

Unfortunately this long-established approach to linguistic change immediately became suspect if Saussure's theoretical premises were sound. For, as Saussure pointed out, it followed from these premises that one could not assume the continuous existence of individual linguistic units over hundreds or thousands of years during which the linguistic system as a whole did *not* remain the same. In other words, it made no sense to suppose that the earlier *b* was 'the same consonant' as its later manifestation *p*, or that 'the same word' appeared in Latin as *causa* but later in French as *chose*. For if linguistic units did not exist except as structural units defined within a single linguistic system, it was impossible for any given unit to 'survive' from one system *A* into a different system *B* at a later point in time. Therefore, concluded Saussure, it was imperative to distinguish within linguistic studies between two quite different points of view. There was what he termed a *synchronic* point of view, from which it was possible to analyse any given *langue* as a system of co-existing units and relations. On the other hand there was also a *diachronic* point of view, from which it was possible to study the changes intervening between a chronological series of such systems succeeding one another in time. For Saussure, the worst mistake that could be made in linguistics was to confuse synchronic facts with diachronic facts: 'The contrast between the two points of view – synchronic and diachronic – is absolute and admits no compromise' (*Cours*: 119). Furthermore, it followed that 'synchronic linguistics' must take precedence over 'diachronic linguistics', since without synchronic systems there could be no diachronic developments. Finally, the absolute separation between synchronic and diachronic studies left no theoretically valid point of view which allowed the identification of linguistic units across systems: hence no possibility of tracing the 'evolutionary' development of a single unit over time, as the Neogrammarians and others had assumed. Thus, at one theoretical stroke, Saussure called in question the entire basis of 19th-century linguistics. Its most important statements (for example of the much acclaimed 'sound laws') were not false but, rather, meaningless.

In spite of his scepticism about 19th-century historical linguistics, however, it would be a mistake to construe Saussure's position as anti-Darwinian. On the contrary, one of the ironies of Saussurean linguistics is that for all its emphasis on synchronic systems it may nevertheless be seen as providing what is in some ways a more convincing interpretation of the Darwinian notion that language is subject to the law of 'survival of the fittest' than the Neogrammarians had ever managed to provide. On the Saussurean view, what 'survive' over time from one linguistic system *A* to another system *B* are elements of linguistic *substance*, but never elements of linguistic *form*; and only those elements of linguistic substance survive which can be accommodated within the new system, i.e. given a new formal role to play in system *B*. This idea is in fact much closer to the biological notion of variations acquiring a useful function than the older interpretation proposed in 1880 by Paul (see Chapter 13), which assumed simply that in language 'survival of the fittest' meant survival of those variants of highest frequency.

Thus the Saussurean explanation of the fact that the phonological system of modern French contains a voiced bilabial nasal consonant (conventionally written *m*, as at the beginning of the word *mer* 'sea'), which does not differ phonetically from its Latin counterpart (also written *m*, as in the Latin word *mare*, from which French *mer* is etymologically derived), is not that the Latin consonant somehow managed to 'remain unchanged' for 2,000 years. On the contrary, according to the Saussurean account what must have happened is that the bundle of phonetic properties which we refer to as 'the consonant *m*' was successfully reintegrated into the whole diachronic series of phonological systems intervening between Latin and contemporary French. It survived because, at each successive stage, it turned out that there was a 'slot' (i.e. a structural position) in the system which could be filled by a consonant having those particular phonetic properties. But the fact that at the beginning and the end of the 2,000-year chain we apparently find this voiced bilabial nasal sound (written in both cases *m*) should not deceive us into concluding that here we have an example of a permanent phonological fixture. For in spite of this apparent identity of phonetic substance, the consonant in question is not 'the same': it enters into a different set of contrastive relations with other consonants in Latin from those which characterize its position in the French system. Consequently, from a Saussurean point of view, in spite of the similarity of pronunciation and in spite of the etymological connection, there is no identity of linguistic form between the consonant *m* of Latin *mare* and the consonant *m* of French *mer*. No other conclusion is possible once we adopt a holistic concept of linguistic systems and their constituent elements.

Exactly parallel Saussurean reasoning applies in morphology. The fact that the French first person pronoun *je* ('I') is etymologically derived from Latin *ego* does not, for Saussure, warrant the conclusion that somehow a particularly tenacious Latin pronoun has managed to survive into French, albeit with a somewhat distorted pronunciation. On the contrary, the pronominal system of French is quite different from the pronominal system of Latin: for not only is the actual inventory of pronouns different, but their syntactic functions are in no way comparable. (The French pronoun *je*, for example, obligatorily accompanies its verb, as in *je vois* 'I see': whereas the Latin for 'I see' is simply the verb form *video*, which does not require an accompanying pronoun *ego*.) Structurally, therefore, there is simply no way of equating French *je* with Latin *ego*. Nevertheless, the etymological 'survival' of the pronouns derived from Latin *ego* can be explained on the assumption that every linguistic system intermediate between Latin and French found a structural position available for them. It should be noted that in this example we are considering not merely the continuity of phonetic substance but also, inasmuch as both *ego* and *je* refer to the speaker ('I'), the continuity of the same idea (i.e. the 'thought substance').

Thus, far from rendering linguistic continuity over time mysteriously inexplicable, Saussure actually provides a view of linguistic change in which the criterion for 'fitness' which determines survival is eminently reasonable. Everything depends on finding a place, 'fitting' into, a succession of structured systems. But linguistics will fail to grasp this as long as it confuses the criteria of identity which are appropriate for synchronic studies with those appropriate for diachronic studies; or, which comes to the same thing, criteria of identity for form (*langue*) with criteria of identity for substance (*parole*). To invoke another of Saussure's metaphors, confusing these quite different sets of criteria is like making the mistake of supposing that the identity of the 8.45 train from Geneva to Paris is determined by its having the same carriages and the same staff (driver, guard, etc.) each day. But this is not so. The 8.45 train is still the 8.45 train even if the entire rolling stock and personnel are replaced overnight:

> the train is identified by its departure time, its route, and any other features which distinguish it from other trains. Whenever the same conditions are fulfilled, the same entities reappear.
>
> (*Cours*: 151)

But this does not mean that the 8.45 train is some kind of 'unreal' abstraction. Such trains as the 8.45 from Geneva to Paris are real enough. Indeed, their 'physical existence is essential to our understanding of what they are' (*Cours*:151–2). So it is too in the case of linguistic signs.

*   *   *

What, then, in practice determines the identity of any given linguistic sign? Certainly not, for Saussure, the existence of a corresponding real-world object. He derides this misconception as taking a 'nomenclaturist' view of languages (*Cours*: 97ff.). The linguistic sign *horse* is *not* constituted by the connection between a certain English monosyllable and a certain animal or class of animals. Consequently the actual existence or non-existence of horses is totally irrelevant to the question. This is not to deny that English speakers typically recognize and talk about real horses, and know when to say of something, for example, 'That is a horse'. But, once again, such considerations for Saussure relate to *parole*, not to *langue*.

The clue to the identity of a linguistic sign is the fact that the relation between its *signifiant* and its *signifié* is arbitrary. Nothing about the monosyllable *horse* determines that it should mean 'horse' rather than 'cow'. We can readily imagine a language identical with English in all respects except that the words *horse* and *cow* have 'changed places': that is, *horse* means 'cow' and *cow* means 'horse'. In this imaginary language, therefore, the phrase *horse-drawn carriage* will refer to a carriage drawn by cows, and a *cowherd* will be a man who looks after horses. However, we should note that in this imaginary language certain relations between words which we are accustomed to in English no longer obtain. These relations are of two kinds, which Saussure terms *syntagmatic* relations and *associative* relations.

Syntagmatic relations are those which hold because in *parole* we string linguistic signs together in linear sequences. Each word will have a unique set of such syntagmatic combinations. For example, *racehorse* is a familiar English combination. But in our imaginary language this will presumably be replaced by *racecow*.

Associative relations, on the other hand, are those which hold because in our minds certain associations obtain between some words which do not obtain between others. Not all these associations will necessarily be different in the case of *horse* and *cow* in our imaginary language. For instance, *horse* will still rhyme with *course*; so to the extent that phrases like *horses for courses* rely on the rhyming association between *horse* and *course* that association will remain. However, it will be weaker to the extent that it is no longer backed up by a sense association (granted that we do not live in a society where cows run round racecourses and have bets placed on them). Thus in our imaginary language *horses for courses* would be a somewhat odd, not to say puzzling, expression. Similarly, the word *cow* is associated by many English speakers with the word *milk*; whereas *horse* has no such association. In our imaginary language, however, this associative situation would presumably be reversed (unless horses suddenly started being farmed for their milk yield, an unlikely eventuality).

The identity of any linguistic sign, on Saussure's account, is determined by the sum total of syntagmatic and associative relations into which it enters with other linguistic signs in the same *langue*. The term Saussure uses for this total set of relations is 'value' (*valeur*); and the term is deliberately chosen because of its economic implications. For Saussure, any *langue* operates in very much the same way as an economic system.

The *Cours de linguistique générale* leaves the reader in little doubt as to Saussure's conception of the parallel between language and economic activity.

... all values appear to be governed by this paradoxical principle. They are always constituted:

(i) by something *dissimilar* which can be exchanged for that which has the value to be determined;

(ii) by *similar* things which can be compared with that which has the value in question.

These two factors are necessary for the existence of a value. Thus in order to determine what a five-franc coin is worth, it is necessary to know: (i) that it can be exchanged for a determinate quantity of something different, for example bread; (ii) that it can be compared with a similar value in the same system, for example a one-franc coin, or with a unit of currency of another system (a dollar, etc.). Likewise a word can be exchanged for something dissimilar: an idea; furthermore, it can be compared with something of like nature: another word. Its value is thus not fixed so long as one goes no further than observing that it can be 'exchanged' for such and such a concept; in addition, it must be compared with similar values, with the other words which may be contrasted with it. Its content is truly determined only by the coexistence of what there is outside it. Belonging to a system, it is endowed not only with a meaning but also and especially with a value, and that is something else again.

(*Cours*: 159–60)

Misinterpretations of Saussure's position are so common that it may be worth making a number of comments by way of clarification of the passage just cited. The coins in this example are not coins of the kind an individual may have at this moment in his pocket, any more than the words in question are the words he may now be hearing, or seeing before him on the printed page. Both coins and words are here envisaged as units of a classification, not as concrete objects or events. They are types, not tokens. This is evident from the insistence on the notion of 'exchange'. For there is no sense in which when A utters a word to B in a given communication situation, he receives the corresponding idea from B; although there is indeed a sense in which when A gives B five francs in a given shop he may get a quantity of bread from B in exchange. But we are not being invited to consider what happens in the real world of transactions. On the contrary, we are dealing with the abstract equivalences which underly such transactions, whether linguistic or commercial. These equivalences belong to 'the system': the *langue* in the linguistic case, and the economy in the commercial case. On a particular occasion, a shopkeeper may refuse to give me the bread in exchange for my five francs, perhaps because he needs the bread himself, or because he does not like me, or for some other reason. But that will not invalidate the notion of 'five francs worth of bread'. It simply means that my attempt to negotiate a particular purchase within the economic system has failed on this occasion. It does not mean that my five-franc coin has suddenly become worthless. The same applies to attempts I might make at the bank to change my five francs into foreign currency.

What Saussure is saying is that transactions presuppose established systems of equivalences, both in the social behaviour we recognize as 'linguistic' and in the social behaviour we recognize as 'economic'. Furthermore, such systems require two different orders of relationship, not just one. There have to be established relationships which systematize the units of exchange as compared both one to another, and also to what else is available in exchange for any such unit. Only when this dual interlocking occurs do the units have a value. Otherwise, we have no stable mode of exchange at all, but at best *ad hoc* bartering (either linguistic or commercial) which exhibits no regularity from one occasion to the next. So if the only answer that could be given to 'What is a five-franc coin worth?' were 'It is worth five times as much as a one-franc coin', we should not be dealing with an economy but merely with a mathematics. And if the only answer that could be given to 'What does the word *five* mean?' were 'It designates the number five', we should not be dealing with a language but merely with a nomenclature.

The whole of the *Cours de linguistique générale* is, in effect, dedicated to arguing that a language is not to be confused with a nomenclature. This confusion Saussure saw – rightly – as a major obstacle to understanding the systematicity of language. It is a confusion which is central to the thesis which is sometimes called 'surrogationalism', which has a venerable history in the Western tradition of theorizing about language. The surrogationalist views words as surrogates or proxies, having meaning by 'standing for' something else of a non-linguistic nature, and the central task of elucidating how language works as consisting in showing the various types of relationship between words and what they stand for. In short, surrogationalism seeks to explain language in terms of relationships between language and what exists independently outside language. For Saussure, surrogationalism embodies a profound misconception of how language works. The systematicity of language cannot be explained simply by seeking correlations between individual linguistic signs and objects, or events, or classes thereof in the world outside. That would be like supposing in economics that an exchange system could be defined simply by seeking correlations between certain coins or currency notes and quantities of goods or services independently available in society. Saussure's economic analogy is in part designed precisely to make the point that the 'independence' of a separate order of entities with which to correlate our units of exchange is an illusion both in linguistic and in commercial behaviour. For the availability of goods and services depends very much on the prevailing exchange system. People do not – if left to their own devices – go on producing or gathering things they can neither eat nor use themselves, with no thought for whether it makes sense to do so. Similarly, where language is concerned, it is not Nature which supplies in advance a fixed inventory of things or events for human beings to find words for, whether they want to or not: but rather human beings who decide, collectively, what verbal distinctions it is useful to draw in order to exchange ideas with one another. In both cases, the exchange system itself is primary, not secondary; and such a system yields values, not just substitutions.

*　　*　　*

At this point two possible objections to the Saussurean picture of language may well be raised. In the first place, does not Saussure's claim that the linguistic sign is arbitrary (in that the relationship between *signifiant* and *signifié* is in no way dependent on factors external to the *langue*) conflict with the whole notion that values are systematic? How can purely arbitrary relations give rise to systematicity in the first place?

Saussure's answer to this is to distinguish between 'absolute' arbitrariness and 'relative' arbitrariness. Saussure does not claim that linguistic structure is in all respects 'absolutely' arbitrary. For example, the French word for 'twenty', *vingt*, is absolutely arbitrary, whereas the word for 'nineteen', *dix-neuf*, is only relatively arbitrary, because we recognize in it the two elements meaning 'ten' (*dix*) and 'nine' (*neuf*) respectively. But this, Saussure would contend, in no way invalidates or compromises the principle of arbitrariness, any more than the fact that five one-franc coins are equal in value to a single five-franc coin means that what they will buy is not arbitrarily determined (within the prevalent system of exchange). Relative arbitrariness is a matter of consistency 'motivated' from within the system. No *langue* exists, he claims, 'in which nothing at all is motivated' (*Cours*: 183)

A second objection might run as follows. If languages are constantly changing, as people have pointed out ever since antiquity, how are these Saussurean values ever established? Does not Saussure have to assume that at some point a language becomes fixed, so that we are in effect dealing with a static system, if only temporarily static?

The problem is again essentially connected with the notion of 'value'. For to fix a value presupposes the stability of certain elements and relations. This is as true in the economic case as in the linguistic. The value of a five-franc coin does not remain the same over a period of years simply because it remains equivalent to five one-franc coins. To suppose that would again be to reduce a system of values to a mere mathematics. But nor does it remain constant simply because, for instance, the price of bread remains constant. For there are many other economic factors involved than the price of one commodity. On the contrary, a fixed price is *eo ipso* no guarantee of anything without considering whether or not it costs more or less to produce the commodity in question than it used to. Analogously in the linguistic case, it proves nothing to show that the word *unfashionable* has at all times in its history been divisible into the same three morphemic units, nor even that it has always been defined as meaning 'not fashionable', if what is at issue is whether there have been changes in the system of lexical values to which it belongs. In short, for Saussure values emerge only from a synchronic perspective, which precludes linguistic change. A diachronic perspective does not yield *changing* values, but rather *no values at all*. For there is no diachronic basis on which one value may be compared with another, diachronically different, value.

For Saussure, therefore, there is no contradiction between systematicity and arbitrariness unless we overlook the basic fact that all values are established contrastively; that is, in virtue of differences between co-existing elements. This was what led him to formulate the view which is perhaps best summed up in the following quotation:

> A linguistic system is a series of phonetic differences matched with a series of conceptual differences
>
> (*Cours*: 166)

It is the emphasis on *differences* which gives this formulation the distinctive signature of Saussurean structuralism.

Thus Saussure in many ways marks the end of the tradition of linguistic thought which began with Socrates, in that he breaks with the basic assumption that we have to understand language by trying to relate, one by one, the many words we use to whatever it is they stand for (whether they are taken to stand for ideas in our minds, or for external things in the world outside). He is the first thinker to issue a radical challenge to the notion that had been prevalent in the Western tradition from Plato onwards; namely, that the core of any language comprises an inventory of names designating things, persons, properties and events already given to human understanding in advance of language. The theoretical task for general linguistics, as Saussure saw it, was to find an alternative set of assumptions on which it would be possible, at last, to erect a genuine science of language.

Bibliography and suggestions for further reading

General

Aarsleff, H. (1982) *From Locke to Saussure*, London: Athlone.
— (1983) *The study of language in England, 1780–1860*, 2nd edn, Minneapolis: University of Minnesota Press.
Diringer, D. (1968) *The alphabet*, 3rd edn, London: Hutchinson.
Havelock, E. A. (1963) *Preface to Plato*, Cambridge, Mass.: Harvard University Press.
Hovdhaugen, E. (1982) *Foundations of Western linguistics*, Oslo: Universitetsforlaget.
Ong, W. J. (1982) *Orality and literacy*, London: Methuen.
Parret, H. (ed.) (1976) *History of linguistic thought and contemporary linguistics*, Berlin: de Gruyter.
Robins, R. H. (1979) *A short history of linguistics*, 2nd edn, London: Longman.
Salus, P. H. (ed.) (1969) *On language: Plato to von Humboldt*, New York: Holt, Rinehard and Winston.
Sebeok, T. A. (ed.) (1975) *Current trends in linguistics*, Vol. 13: *Historiography of linguistics*, The Hague: Mouton.

Chapter 1

The translation of Plato's *Cratylus* is that of H. N. Fowler in the Loeb Classical Library, which also gives the Greek text (London: Heinemann, 1926).

F. M. Cornford in *Plato's theory of knowledge* (London: Routledge and Kegan Paul, 1935) has an excellent discussion of the linguistic implications of Plato's doctrine of forms.

Chapter 2

The translations of Aristotle's works cited are: *Poetics*: I. Bywater (Oxford: Clarendon Press, 1920); *De Interpretatione* and *Categories*: H. P. Cook (London: Heinemann, Loeb Classical Library, 1938).

The latter also gives the Greek text of both treatises.

An edition of the Greek text of the *Poetics*, with copious notes, is that of D. W. Lucas (Oxford: Clarendon Press, 1968).

A wide-ranging collection of essays on the problem of metaphor is to be found in the volume *Metaphor and thought*, edited by A. Ortony (Cambridge: Cambridge University Press, 1979).

Chapter 3

The Bible translation quoted is the 1611 King James version.

The passage from St Augustine's Confessions is quoted in L. Wittgenstein, *Philosophische Untersuchungen*, edited and translated by G. E. M. Anscombe (Oxford: Blackwell, 1953).

The passage by Bertrand Russell comes from his book *An outline of philosophy* (London: Allen and Unwin, 1927).

Chapter 4

The translation of *De Lingua Latina* is by R. G. Kent in the Loeb Classical Library, which also gives the Latin text (London: Heinemann, 1938).

A detailed discussion of Varro's view of language is D. J. Taylor's *Declinatio. A study of the linguistic theory of Marcus Terentius Varro* (Amsterdam: Benjamins, 1974).

There is an edition of the Greek text of Dionysius Thrax by G. Ühlig, *Dionysii Thracis ars grammatica* (Leipzig: Teubner, 1883). R. H. Robins in an article entitled 'Dionysius Thrax and the Western grammatical tradition' (*Transactions of the Philological Society*, 1957), and J. Pinborg's survey 'Classical Antiquity: Greece' (in Sebeok 1975) both discuss the role played by Dionysius in early linguistic thought.

Donatus' *Ars Minor* is translated by W. J. Chase (Wisconsin: University of Wisconsin Press, 1926: reprinted in Salus 1969). The Latin text is printed in H. Keil (ed.) (1868) *Grammatici Latini*, vol.V (Leipzig: Teubner; reprinted 1961, Hildesheim: Olms).

Chapter 5

Quintilian's *Institutio Oratoria* is translated by H. E. Butler in the Loeb Classical Library, which also gives the Latin text (London: Heinemann, 1920).

Aristotle's *Rhetoric* is translated by H. H. Freese in the Loeb Classical Library, which also gives the Greek text (London: Heinemann, 1926).

A comprehensive survey of Greek and Roman rhetoric is provided by G. Kennedy in two books: *The art of persuasion in Greece* (Princeton: Princeton University Press, 1963) and *The art of rhetoric in the Roman world* (Princeton: Princeton University Press, 1973).

Chapter 6

Thomas of Erfurt's Latin text is edited and translated by G. L. Bursill-Hall
(London: Longman, 1972), who also gives a general survey of medieval
linguistics in his paper 'The Middle Ages' (printed in Sebeok 1975).

A good introduction to modistic grammar is M. A. Covington *Syntactic
theory in the high middle ages* (Cambridge: Cambridge University Press,
1984).

Chapter 7

The Prologue to Caxton's translation of *Eneydos* is reprinted in W. A.
Craigie, *The critique of pure English from Caxton to Smollett* (Oxford:
Clarendon Press, Society for Pure English Tract LXV, 1946), and also in
W. F. Bolton *The English language* (Cambridge: Cambridge University
Press, 1966).

The standard edition of du Bellay's *Deffence* is that of H. Chamard
(Paris: Didier, repr. 1970). The French text is translated by G. M. Turquet
(London: Dent, 1939).

There is an article by W. K. Percival on 'The grammatical tradition and
the rise of the vernaculars' in Sebeok 1975.

Chapter 8

The best available translation of the *Grammaire générale et raisonnée* is
that by Jacques Rieux and Bernard E. Rollin under the title *General and
rational grammar: the Port-Royal grammar* (The Hague: Mouton, 1975).
This includes a Preface by Arthur Danto, a useful Translators'
Introduction, and an appended Critical Essay by Norman Kretzmann.

The English translation of the Port-Royal Logic is published under the
title *The art of thinking: the Port-Royal logic*, translated by James Dickoff
and Patricia James (New York: Bobbs-Merrill, 1964). There is an
explanatory Foreword by Charles Hendel.

An excellent English-language discussion of Port-Royal ideas appears in
*Grammatical theory in Western Europe: 1500–1700. Trends in vernacular
grammar I* by G. A. Padley (Cambridge: Cambridge University Press, 1985).

Noam Chomsky's *Cartesian linguistics* (New York: Harper and Row,
1966) contains a controversial interpretation of the aims of the Port-Royal
Grammar, seen from the perspective of Chomsky's generative grammar. A
rebuttal of Chomsky's interpretation may be found in 'The history of
linguistics and Professor Chomsky' by Hans Aarsleff (reprinted in Aarsleff
1982).

Chapter 9

The best edition of Locke's *Essay concerning human understanding* is that
by P. H. Nidditch (Oxford: Oxford University Press, 1975).

Locke's philosophy of language is discussed in Chapter 2 of Stephen K.

Land's *The philosophy of language in Britain* (New York: A.M.S. Press, 1986).

An important article is Norman Kretzmann's 'The main thesis of Locke's semantic theory', in *Locke on human understanding* (ed.) I. Tipton (Oxford: Oxford University Press, 1977).

The influence of Locke's philosophy of language on the eighteenth and nineteenth centuries is discussed at length in Aarsleff 1982 and Aarsleff 1983.

Chapter 10

A reprint of the 1756 translation of the *Essai* by Thomas Nugent is found in *Essay on the origin of human knowledge* (New York: A.M.S. Press, 1974). *Philosophical writings of Etienne Bonnot, Abbé de Condillac* includes a translation of Condillac's *Logic* by Franklin Philip with the collaboration of Harlan Lane (Hillsdale, N.J.: Lawrence Erlbaum, 1982). There is not an available translation of Condillac's *Grammaire* nor of the other works mentioned in the text. These may be found in French in the *Oeuvres complètes*, reprinted by Editions Slatkine (Geneva, 1970).

Aarsleff 1982 contains an excellent discussion of Condillac's contribution to the history of linguistic thought. Condillac is also discussed in Stephen K. Land's *From signs to propositions* (London: Longman, 1974) and in G. A. Wells' *The origin of language* (La Salle, Ill.: Open Court, 1987). Condillac's work is situated in the context of 18th-century French linguistic thought by Pierre Swiggers in *A world of words* (London: Routledge, forthcoming).

Chapter 11

The edition of *The diversions of Purley* referred to in the text is that of 1857, including the *Letter to Mr Dunning*.

The best discussion of Horne Tooke's place in linguistic thought is in Aarsleff 1983. Complementary discussions may be found in Stephen K. Land's *From signs to propositions* (London: Longman, 1974), in Olivia Smith's *The politics of language 1791–1819* (Oxford: Oxford University Press, 1984), and in an article by Patrice Bergheaud 'Empiricism and linguistics in 18th-century Great Britain' (*Topoi*, 4 (1985)).

Chapter 12

The best translation of Humboldt's 1836 introduction to the *Kawisprache* is that by Peter Heath under the title of *On language: the diversity of human language-structure and its influence on the mental development of mankind* (Cambridge: Cambridge University Press, 1988). This contains an introduction by Hans Aarsleff in which Humboldt's place in 18th- and 19th-century linguistic thought is examined.

The philosophical foundations of Humboldt's linguistic doctrines by Martin Manchester provides an excellent book-length introduction to and analysis of Humboldtian thought (Amsterdam: Benjamins, 1986).

Chapter 13

F. M. Müller's *Lectures on the science of language* were published in two volumes (London: Longmans, Green, 1861, 1864).

H. Paul's *Principien der Sprachgeschichte* (1st edn 1880) was translated by H. A. Strong *Principles of the history of language* (London: Longmans, Green, 1891).

Charles Darwin's *The origin of species* (1859) went through a number of editions during the author's lifetime. The sixth edition is reprinted in the Everyman's University Library (1971), with an Introduction by L. H. Matthews.

J. W. Spargo's translation of H. Pedersen's survey of nineteenth-century linguistics, *The discovery of language. Linguistic science in the nineteenth century*, 2nd edn (Bloomington: Indiana University Press, 1962), gives useful background material.

Chapter 14

The fifth edition of Saussure's *Cours de linguistique générale* (1916) is published with an Introduction and notes by T. de Mauro (Paris: Payot, 1972). It is translated by R. Harris, *F. de Saussure, Course in general linguistics* (London: Duckworth, 1983). A full-length commentary is provided in R. Harris, *Reading Saussure* (London: Duckworth, 1987). A briefer analysis of Saussure's contribution to modern linguistics is J. Culler's *Saussure* (London: Fontana, 1976).

Index

Aarsleff, H. ix, 45
abbreviations 101f., 106, 143ff.
Adam 36ff., 77
Aelfric xiv
Aesop 73
Alcuin xiv
Alexander xii, 21, 52
alphabet xii, 51, 64f., 69, 78, 89
analogists xiii
analogy 31, 34, 37, 50, 54, 70f., 73, 105, 129ff., 142, 171f.; *see also* regularity
anomalists xiii
anomaly 46f., 49, 56
arbitrariness 113ff., 122, 124, 129ff., 142, 185, 189f.
Aristarchus 50
Aristotle 20–34, 39, 49ff., 54, 60f., 73, 75ff., 82, 84f., 87, 113, 119, 135, 179
Arnauld 94–107, 147
Ascham 87
associative relations 185f.
Augustine 39f., 98

Babel 36, 41ff., 77
Bacon 113
Beauzée 44
Bede xiv
behaviourism 40
Bible xiii, 35–45, 76f., 85, 169, 174
bilingualism xiv, 63f.
Boethius 80
Bopp xviii
Braune 168

Brugmann 168, 171
Burnett, James (Lord Monboddo) 134

Cadmus xii
Caesar 48, 73
categories 26f., 97ff., 149, 163; *see also* parts of speech
Caxton 86–93
Chaucer 88
Chrysippus 49, 63
Cicero xiii, 48, 70, 91
Comparative Philology xviii, 166ff., 181
Condillac xvii, 120–34, 141f., 147, 154, 157f.
conventionalism xiii, 3f., 16f., 22, 25, 27, 32ff., 76, 92, 100, 104f., 157, 165
correct language xiv, 6, 46f., 53, 63f., 67ff., 152
correctness of names 1–19, 22f., 26, 36
Cratylus 1–20, 22, 35, 37, 47, 51, 53, 92

Dalgarno xvii, 58
Darwin xviii, 165ff., 181f.
definitions 116f.,121
democracy 18f., 138
Demosthenes 87, 91
Descartes xvi, 98, 110, 175
diachronic linguistics 182, 190
dialectic *see* logic
dialects xii, 86–93, 167, 169

dictionaries xvii, 92, 179
Diderot 134, 154
Diogenes of Babylon 49
Dionysius Thrax 49ff., 63, 66
Domitius Afer 60
Donatus xivff., 53f., 76, 80
du Bellay 91f.
Durkheim 180

Ehrenfels 181
Epicurus 165
Erasmus xvi
Esperanto 58
etymology xii, 8f., 22, 42f., 48ff., 57,
    70, 118f., 135, 136–50, 183
euphony 8, 152

Frege viii

Genesis 35–45
Gestalt psychology 181
grammar xiii, xv, 15, 49ff., 63, 66ff.,
    72ff., 75ff., 92, 94–107, 130, 140,
    145, 156, 160ff.
Grimm xviii, 169f.
Grimm's Law 170, 173, 181
Gutenberg xvi

Harris, James xvi
Hazlitt 150
Henry V 88
Herder xvii, 134f.
Herodotus xii
Hesiod 8
Hobbes 113
Homer xii, 8, 51ff., 72, 87, 91
Humboldt xvii, 135, 151–64, 165

imperfections of language 108–19,
    121, 142f., 152, 154, 162, 164
inflection 55f., 161ff.
Isocrates xi

Jerome xiii
Johnson, Samuel 117, 137
Jones, Sir W. xviif.
Justinian xiii

Lancelot 94–107, 147
language typology 55f., 161ff.
langue 47, 177ff., 184ff.
Leibniz xvi, 37
Leskien 168, 171
linearity 120, 125, 128, 130
linguistic change xii, 8, 25, 69, 71,
    89, 165–75, 181ff., 189
linguistic rationalism 98ff., 135, 141,
    159f.
linguistic relativism 159f.
Locke xvii, 37f., 108–19, 121ff.,
    132ff., 138, 140ff., 148, 158, 175,
    177
logic xiii, xv, 22, 24f., 49, 60f., 76,
    79, 84f., 106, 130
logos xi, xiii, 22, 25, 27f., 43, 49, 56,
    174f., 177f.
Lyell 169

Maupertuis 134
metaphor 20–34, 118f., 132
modes of signifying 75–85
modistae see speculative gram-
    marians
Müller xviii, 56, 165–75

names 1–20, 22ff., 35–45, 57, 134,
    142, 147, 190
natural selection 165ff.
natural signs 124ff.
naturalism xiii, 1, 4, 8, 11f., 14ff., 34,
    36f., 41, 100, 124ff., 142
Neogrammarians xviii, 168ff., 182
Newton 24
Nicole 96, 100
nomenclatures 26, 36ff., 57, 77, 188
nominalists xv

onoma 3, 27, 30, 54
oratory xii, 46f., 59–74
origin of language xii, xvii, 7, 10ff.,
    17, 35–45, 120–34, 141ff., 155f.,
    174
Osthoff 168, 171

Parmenides 1
parole 47, 178ff., 184f.

parts of speech xiii, 2ff., 27, 30, 53f., 56, 69, 73, 78f., 84, 96ff., 141, 146ff., 160ff.
Pascal 98
Paul 168, 172ff., 183
Philip of Macedon 21
phonetics 78
Plato xii, 1–23, 27, 32, 36f., 40f., 47, 50f., 53, 60, 73, 87, 92, 190
Pliny 59
poetry xi, xiii, 20, 28ff., 46f., 50ff., 67, 72f., 156f.
Pompey 48
Port-Royal xvi, 94–107, 135, 159
prescriptivism 72, 117, 160
printing xvi, 87ff.
Priscian xiiiff., 76, 80
Protagoras 18
Psammetichos xii
puns 2f.

Quintilian 59–74

Ramus xvi
Rask xviii, 170
reading 53, 64, 66f., 72f.
realists xv, 19, 77, 84f.,145
regularity xiii, 46–58, 104ff., 152, 172
    see also analogy
Remmius Palaemon 59f.
Renaissance viii, xiii, xv, 45, 87ff.
rhēma 3, 27, 30
rhetoric xiii, xv, 59–74, 106
Rousseau 134
Russell viii, 27

Sanctius xvi, 98
Saussure viii, xviii, 47, 167f., 176–90
Scaliger xvi
Schlegel 55
Schleicher 166
Schleyer 58
scientific method 167ff.
semiology 177
Seneca 59
Sextus Empiricus viii
Sievers 168

signifiant 177, 185, 189
signifié 177, 185, 189
Smith, Adam 134
Socrates xii, 1–20, 22ff., 35, 37, 40, 190
Sophists xii, 18f.
sound laws xviii, 170f., 182
speculative grammarians xv, 75–85, 98, 104
spelling 8, 15, 66, 69, 72, 89
Spencer 181
Speroni 92
Stoics viii, 49, 73
structuralism xviii, 178ff.
surrogationalism 38ff., 76, 84, 188
Swiggers, P. ix
syllables 11, 64ff.
syllogism 24f., 27, 49, 80
synchronic linguistics 182, 190
syntagmatic relations 185f.
syntax 48, 54, 82ff., 107

telementation 33, 110ff., 119, 142
Thomas of Erfurt 75–85
Tooke xvii, 118, 135, 136–50
trivium xv
truth 5, 12ff., 23, 27f., 38, 76, 135, 140

usage 4, 46f., 50, 71f., 89, 104ff., 172ff.

valeur 186ff.
Varro 46–58, 70
Vespasian 59
Virgil xiii, 72, 91
Volapük 58

Wertheimer 181
Wilkins xvii, 58
Wittgenstein viii, 39, 44
Wolf, G. ix
writing xii, 21, 51ff., 65ff., 73f., 96
Wundt 181

Zamenhof 58